HOW TO
WATCH BASKETBALL
LIKE A GENIUS

HOW TO
WATCH BASKETBALL
LIKE A GENIUS

What Game Designers,

Economists, Ballet Choreographers,

and Theoretical Astrophysicists

Reveal About the

Greatest Game on Earth

NICK GREENE

Abrams Press, New York

Library of Congress Control Number: 2020944848

ISBN: 978-1-4197-4480-8
eISBN: 978-1-68335-920-3

Printed and bound in the United States
10 9 8 7 6 5 4 3 2 1

Abrams books are available at special discounts when purchased in quantity for premiums and promotions as well as fundraising or educational use. Special editions can also be created to specification. For details, contact specialsales@abramsbooks.com or the address below.

Abrams Press® is a registered trademark of Harry N. Abrams, Inc.

ABRAMS The Art of Books
195 Broadway, New York, NY 10007
abramsbooks.com

For Laura

Section Three: Making That Dream Work

PROLOGUE
It comes in peace

I N JULY 2020, the *New York Times* published a report suggesting the United States military is in possession of alien technologies, including materials retrieved from UFO crash sites. An astrophysicist working with the Pentagon went on record and said that he had issued a classified briefing in March, asserting the recovered materials were from "off-world vehicles not made on this earth." You may have missed this story about a potential interplanetary Cold War. I know I did. It came out in the middle of a summer beset by plague and chaos and got lost in the shuffle. America was exhausted. The aliens would have to check back in with us later.

The *Times* published a short follow-up piece, essentially to say, "We can't believe we have to reiterate the alien news to you people." It didn't contain much new info, but the reporters further explained their sourcing: "Numerous associates of the Pentagon program, with high security clearances and decades of involvement with official UFO investigations, told us they were convinced such crashes have occurred, based on their access to classified information. But the retrieved materials themselves, and any data about them, are completely off-limits to anyone without clearances and a need to know."

How, exactly, do they decide who gets to take a gander at this alien junk? I'm not talking about security clearances, but rather the specific kinds of expertise deemed appropriate to the task of combing through the detritus of an extraterrestrial crash site. Physicists and materials scientists are obvious and necessary participants, as they are prepared to analyze the alloys or polymers or whatever this stuff may be, but the mystery goes beyond simply identifying properties of matter. As a species, we are very new to this sort of thing. I'd hate to see us limit our options.

What if the aliens were moving to a new planet when an armoire fell out of their spacecraft and tumbled to Earth? Maybe a glowing heap at a crash site is actually a pile of otherworldly pants and overalls, but we have no clue because the military didn't ask a fashion designer or textile manufacturer to weigh in with their thoughts. Are the Pentagon's astrophysicists prepared to identify a pair of jaunty culottes? This is a legitimate concern.

Think for a moment about the reverse scenario. Humans haven't sent any physical objects far enough to realistically believe that they'll bump into the home planets of other intelligent beings, but our radio and television signals travel at high enough speeds to reach thousands of nearby star systems. It is a very real possibility that aliens living light-years away are just starting to enjoy our old programming. They might be tuning into Game 7 of the 1984 NBA Finals as you read this.

How would those extraterrestrials approach basketball? Barring the extreme cosmic coincidence that they developed an identical version of the sport independently and without our influence, the aliens wouldn't have any hoops analysts or former players to help explain what's happening. They'd be forced to formulate their budding expertise regarding crossovers, reverse layups, and three-pointers on observation alone. I hope the alien powers that be let everyone, and not just their most esteemed scientists, watch hoops. The game was designed to be enjoyed by all.

Basketball is a relatively recent invention. It didn't crash-land on Earth until the late nineteenth century, and it didn't arrive fully formed. The sport has undergone constant changes throughout its brief life, many of which were thought up by people who could not be described as "basketball experts." (Especially in its early days, when that distinction did not yet exist.) Despite its ever-evolving form, there remains a unique pull to the game that transcends routine fandom. Much like the Beatles' discography or Sandra Bullock's performance in *Speed*, basketball is maximally appealing to a staggeringly large audience. It's as if we're preconditioned in the womb to embrace it. While I can't remember the first time I saw the game being played,

I am confident that my underdeveloped cerebral cortex responded, warmly: *This must be basketball. It's rather nice.*

I live in the Bay Area, which was the center of the basketball universe for the better part of a decade thanks to the success of the Golden State Warriors. Naturally, all anyone wants to talk about is basketball. I tend to cover sports for work, but I've long balanced that beat with writing on a whole slew of topics. As a result, I have found myself discussing hoops with concert harpists, cat behaviorists, and plasma physicists. I initially considered this to be small talk—common ground to explore before we got to the nitty-gritty of their respective fields—but it quickly became apparent that, if they had their druthers, we'd spend hours talking about Steph Curry.

These are people who don't think like the athletes playing the sport or like the writers covering it. For example, a wine critic once told me she thought that noted oenophile LeBron James would make a good vineyard owner because he's a multitasker who prefers to delegate on the fly, and that his history with erratic teammates like J. R. Smith would come in handy when harvesting in unpredictable weather. This hypothetical vineyard stewardship was some of the most apt analysis I've encountered in all my years following basketball. Score one for viticulture.

We all watch basketball differently. Not only did this realization help me build a greater appreciation for what had already been my favorite sport, but it also sparked the idea for this book. If one person's unique perspective on the game can help expand my own, what else have I been missing? I'm no genius, but I knew well enough to assume there was much more to learn.

This book will not make you a better basketball player. How could it? Its author can barely dribble to his left, and I want to get that embarrassing fact out of the way early lest anyone who is familiar with my handles comes forward to initiate a public shaming. Nevertheless, I still *love* the sport. It just works. Whether as a whole or broken down to its disparate parts, basketball has something for everyone.

The question of how and why the game remains compelling cannot be answered from a single point of view. The NBA may never invite a ballet choreographer to judge its annual Slam Dunk Contest, and you probably won't hear a magician analyze Kyrie Irving's handles on *SportsCenter*, but these surprising founts of basketball wisdom are worth listening to. With this in mind, I sought out some of the smartest and most interesting people I could find and approached them with the same simple request: *Would you like to talk about basketball?*

I'm unsure whether the chemists, professors, casting directors, philosophers, and everyone else who agreed to chat about hoops thought they were going to greatly broaden my own understanding of how the game works, but each and every one managed to do just that. What follows is an attempt to collect and contextualize all those little epiphanies so that I can share them with you.

Who knows? If this goes well, maybe they'll let us take a crack at those UFOs, too.

THE SHAPE OF THE GAME

TOPICS DISCUSSED IN THIS SECTION:

Where basketball
   comes from
Grievous bodily harm
Reese's Puffs cereal
Board games
Facial hair
Nominalism
Dribbling
Close-up magic
Cheating

Chain-smoking
The shot clock
Bowling alleys
PBA Rule 17.6.2.b
Superman
School dances
Maps
Faith Baptist Bible College
Management consulting
Traffic signals

TOPICS NOT DISCUSSED IN THIS SECTION:

Where babies come from
The 1988 Democratic
   Convention
Fly-fishing
Bubble tea
Acupuncture
Pangea
Artificial intelligence
Millinery
Wheat allergies
Calligraphy

The Olestra diarrhea panic
   of 1996
Pointillism
Rick Steves' Europe
Baccarat
Pliny the Elder
Foghat
Pliny the Younger
Train ferries
The different types
   of clouds

AN INTRODUCTORY CLASS

Naismith's original thirteen rules for basketball

THERE ARE TWO wildly dissimilar stories about the first-ever basketball game. In one telling, it went off without a hitch. In the other, players were nearly murdered. It's important to consider sourcing when assessing validity, but that only confuses things here because both versions come from the same guy: James Naismith, the man who invented the sport.

Let's start with the murder story because it's obviously more interesting. In 1939, Naismith was interviewed about the birth of basketball for a radio program called *We the People*. The audio, which was unearthed from the WOR-AM archives in 2015, remains the only known recording of Naismith's voice. He was seventy-seven at the time of his appearance and sounds grandfatherly and kind. (Sadly, he died ten months after the interview.) It's a rather polished performance, and Naismith regales the studio audience with the story of how he tamed a class of "incorrigibles" he was tasked with teaching at the YMCA Training School in Springfield, Massachusetts, on December 21, 1891.

"We had a real New England blizzard," Naismith says. "For days the students couldn't go outdoors, so they began roughhousing in the halls." He then explains how, after an unsuccessful attempt at indoor football, he came up with a totally fresh sport for the cooped-up students to play: basketball.

"What rules did you have for your new game, Dr. Naismith?" asks Gabriel Heatter, the show's host.

"Well, I didn't have enough, and that's where I made my big mistake," Naismith says. "The boys began tackling, kicking, and punching. . . . They ended up in a free-for-all in the middle of the gym floor. Before I could pull them apart, one boy was knocked out, several of them had black eyes, and one had a dislocated shoulder. It certainly was murder." Heatter chuckles, and Naismith continues, "After that first match, I thought they'd kill each other. But they kept nagging me to let them play again."

Naismith explains that, thanks to the addition of a few rules, basketball became the "fine, clean sport" that would soon take the world by storm. "I guess it just goes to show what you can do if you have to," he says. The audience then bursts into applause and the orchestra plays him out.

It's a lively story, but it's difficult to reconcile with what he wrote in his memoir, which was published two years after his death (and three years after that radio appearance): "The game was a success from the first time that ball was tossed up."

We know that *some* elements of his violent *We the People* story are true. Naismith really was tasked with keeping a class of rowdy jerks dubbed "the incorrigibles" active and entertained. Their previous physical education teacher (a retired circus performer) failed to get the students interested in calisthenics and gymnastics, and Naismith theorized that the young men craved competition and needed to fulfill a "play instinct." He tried to modify football and soccer for the indoors, but the former was too violent and the latter led to errant kicks that frequently knocked dumbbells off their wall racks. (It was a "practical lesson in first aid," Naismith wrote.) His solution was a game that involved tossing a ball into peach baskets nailed to the gym's balcony.

Naismith does allude to violence in his book. He had struggled to come up with a method to start each basketball game, and, in writing about his invention of the opening tip-off, he recalls that he had figured "there would be little chance for roughness" if he selected one player per side. Despite it being "the fairest way to start," he admits he "seriously underestimated the ingenuity of the American boy." Could those early tip-offs have inspired the brutal, *Braveheart*-like battle he describes on the radio? The book contains no mention of unconscious students or shoulders pulled from sockets, and while good writing may be concise, the omission of such juicy details would frustrate even the most succinct stylists.

It's possible that Naismith, in an attempt to tell an entertaining tale on the radio, embellished the roughhousing that transpired and condensed it into an allegorical fable about rules facilitating peace. Besides being a teacher and a medical doctor, Naismith was also a Presbyterian minister, and it's easy to imagine why that kind of story would appeal to him.

The embellishment may have also been down to the fact that the first game was extremely boring. It finished with a score of 1–0, and a student named William Chase hit the only basket on a desperate heave from twenty-five feet (all shots were worth one point). The gymnasium floor measured thirty-five by fifty-four feet, meaning the first successful shot in hoops history was from nearly mid-court. Besides this Steph Curry–like anomaly, that inaugural game was clumsy, if not entirely chaotic. "There was no teamwork, but each man did his best," Naismith wrote of his guinea pigs.

His students greatly enjoyed the new sport, even if they stunk at it. In other words, if you ever obtain access to a time machine, don't waste it on a trip to Springfield, Massachusetts, in 1891 to watch the first basketball game. Go somewhere warm instead. (Florida before it became Florida, perhaps?) If you *really* want to bear witness to the birth of basketball, you'll have to use your imagination. Here are a few key visual cues that may help paint a picture of this particular New England moment.

Amazing facial hair, including a good number of jaunty walrus mustaches. Descriptions of the Springfield affair sometimes juvenilize the students, but they were hardly "boys," as Naismith called them during his radio appearance. The class was full of scruffy college-aged men who were studying to be YMCA secretaries. In the 1930s, a committee of physical education administrators wanted to re-create that first game at a convention, but Naismith thought they would have trouble finding "eighteen young men with the proper facial adornment" in those modern times and denied permission. They, too, would have to settle for their imaginations.

An extremely crowded court. Each team had nine men per side, and everyone played at the same time. Substitutions weren't invented until the following year, after a game at Cornell featured more than a hundred players on the floor at once. The teacher there cut the contest short because, as Naismith writes, "there was a danger of serious damage to the building."

Those peach baskets. Naismith wanted boxes, eighteen inches square, but the YMCA building superintendent could only supply two round baskets from the storeroom. Naismith nailed them to the lower balcony railings on each side of the gym. They happened to be ten feet high, and that measurement is one of the only facets of the game that has remained consistent throughout the sport's history. (Modern rims, as a matter of coincidence, are eighteen inches in diameter.)

A stepladder propped up against the wall. The baskets lacked holes in their bottoms and, in the event of a made shot, Naismith's assistant would climb a small ladder to retrieve the ball. Successful shots were a rarity in basketball's early days, and there is at least one recorded instance of a ball retriever becoming so bored during a game that he left the gym and caused a delay.

The game itself. It was static and looked nothing like basketball as we know it. Seems odd, but that's exactly how Naismith drew it up.

Naismith's game sprouted from a restriction. He believed the best way to curtail violence was to prevent players from moving when in possession of the ball. In his book he describes this realization as a eureka moment that begat the rest of his sport:

I sat erect at my desk and said aloud: "If he can't run with the ball, we don't have to tackle; and if we don't have to tackle, the roughness will be eliminated." I can still recall how I snapped my fingers and shouted, "I've got it!"

You'll probably notice that this epiphany is in direct opposition to the spirit of modern basketball. In fact, only a few of Naismith's original rules are essential or even applicable to the game as it is played today. The "no running" edict became Rule 3, and everything else grew from there. It took Naismith about an hour to jot down the outline for his invention, and he pinned the list of rules to the gymnasium's bulletin board before the incorrigibles gathered for their 11:30 A.M. class:

1. The ball may be thrown in any direction with one or both hands.

2. The ball may be batted in any direction with one or both hands (never with the fist).

3. A player cannot run with the ball. The player must throw it from the spot on which he catches it; allowance to be made for a man who catches the ball when running at a good speed.

4. The ball must be held in or between the hands; the arms or body must not be used for holding it.

5. No shouldering, holding, pushing, tripping, or striking in any way the person of an opponent shall be allowed; the first infringement of this rule by any player shall count as a foul, the second shall disqualify him until the next goal is made, or, if there was evident intent to injure the person, for the whole of the game, no substitute allowed.

6. A foul is striking at the ball with the fist, violation of Rules 3, 4, and such as described in Rule 5.

7. If either side makes three consecutive fouls, it shall count as a goal for the opponents (consecutive means without the opponents in the mean time making a foul).

8. A goal shall be made when the ball is thrown or batted from the grounds into the basket and stays there, providing those defending the goal do not touch or disturb the goal. If the ball rests on the edge and the opponent moves the basket, it shall count as a goal.

9. When the ball goes out of bounds, it shall be thrown into the field of play by the person first touching it. In case of a dispute, the umpire shall throw it straight into the field. The thrower-in is allowed five seconds; if he holds it longer, it shall go to the opponent. If any side persists in delaying the game, the umpire shall call a foul on that side.

10. The umpire shall be judge of the men and shall note the fouls and notify the referee when three consecutive fouls have been made. He shall have power to disqualify men according to Rule 5.

11. The referee shall be judge of the ball and shall decide when the ball is in play, in bounds, to which side it belongs, and shall keep the time. He shall decide when a goal has been made, and keep account of the goals with any other duties that are usually performed by a referee.

12. The time shall be two 15-minute halves, with five minutes' rest between.

13. The side making the most goals in that time shall be declared the winner. In case of a draw, the game may, by agreement of the captains, be continued until another goal is made.

Let's ignore the content of these rules for a moment so we can better appreciate them as a historical document. What Naismith accomplished is truly astounding. Football, baseball, soccer, and hockey all evolved over centuries

from various folk games. Basketball, meanwhile, sprouted from the brain of a thirty-year-old Canadian gym teacher shortly after breakfast. Even the world's most seductive religions and cults would envy how fast and far Naismith's game has spread. Basketball is the second most popular sport in the world to play. In 2017, nearly 190 million people watched the NBA Finals in China, and that number only accounts for those who viewed the games on their mobile phones. Not bad for a guy who was just trying to keep eighteen mustachioed jerks entertained for an hour.

The incorrigibles were the first to fall in love with basketball, and they took to the sport immediately. The students introduced it to friends at home during winter break, and requests soon filtered in from around the country for the official rules. In January 1982, the YMCA newspaper the *Triangle* printed Naismith's instructions under the headline, "A New Game." More requests came in, but this time they were for clarification: the *Triangle*'s editors forgot to specify the kind of ball that should be used. (It was a soccer ball.) They also left out the court's measurements and the fact that the baskets were to be elevated. Who knows what kind of bizarre games were being played in YMCAs across the country before those omissions were corrected? But none of it mattered in the long run. The game was an instant hit. Somehow.

Put yourself in the position of a YMCA administrator or student in the late nineteenth century. You open the newspaper and read Naismith's rules. Do they make you want to drop what you're doing, pick up an unspecified ball, and, in the words of its creator, "bat it from the grounds into a basket"?

I must admit that, to my untrained eyes, Naismith's original game doesn't exactly capture the imagination. It's halting. There are too many ejections. The umpire essentially maintains power of attorney over the players. Surely, I must be missing something, for Aristotelian logic *proves* that Naismith's original rules were engaging:

1. Students at the YMCA would have stopped playing basketball if they weren't having fun.

2. That was in 1891. It is currently the twenty-first century and I am writing a book about basketball.

3. Therefore, basketball was fun in 1891.

As countless ancient Athenians can attest, there's no use in arguing with Aristotle. I'm clearly reading the rules incorrectly; even the incorrigibles were able to properly interpret and turn them into a good time. What about Naismith's design, exactly, was divine?

• • •

GAMES ARE PECULIAR things. They are the only pursuit in which rules are used to facilitate fun. That's the goal, and those who create games must dole and winnow restrictions like a chef picking ingredients.

Game designer as a job title didn't exist in 1891, but Naismith fit that description to a T. College students can major in game design nowadays and, if they do, Eric Zimmerman might be one of their professors. He teaches at NYU's Game Center and is a cofounder and the CEO of Gamelab, the first video game studio to receive a grant from the MacArthur Foundation. Zimmerman rose to prominence designing computer games (his most famous creation is the mid-aughts PC hit *Diner Dash*), but he teaches his students how to make games in all types of media, starting with basic board games.

I sent him the original thirteen rules for basketball to gauge whether or not Naismith nailed it on his first try. "From a design point of view, I think it's interesting," Zimmerman says. "From a presentational point of view, if a student turned this in, I would tell them they need to do some work on these. If you think about a tabletop game, the rulebook is a whole experience."

True, the list Naismith pinned to the YMCA bulletin board was hardly eye-catching. But he wasn't interested in art—he just wanted to keep his students from coldcocking each other. "I'm not criticizing him," Zimmerman says. "I'm just making an observation that these rules are clearly functional in that sense." For a game designer, the word "functional" sheds its utilitarian connotation and instead refers to something much more enjoyable.

"One of the paradoxes of game design is that the creativity of play is made possible by play's opposite, which are rules," he says. "Rules are in essence constraints, but games don't feel that way. Basketball is an amazing example of this. When the rules are activated, what follows is fluid, unpredictable magic. If you read the rules, you would never guess that's what emerges." But Naismith's original rules resulted in clumsy, low scoring affairs. Where does the magic come in?

Zimmerman gives his classes an assignment where they try to improve tic-tac-toe. He asks them to write out the game's existing rules on the whiteboard and then has them brainstorm gameplay adjustments that will ideally create a totally new experience. "My favorite variation was when the students altered just one rule: If you get three in a row, you lose. It was a small tweak, but it completely changed everything. I just thought it was so elegant."

A game becomes exponentially more fun once its players learn to get creative within its boundaries. It's less about following the rules and more about filling in the gaps that exist between them. Zimmerman uses poker as an example. "There's nothing in the rules about bluffing," he says. "There's not a rule that says you can lie if you don't have a good hand. It's intrinsic to the system. Bluffing is an emergent property that appears out of the negative space of the rules." For a game designer, this is *everything*. It's how a snow-day diversion evolves into a global phenomenon. "I'm getting chills just talking about it," he says.

With his background in video game design, Zimmerman is attuned to seeing games as products, and basketball's journey through the marketplace follows a familiar path. "If you think about it, the YMCA was the platform for that game in the way that a Nintendo Switch is a platform for a piece of software," he says. "As we say in the game industry, there was an embedded base." Had Naismith invented basketball outside the purview of the YMCA's worldwide network, it could have remained a regional curiosity and fizzled into obscurity.

Nevertheless, some YMCAs weren't prepared to handle this incredibly popular new game. The Philadelphia chapter banned basketball because participants and spectators overcrowded its facilities. Administrators eventually reinstated the sport when they realized it also functioned as their most successful recruitment tool.

This early reach wasn't limited to America. One of Naismith's classmates at the training school, Genzabaro Ishakawa, was from Japan, and he returned home with a guide to basketball. There is evidence that the game was played there as early as 1900. China, meanwhile, enjoyed the sport even before Japan, and it was introduced to the country in 1895 after a YMCA opened in Tianjin.

When basketball first appeared in the Olympics, in 1936, a Chinese referee officiated the gold medal game between Canada and the United States. Naismith was in attendance in Berlin and happily noted that "there was not a single questioning of [the official's] rulings" by the players. It was one of his favorite aspects of what must have been a surreal event for Naismith. Here was a referee who was born seven thousand miles away from the Springfield YMCA, and he's interpreting a version of the game rules Naismith had jotted down forty-five years before that trip to Europe. That moment of harmony also served as a sort of spiritual opposition to the horrendous backdrop of those Olympics. Nothing in Naismith's personal life would suggest that his journey to Germany was in any way an endorsement of the event's hosts. Back home he had long been staunchly against segregation and personally mentored John McLendon, University of Kansas's first black physical education major and the man who would eventually break the color barrier as a professional basketball coach.

To Naismith, the Olympics were above all a profoundly personal experience, and he couldn't hide his tears when teams from the Philippines, Uruguay, Estonia, and other nations took turns applauding him in the stands during a tip-off ceremony.

"Basketball is kind of a turning point in the history of games," Zimmerman says. "It occurred at a pivotal moment. In the twentieth century games gradually became authored media. They became something that's ascribed to a person or a team of people who made it."

Naismith had none of this in mind when he introduced the sport to his students on that snowy day in Springfield. In his book, he recalls that Frank Mahan, one of the rowdier incorrigibles, suggested the game be called "Naismith Ball." The teacher demurred and joked that this would immediately kill any interest in the activity.

"Why not call it basketball?" the student asked. He nailed it.

• • •

COLLEEN MACKLIN LOVES Naismith's first rule—"The ball may be thrown in any direction with one or both hands." She is a professor at the Parsons School of Design and the director of PETLab, an organization that develops experimental games for learning. It's some pretty heady stuff, which seems to be her specialty. "Lately I've been trying to make games that are ambient or in the background," she says. "I'm currently working on a game you play when you're not playing anything. You basically take weird topics and try to subtly weave them into conversation without anyone realizing it." I don't think she uses our phone call as an opportunity to play her creation, unless that means that I have already lost the game.

I read her basketball's first rule and the wheels start spinning. "Already I'm thinking about what I can do," she says. The rule follows a durable tenet of game design, one she credits to USC professor Tracy Fullerton: Begin with *What does a player get to do.* "What you're looking for with a game is spontaneity," Macklin says. "You want players to do things you didn't expect. Surprise is fun."

Naismith loved it when his students got creative (so long as they didn't knock each other unconscious), and he thought that basketball was uniquely suited to improve a person's ability to react to the unknown. "It is impossible to tell what an expert opponent will do," he writes in his book. "A player must react to the conditions without time for deliberation. He can not depend on the coach, but must face the emergency himself."

Both Zimmerman and Macklin refer me to "The Heresy of Zone Defense," an essay by art critic Dave Hickey that is especially revered by game designers. (Zimmerman says it's one of the best things ever written on the subject.) What does an art critic think about basketball? Well, for one thing, Hickey wishes art was more like Naismith's sport. In writing about Julius Erving's famous behind-the-backboard layup from the 1980 NBA Finals, he examines how this spontaneous response to restrictive elements of the game (defense, the backboard, the out-of-bounds borders, etc.) created a moment of joy. Fans witnessed "the triumph of civil society in an act that was clearly the product of talent and will accommodating itself to liberating rules." Hickey flows from Dr. J to Jackson Pollock's drip paintings and explains how the latter artist's act of defiance eventually became a "prohibitive, institutional edict" taught in art schools. Following the rules can be groovy, but only if they're enforced for the right reasons.

"The trick of civilization lies in recognizing the moment when a rule ceases to liberate and begins to govern," Hickey writes. "Basketball has been supreme in recognizing this moment of portending government and in deflecting it." In evolving to welcome these liberating forces, Naismith's sport manages to out-avant-garde the avant-garde. "Once you learn what to watch in this game (basically, everything), it is civilized complexity incarnate—quite literally made flesh," Hickey argues. "This is not to say that basketball is a religion. It is better than a religion."

As such, a successful game welcomes change. Macklin and Zimmerman worked together, along with John Sharp, to create the Metagame, a card game about games that was originally intended to be played by game designers at a game design conference. (Hence, "meta.") In some ways, it's the opposite of basketball. Whereas Naismith wrote his rules by purposefully avoiding or countering specific aspects of other sports, the Metagame absorbs and pays homage to a myriad of different titles. Naismith removed the contact from football and the kicking from soccer, and while he momentarily considered using a lacrosse net, he instead opted for the goal to be on a horizontal plane in order to encourage delicate, parabolic throws. The Metagame, meanwhile, can incorporate the guessing of charades, the questions of Trivial Pursuit, and the subjective zaniness of Apples to Apples. Macklin and Zimmerman worked on this creation for about a decade, and they still release updates online. "We have one hundred versions," Macklin tells me. "Literally." The

start of the design process was clear, but when, exactly, is it finished? When is any game finished?

"What you're trying to do is carve a narrow set of rules out of a possibility space that's multidimensional, so it's pretty challenging to get to the point where something is 'done,' " Macklin says. "You know when a game is done when the date comes that you've promised to deliver it. Kind of a facetious answer, but it's actually true." In fact, the director of the Springfield YMCA gave Naismith two weeks to tame the incorrigibles, and he wrote the rules for basketball right at the end of his deadline.

While Naismith's project was delivered on time, it will never be finished. It is with this thought that Macklin mentions Dave Hickey's wonderful essay about Dr. J, art, and religion. The art critic argues that the perpetual evolution of basketball and its rules is special because the changes are usually "made in the interest of aesthetics."

"That is amazing when you think about it," Macklin says. "A lot of game rules are modified or changed based on what the player wants. Basketball rules are modified in order to make the game more interesting to the spectator." When she watches basketball, she sees players both following and exploiting rules for the benefit of us fans. The result, she says, is "one of the most beautiful things you can see."

Macklin loves Hickey's example of the Dr. J behind-the-backboard layup, as it alludes to the kinds of decisions game designers must make. "When it happened," she says, "everyone was like, 'Oh my God, we've never seen such a graceful move before.' And so you have a choice there. The NBA could either say it's not allowed, or they could be like, 'Yeah, let's let that happen.' The right choice is obviously 'let's let that happen.' "

Despite his humble expectations, Naismith always wanted to create something that was pleasing to the eye. Basketball would have "a definite place in a program of physical education," he wrote, "first, because it is attractive."

It worked. Within two weeks of the first game, around two hundred spectators filled the YMCA gallery to watch Naismith's class. Backboards—the impediment Dr. J so gracefully transcended—were actually invented in response to the sport's overwhelming popularity. Obnoxious fans so frequently reached over the balcony to swat away goal-bound shots that physical blockades had to be installed. By interfering with games in the 1890s, fans inadvertently established the conditions under which one of the sport's most incredible moments could occur nearly a hundred years in the future. That's one hell of an assist.

Not all of Naismith's ideas were winners and, as we're chatting, Zimmerman zeroes in on an obvious dud. "One of the rules that struck me was, 'When the ball goes out of bounds, it shall be thrown into the field and played by the person first touching it.' Does that mean that you just go running for the ball?"

He is referring to Rule 9, which is indeed a juicy slice of madness. Considering the explicitly stated goal of basketball was to keep players from colliding into one another, it's rather surprising that there would be a rule that calls for a total melee whenever the ball leaves the field of play. In his book, Naismith wrote about the pitfalls of this rule and how a student named Lloyd Ware took "great pleasure, when in a jovial mood, in exhibiting a scar that he got when he dived for the ball and came into contact with the sharp corner of a radiator."

During an early YMCA game, the ball landed in the balcony and one team sprinted up the stairwell to go get it. As Naismith remembered it, "two of the players on the other team boosted one of their mates up until he could catch the lower part of the balcony, swing himself up, and regain the out-of-bounds ball."

The rule was soon tweaked to award possession to the player *holding* the ball (rather than merely touching it), but this only accelerated the violence. "During that year there were so many fights that the rules committee returned to the original wording of the rule," Naismith wrote. For a considerable chunk of basketball's adolescence, the problem was solved by erecting cages around the courts.

A version of the current out-of-bounds rule wouldn't be established until 1913, but this obvious flaw didn't slow the sport's growth. "You can tell that Naismith was thinking about exceptions," Zimmerman says of that first set of rules. "Trying to figure out the loopholes players will try to exploit." But the exploitation of rules is vital to a game's evolution. Essentially everything related to basketball that isn't contained within its original thirteen rules developed because some player somewhere at some time fudged with them.

Game designers encourage this type of behavior and establish conditions where players can freely experiment within (and with) the rules. These are called "playtests," and they are used to gather feedback before a game is sold commercially. Basketball has been in the throes of an ongoing playtest for more than a hundred years. The sport has always been fun to play, but it is worth watching because players are constantly experimenting within its constraints, bending (or outright ignoring) them when needed. That the game still manages to surprise us is a testament to its good design.

• • •

THE SHIP OF Theseus is an extremely straightforward thought experiment, as far as metaphysics goes. There is a boat. When its crew spots a few rusted bolts, they swap them out for fresh ones. Later, a rotted piece of the hull is pried free and they patch over the space with a new plank. This process gets repeated over time until, one day, each and every component of the ship has been replaced. Is it still the same boat?

It's a fun little parable that can apply to all types of scenarios, hence my propensity to blurt out "Ah yes, just like the Ship of Theseus" whenever I happen to find myself in a conversation about philosophy. It doesn't always track, but Francisco Javier López Frías understands what I'm getting at.

Frías teaches kinesiology and philosophy at Penn State and dedicates much of his research to understanding ethical and philosophical quandaries as they relate to sports. We're talking about basketball, and I have been trying to reconcile the sport we watch today with the one Naismith invented in 1891. It is highly unlikely the two would ever be mistaken for each other, but we nevertheless understand them to be materially one and the same. What, exactly, makes basketball *basketball*? The whole thing is a little confusing. You know, just like the Ship of Theseus.

It's not just basketball. Most sports undergo observable changes over time. Frías mentions soccer, which sprouted from various ancient games but is still evolving. When he watches matches from the 1950s and 1960s, he can't ignore that they appear to be, by his estimation, "at least 80 percent" different from their modern iterations. "How do we determine that that sport is still soccer?"

Some philosophers take the "nominalistic" route with this quandary. "We give that sport a name, and as long as people identify it with that name and call it that name, then it is that sport," Frías says. "I don't agree with that position." The approach is a pretty simplistic one, and we're not even taking into account the obvious wrinkle that "soccer" is known as "football" pretty much everywhere else in the world. Consider that an own goal for nominalism.

"My take on it would be that soccer is still soccer or basketball is still basketball because the basic set of skills or the basic set of experiences are still the same," he says. "In basketball, you have to pass and shoot in order to score more points than the opponent. In soccer, you still have to kick the ball around and combine with your teammates. The number of teammates or number of players on the field can vary depending on the type of soccer you are playing, but the basic abilities or the basic experiences upon which the sport is built are the same ones."

Frías argues this maintains cohesion not just over time but across skill sets as well. "You can look at pickup friendly games. You can look at high-level professional games. You ask practitioners, players, they all are going to tell you that one of the reasons why they engage with the sport is because that sport provides them with experiences they cannot find anywhere else," he says. "There are the things you have to do with your body, I call them 'embodied' or 'bodied' experiences that you can only get in a specific sport. It is based on those experiences that we try to change the rules or try to adjust the sport so we can get more valuable or richer experiences."

Someone blessed with a more refined philosophical mind than my own would perhaps use this moment to peel away the layers of this metaphysical onion known as "experience," but I'm still stuck on the boat thing. What if the rudder is not merely replaced, but upgraded? What if its cloth sails are swapped out for ones made from durable polymers? What if . . . I don't know any other nautical terms?

"Even though the different parts of the ship have changed, it is still the ship." Frías says. "The question is, is it the same ship?" He takes the briefest of pauses before answering his own query. "If the people who have made the changes to the ship still think about the ship as being the same ship and nothing essential has changed, well, it is roughly the same ship. I would say the same thing about the sport."

You don't need to understand all the specific things that make basketball *basketball*; you just need to appreciate how they work together.

When Naismith wrote his book, he proudly stated that the "fundamental principles on which the game was founded" remained intact. "When the question is asked, 'What is the biggest change in basketball?' it is easy for me to answer. There is no doubt in my mind that it is the skill of the players and the kinds of plays that have been adopted."

The boat may have looked different after all that time, but Naismith still recognized it as the one he had built. He didn't much object to the direction in which it was sailing, either.

• • •

LET'S TALK ABOUT Naismith's book for a moment. *Basketball: Its Origin and Development* was published in December 1941 to coincide with the fiftieth anniversary of the sport's invention. You may notice that this is the same month the Empire of Japan attacked Pearl Harbor and thrust the United States into World War II. With America at the fulcrum of history, James Naismith's little book about basketball wound up getting completely ignored.

It was a tough break for a first-time author who had spent his final years putting the details of his legacy to paper. The text is concise and clear, though that is a clue that Naismith didn't write it himself. In the introduction to a 1996 edition, history professor William J. Baker writes that Naismith was "literarily disinclined" and that his "spelling and grammar were poor." Naismith's oldest son Jack attempted to transcribe the memoir for him but couldn't deal with his father's meandering, repetitive speaking style and instead outsourced the task to one of his English professors for $150. (She is not credited by name anywhere in the text.)

Despite her help, *Basketball: Its Origin and Development* feels a little lopsided in parts. There is no mention of the score from that first-ever game, but there is a lengthy section later in the book featuring data from a 1925 high school basketball tournament, included in which is a detailed table documenting the teenagers' urinalysis results. (Naismith's assistant, a Mr. C. E. Rowe, collected samples from every winning team over a four-day span. "His work was invaluable," Naismith recalls.)

I mention all this because, while his book purports to be the definitive story of the earliest days of basketball, it is actually a heavily edited retelling that's twice removed from its original source. It serves as a decent metaphor for basketball itself—a sport that, in its current form, looks absolutely nothing like the game Naismith invented.

I realize that I have been a little tough on our old friend James. I've described him as a barely literate fabulist, and that is a terribly unfair assessment. Naismith was, by all accounts, a kindhearted man who was genuinely concerned about the education and well-being of young people. In fact, basketball's popularity is a direct result of his generous and egalitarian nature. Were he just a hair less humble, he would have exerted more ownership over the invention and stifled its growth. He never patented his game and expressed no interest in making money from it. When a lawyer suggested he could claim a percentage of the profits from tickets sold to every basketball game, Naismith chased the man out of his office.

Naismith will slowly fade in the rearview as we venture beyond the environs of the Springfield YMCA. This is a shame, as I've grown rather fond of him. He was a delightfully odd man, the kind of sweet eccentric who brought his dog along on his honeymoon. The honeymoon took place aboard a twenty-two-foot boat, and both wife and dog were seasick for the entire trip.

Here's another example of just how weird James Naismith was: Despite inventing basketball, he only played the sport two times in his entire life. His team in one of those games, the YMCA teachers, lost 5–1. Their lone basket came from Naismith's friend A. A. Stagg, a man who would go on to become a pioneer of American football. (Naismith and his wife Maude invented an early flannel version of the football helmet. It was an attempt to prevent cauliflower ear, an ailment Naismith picked up while playing center for the YMCA Training School's gridiron squad.) When University of Kansas was looking for a director for its physical education department in 1898, Stagg suggested Naismith, whom he described as the "inventor of basket-ball, medical doctor, Presbyterian minister, tee-totaler, all-around athlete, non-smoker, and owner of a vocabulary without cuss words."

Naismith also agreed to coach University of Kansas's basketball team, even though he thought players should be left to their own devices while on the court. He called coaches who micromanaged "evil," and he more or less allowed his team to do as they pleased.

He refereed many of his own team's games during those early years and was unflinchingly fair. Kansas lost a good number of these self-officiated contests, including the university's first-ever game, a 16–5 defeat to the Kansas City YMCA. Their opponents played rough, but when Naismith called fouls on them, the young men from Kansas City told him he was mistaken and then kept on playing without punishment.

In his final year as head coach, an article in the *University Daily Kansan* questioned his commitment to success. "Dr. James Naismith, the inventor of the game, is so busy with his work as athletic director that he rarely finds time to give the men thorough training." He never thought winning was all that important, and his record during his nine-season run as Kansas's coach reflected this: 55 wins, 60 losses.

Kansas became a basketball powerhouse soon after Naismith stepped away from the sidelines. According to Rob Rains's biography of Naismith, he spent his post-coaching years teaching and working on medical experiments. These included a sobriety-tester and a proprietary method for determining whether or not someone was a natural athlete. According to a former student, Naismith blindfolded his subjects, clogged their ears, and put them behind the wheel of a car. If they could sustain a speed of thirty-five miles per hour, that meant they had "great kinesthetic sense." Read into this what you will, but Naismith himself was a terrible driver, with or without the blindfold.

Naismith also invented a medieval rack-like machine that he believed would make people taller. He told the school newspaper that babies between the ages of five months and one year should be stretched on the device. His only concern, he said, was that the children may never stop growing.

Unlike his baby torturing machine, basketball actually works. It's a stupendous invention, though it didn't gain him ubiquitous recognition as a household name. Once, when visiting his son in Iowa, Naismith popped into a gym at Morningside College to watch a pickup game. The boys needed a referee, and one suggested the quiet, bespectacled man with the center-part for the job. "Come on! That old duffer never saw a game of basketball," exclaimed another student. Naismith found the ordeal hilarious.

Nearly a decade after Naismith's death, his daughter wrote to legendary Kansas basketball coach and Naismith protégé Phog Allen to complain about the glaring lack of recognition on campus for her father. There wasn't so much as a plaque to commemorate his accomplishments. Allen wrote back that he had suggested dedicating the new stadium to her father, but the idea was rejected by university officials. A few years later, Allen Fieldhouse, named for Phog, opened to great fanfare. A tough break, but I don't think Naismith would have been too bothered by it. Going by his own words, "There is no place in basketball for the egotist."

• • •

I CAN TRUST game designers to approach Naismith's rules from a different place than I normally would. This led to the discovery that their own understanding of rules in general has been shaped, in part, by an art critic's essay about Dr. J. Passionate and smart people tend to be excited and informed about more than just their jobs, and basketball provides some surprisingly bountiful ground on which to excavate these observations. I may not be the smartest guy in the room (any room, you pick), but at least I can always talk about basketball. After all, Naismith intended for it to be enjoyed by everyone.

During basketball's earliest days, a group of female teachers from the Buckingham Grade School for girls wandered into the YMCA and watched the incorrigibles shoot at those peach baskets. When they asked Naismith whether girls could play, he reserved time at the gym and invited them to try it out with their students. As such, one of the first basketball games in history was played by young women, and this happened at a time when girls were otherwise prohibited from participating in team sports at all.

Naismith helped organize the first women's basketball tournament in 1892, and through it he met a star on a team of YMCA stenographers named Maude who would later become his wife. (Had Maude known that she'd eventually have to share her honeymoon quarters with a seasick dog, she might have reconsidered her decision.) Naismith actively promoted the women's game throughout his life, and in his book he proudly states that "girls have made far greater strides in physical education in the past twenty-five years than boys." After attending a women's tournament in Wichita, Kansas, in the 1930s, Naismith noted that he "had not seen a boys' game during the entire season that would compare in speed, accuracy of passing, and teamwork with that of the girls."

Basketball has a wide appeal, and that is precisely what Naismith intended for his game. Given what we know about the sport evolving in response to the whims of its players, it surely benefited from its uniquely diverse pool of influence. Celebrating this is a fine way to promote Naismith's legacy. At the very least, we know it's more effective than releasing his book right after Pearl Harbor.

• • •

NAISMITH DIDN'T LOVE *all* the changes to his sport. Roughness had found its way into basketball shortly after he stopped coaching and, upon watching a foul-heavy 1910 contest between Kansas and Missouri, Naismith reportedly exclaimed, "They are killing my game!" He felt the referees needed to be more authoritative, perhaps forgetting that he had let a team of young men from the Kansas City YMCA ignore his foul calls back when he was moonlighting as an official.

One of his more prescient concerns had little to do with on-court action. In 1911, Naismith published an editorial in a Kansas magazine lambasting "commercialization in sports." He adamantly opposed money's role in collegiate basketball and abhorred the "worship of the dollar in the field of athletics." He had invented his game to be a "laboratory in which the great moral lessons of fair play and the square deal are . . . taught," and he believed these to be incompatible with capitalistic greed. In other words, were he alive today, Naismith would probably choose to avoid the Capital One® NCAA® March Madness® Bracket Challenge.

But the sport was at the mercy of the unknown from the moment those students picked up the ball. To his credit, Naismith was open to growth. "I am not worried about the future of basketball," he wrote in his book. "The game itself is interesting no matter how you fool with it."

That may be true, but the sport is also interesting *because* you fool with it. Just ask a game designer. "Games are the democratic art form," Colleen

Macklin tells me. "That is the beauty of a physical game. You don't have to be a programmer or an artist to make changes. The rules can be modified and tweaked and played with by regular humans."

There's some nice irony to all of this. While basketball is the only major sport that can be traced to a single person, that person's most important contribution was that he relinquished control of his invention. The game has never been perfect. That was the case on day one, whether or not Naismith's students ripped each other's limbs off. It continues to be a work in progress, and, as far as group projects go, it has been miraculously successful.

Can basketball teach us anything about the world? What about the inverse—is there some unified wisdom that has telescoped itself to fit through a burnt-orange hoop? This book doesn't purport to answer either of those questions, but feel free to fill in the negative spaces as you would with those between the rules of a game.

I'm confident that basketball can provide us with at least one valuable lesson, which is that you can keep a bunch of rowdy brats from beating on each other by giving them a ball and two peach baskets. If the game can teach us *two* valuable lessons, consider what Naismith learned: There's no way of knowing what will happen to the things we make. The fun is in the surprise.

My favorite example of this comes from Naismith's wonderfully imperfect book. He recalls walking through the Springfield YMCA gymnasium and seeing a young man "toss the ball toward the basket, recover it, and toss it again." When he returned about an hour later, the student was still at it. Puzzled, Naismith asked what he was doing. "The boy answered that he did not know, but that he just liked to see if he could make a basket every time he threw the ball."

It hadn't occurred to Naismith that people would actually practice his game. Foresight, it turns out, is not an essential quality in an inventor.

MAKING A BAD RULE DISAPPEAR

Dribbling's outlaw illusionists

L IKE THE LIFEGUARD at a public pool, James Naismith had a crystal-clear policy regarding running. It was Rule 3—"A player cannot run with the ball"—and he structured the entire sport of basketball around it. Ignoring this command would be an affront to the original spirit of his game, and only the most self-involved and petulant would dare transgress such a clear edict without guilt or shame. Sounds like a job for Yale.

The Yale basketball team didn't acknowledge that they were breaking the rules when they started dribbling. This was around 1896, and they did it under the guise of "passing to themselves." It was a clever workaround, the kind of sly approach you would expect from a team of future white-shoe litigators and society page heavies. Those early Yale squads were among college basketball's most successful, and one can't help but wonder what their opponents thought as they jauntily bounced around the gym and toward victory.

The story of dribbling could have ended right there as a simple morality play about Ivy League entitlement but for the fact that dribbling was a *fantastic* idea. Naismith gave it a hearty endorsement, calling it "one of the most spectacular and exciting maneuvers in basketball."

Those Yalies weren't the first people to come up with a workaround for Rule 3, but theirs was far better than the era's other clumsy attempts to bring movement to the game. As Naismith notes in his book, players who found themselves cornered would "lose possession of the ball voluntarily" and roll it to a space where they had a decent chance of retrieving it. Dribbling was a refined extension of this strategic attrition, though new rules had to be put in place to assure it didn't get out of hand. According to Naismith, "It was not uncommon to see a player running down the floor, juggling the ball a few inches above his head." (Picture a child trying to keep a beach balloon airborne while she sprints across the sand and you'll get the idea.)

All's well that ends well and whatnot, but can we really ignore the glaringly unavoidable truth at the heart of this whole dribbling affair? Rule 3 is clear and Yale broke it. What can you call that other than "cheating"?

"It is a subversion," Dr. Shawn Klein, a philosophy lecturer at Arizona State University, tells me. Klein specializes in the ethics of sport, and I reached out to him to better understand the moral (or amoral) underpinnings of dribbling. "That's probably the best word for it. They were adhering to the rules, but they were subverting the expectations of how those rules would be followed."

We're more than a century removed from its invention, so I think it's safe to say that basketball is objectively better thanks to dribbling. "In the creation of any game, there are gaps," Klein says. "The players discover these ambiguities and vaguenesses in the rules. It's a way that the game evolves." While board games may come to mind for some, Klein cites high jumper Dick Fosbury, who shocked the track and field world at the 1968 Summer Olympics when he cleared the bar backward. He won gold, and the "Fosbury Flop" became the standard technique used throughout the sport.

"Not being allowed to move with the ball was probably a glaring problem with basketball early on," Klein says. "The sport wouldn't still exist and be successful without that subversion." But for the game to really evolve, changes had to be made to more than just the rules.

Basketball was originally played with a soccer ball, and Naismith asked former baseball pitcher A. G. Spalding to create a ball specifically for his new sport in 1894. With a suture of thick threads, his design looked like it had escaped from Dr. Frankenstein's laboratory. The stitched gash greatly affected how the ball moved, and Spalding's monster would have had to have been deliberately bounced on its smoother panels to prevent it from careening in unintended directions. Dribbling was hardly a natural maneuver, and this remained the case until the invention of the seam-free basketball in 1929. Still wary of that once-unruly sphere, players tended to bounce with caution, but a few rogue souls experimented with "trick" dribbling—crisscrosses and other moves that are now considered normal but were perceived as a kind of sorcery back then.

Of those show-offs, Marques Haynes was a dribbler without equal. Haynes rose to prominence with the Harlem Globetrotters in the late 1940s before splintering off to create his own team of barnstormers, the Fabulous Magicians. The name was neither exaggeration nor shallow homage, for he and his squad entertained audiences and baffled hapless opponents with feats of basketball sleight-of-hand. A *Boys' Life* article from the time describes a Magicians' performance in an exhibition game against a high school alumni team from Plainfield, New Jersey:

[Haynes] started to dribble. The player guarding him darted for the ball and presto! the ball and dribbler were gone, both working their magic on another victim across the court. . . . The crowd screamed and applauded and stamped its feet. Strangers looked at each other, shook their heads and smiled. They had heard about the man and his dribbling, and hadn't believed it. Now they had seen for themselves, and they still didn't believe it.

Haynes confided to the *Boys' Life* reporter that, despite the audience's reaction, the Magicians' show was a bit of a disappointment. "I could have done more against a more experienced team," he said. Haynes's opponents weren't good enough to convincingly pursue all his feints and misdirections. "These boys just weren't in shape."

Haynes elevated ballhandling to a form of stagecraft, though this style of dribbling has become so common we now expect to see it at all levels of the game. If a point guard can't shake a defender with a little misdirection, then she really isn't much of a point guard. Today, dribbling exists as a means of moving with the ball much like a dazzling assistant exists to provide help onstage. There's nothing inherently deceitful about it, but if she happens to get sawed in half . . . well, that's just part of the gig.

According to magician Jamy Ian Swiss's book *Shattering Illusions*, the "basic definition of magic" is to "fool the audience." Assuming you consider your opponent to be your audience, then a decent crossover can be a heck of a magic trick.

It also helps that basketballs happen to be preternaturally distracting. In a video made by the Visual Cognition Laboratory at the University of Illinois, six people dribble and toss basketballs to each other. Test subjects watching the footage were asked to do something trivial, like count the number of bounces and report back to the researchers with a summary of what they saw. The neuroscientists weren't interested in how many dribbles they were able to tally—they were curious as to whether or not the respondents noticed the person wandering in the background wearing a gorilla suit. Those who didn't notice the intrusive ape were too busy focusing on the basketball.

• • •

THE PREDICTABILITY OF a basketball's bounce—something that didn't exist with Spalding's early model—is key to its effectiveness as a tool for misdirection. A defender assumes to know where the ball is going, thus putting himself at risk for humiliation. When those Yale students first started dribbling, it was anyone's guess as to where the ball would end up, and ball handlers didn't gain a real advantage until all the seams were ironed out. Appropriately, the most recent advancement in trick dribbling came as a result of a basketball that didn't quite behave as players expected it to.

In 2006, the NBA unveiled a revamped official ball that was made out of synthetic materials. Spalding (the corporate descendant of Naismith's old pal) promised more grip with its "Cross Traxxion" microfiber, and the company wasn't kidding. "The ball tears my fingers apart," Phoenix Suns point guard Steve Nash said, his bandaged hands evidence for all to see. Sharpshooter Ray Allen, meanwhile, resorted to heavy lotion use. "My fingers are cracking and it's causing splits on my fingertips," he told reporters. The league finally withdrew the ball after two months of player complaints, but one part of its legacy stuck.

During preseason that year, point guard Chris Paul (then with the New Orleans Hornets) noticed that he could take advantage of the new ball in strange ways. "I could actually throw it out away, really far from me, and it

The yo-yo ball trick.

1.
2.
3.
4.

can still come back," he later recalled. The ball would begin its journey looking like a bounce pass but then spin back to Paul, allowing him to continue his dribble. Defenders scrambled to intercept the pass but, by the time they got to their spot, the ball was already back in Paul's hands. "I'm not dunking over anybody," the six-foot Paul said, "so I've got to come up with little tricks like that."

The move briefly disappeared when the league stopped using the synthetic ball, but Paul kept practicing and learned how to perform a version of the "Yo-Yo Dribble" with the NBA's reinstated equipment. Other players have added the move to their repertoires to varying degrees of success. "I realized how hard it was," Damian Lillard of the Portland Trail Blazers said. "So I was like, 'I ain't even gonna mess with it.' "

When executed with enough dexterity, the Yo-Yo Dribble can fool even the most stout defenders. But is it magic? I posed this question to Joe Pon, owner of Misdirections Magic Shop in San Francisco's Sunset District. Pon is considered to be something of a Jedi Master within the magic community. Professional and amateur magicians from around the globe travel to California to seek his advice, and the walls of his shop are plastered with pictures of him hanging out with famous illusionists. When I visit, he's helping a man who describes himself as "The Silicon Valley Magician" refine a trick that involves an array of cards. I'm second in line, behind a Frenchman who patiently puffs on his vape pen.

"Open your eyes!" the Silicon Valley Magician says with a burst of gusto. "One of the cards is gone!"

"Ehh," Pon mutters. "Stay quiet. She should discover the missing card herself."

"But what if someone in the audience says something?"

Pon shoos me and the Frenchman away from the counter so he can counsel his charge in private. The two men exchange whispers and the Silicon Valley Magician stiffens. "I don't want to lie to them," he exclaims.

It's going to be a long lesson.

The shop is small and organized in varying degrees of clutter. The first thing you see is merchandise intended for tourists. More pranks than magic, these are the fart powders, exploding golf balls, and squirting lapel pins displayed neatly in the front and along the side wall. (I spent a considerable amount of time browsing this section.) Inside the glass counters are magic kits and accoutrements dedicated to the craft—decks of cards, suspicious coins, stainless steel rings—laid out haphazardly atop black velvet.

Behind the counters and sectioned off from civilians is the area where Pon keeps the good stuff. Orbs and jewels crowd the shelves, the dustiness only adding to their mystique. There's an electric saw jutting out from an assistant-size box, and its power cord dangles tantalizingly close to an outlet on the wall. Mostly, though, there are books, and these are organized with their spines facing in. I have no clue how Pon knows which ones are which.

The Silicon Valley Magician finishes yet another trick. Pon looks for the vaping Frenchman, but he has excused himself to puff outside and I am invited up to the counter.

Pon is a basketball fan, but he says he hasn't heard of the Yo-Yo Dribble before. I show him a video on my phone of Paul performing it during a game. Pon chuckles and asks to see it again. It's certainly cool, but is it a magic trick?

"No," he says. "I would consider it a technique. In basketball it's about how I'm going to get to one side of the court to the other side. How am I going to get around my defender? Am I going to feint? Am I going to dribble between my legs? This is just one technique."

Pon was an acquaintance of Dr. Robert Albo, who was the Golden State Warriors' team physician for nearly forty years. Albo also happened to own the largest private collection of magic artifacts and tricks in the world, and the majority of these items were sold to David Copperfield after Albo's death in 2011. Albo was a standout basketball player at the University of California, though he didn't perform any sleight-of-hand on the court. A tough power forward, his value to the team was in his rebounding and grunt work. "He wasn't a great magician, either," Pon adds. "But he loved magic."

"There are no secrets in magic," Albo told the *San Francisco Examiner* in 1986. "Everything you see in magic today is simply an adaptation of an old principle." The same goes for basketball. Paul's Yo-Yo Dribble is an extension of the "Shammgod," a move in which a player performs a hard dribble forward and then pulls it back with his opposite hand before segueing into a crossover. It's named after its inventor, legendary New York streetballer God Shammgod. Shammgod only played twenty games in the NBA, but elite players still use his move to shake defenders and wow crowds. I show Pon a video of Brooklyn Nets guard D'Angelo Russell pulling off the Shammgod to gauge his reaction.

"Hmm. Still a technique."

"What would he have to do in order for you to consider it a magic trick?" I ask.

"Make the ball disappear," Pon deadpans.

The vaping Frenchman has returned, and, in the corner, the Silicon Valley Magician practices a numbers-guessing routine on him. I interrupt to show him the video of Russell.

"Not a magic trick," he says. "But he does use misdirection."

"He's using sleight-of-hand technique," adds Pon. "His opponent recognizes what's happening. See? He's too late, but he knows what's going on. That's not a magic trick."

I express some confusion, firmly outing myself as the only non-magician in Misdirections.

"I can make a coin disappear in twenty different ways," Pon says. "To a layperson, I just made a coin disappear. It's all the same to them, no matter how I do it." But if that person learns how it's performed? Then it's no longer a magic trick. "Now that you know the technique, I have no choice but to try and fool you in a different way."

The Silicon Valley Magician wants to show me a trick. "I just did this one for Google," he says. It's standard "pick a card, any card" fare, and, after a couple rounds of shuffling, he produces my seven of clubs. I'm entertained, but Pon isn't impressed.

"What's the hook?" he asks.

"I'm still developing it," the Silicon Valley Magician says. "Google liked it."

Pon pulls a copy of *Shattering Illusions* from a bookshelf behind the counter, and the cover earns an "ooooh" from the Silicon Valley Magician. This is the book I mentioned a few pages ago, the one that lists the basic definition of magic as "fooling the audience." That was a little bit of misdirection on my part, as I didn't provide the full context. Namely, what Jamy Ian Swiss writes immediately afterward: "But the problem is that for far too long magicians have stopped at that [definition] and gone no further. . . . A magician who has learned to fool the audience is little more than an actor who has learned to remember his lines and not bump into the furniture. It is a beginning."

Swiss's book is packed with bon mots and aphorisms. "I probably went a bit overboard with the epigraphs," he tells me over the phone. Swiss is prone to speaking in epigraphs as well ("Like my friend Max Maven says, 'All art embraces mystery but only magic is at its core fundamentally about mystery' "; "In the words of my friend Michael Weber, 'We don't keep secrets from you, we keep secrets for you' "). But Swiss is more than capable of being frank when he wants to be, as is the case when I ask about the connection between magic and basketball.

"I'm gonna blow your balloon here," he says. "Magic is magic. It's not anything else."

Swiss's son is a basketball fanatic, and the magician has been watching the sport with renewed interest lately. "There's a lot of deception to overcome defense," he says. "Make the guy think you're going one way and you open a hole and go the other way. But there are a lot of things in the world that involve deception that are not magic."

According to Swiss, "You can find hundreds of magicians who'll tell you that any deception is a form of magic." He's just not one of them. "Magic doesn't happen in the hands," he says. "It doesn't happen in the prop. It only happens in one place: the viewer's mind."

Marques Haynes of the Fabulous Magicians knew this. Enchantment was the goal, and his dribbling shows weren't about scoring points. If that were the case, he would have been thrilled at the prospect of facing an out-of-shape alumni team. His opponents were unwitting elements of an extended illusion, but in that specific show they weren't good enough (in Haynes's opinion) to convincingly sell the tricks. He still managed to wow the crowd, however. A magician always holds himself to a higher standard than his audience does.

Dribbling and magic both require dexterity and some level of misdirection, but being good at one skill doesn't necessarily translate to success with the other. Ricky Jay was widely considered to be one of the greatest close-up magicians in history, but as a kid his jump shot routinely threatened to dent his house's aluminum siding. It drove his mother nuts. Dr. Robert Albo dedicated his life to both magic and basketball, and while he saw similarities between the two, he found one to be more accessible than the other. "I can teach you how to do magic," he told the *San Francisco Examiner*. "I can't teach you to dribble between your legs and dunk unless you already have that ability."

Swiss tells me about a well-regarded magician who cut his teeth as a juggler. "The skills he had as a juggler are much more similar to those he'd use in basketball than they are in magic. And, you know, he's not that great of a sleight-of-hand artist." He catches himself and asks me not to reveal this juggler-magician's identity. "He's actually a fine sleight-of-hand magician. I don't want this getting out, me saying he's shit."

In a *New Yorker* profile of Swiss, Adam Gopnik writes that the magician has "one of the masterly sleight-of-hand techniques in the world today." Swiss agrees, though it takes him a few sentences to build steam and reach this conclusion: "I'm a prominent sleight-of-hand artist. I'm a pretty good sleight-of-hand technician. I'm one of the better sleight-of-hand artists in the world and of my generation."

I ask Swiss if, with all his dexterity and carpal suppleness, he had ever found success playing basketball.

"Fuck no," he says. "I had all the traits to excel in magic. I was a fat, four-eyed kid with a speech impediment."

Swiss is militant in his belief that magic is a singular experience. "Some narrative arts remind me of magic," he says. "Where there's deliberate plotting and an intent to elicit emotion. Basketball doesn't do that." While everyone is permitted to one's own opinion, I can't help but disagree. Basketball, whether by design or accident, elicits emotion. For example, no one *needs* to dunk—the move exists for the purposes of thrilling fans and leaving opponents despondent. The same can be said for certain kinds of dribbles that aren't explicitly for the purposes of moving between points A and B.

Nevertheless, Swiss's claim has me thinking. In magic, we know that *something* will occur, but the specific surprise is plotted for the audience long before the magician ever steps on stage. The outcome of a basketball game, meanwhile, depends on randomness and improvisation; we watch because anything can happen. I run this by Swiss and, in what can only be described as a monumental moment in our brief relationship, he finally agrees with me.

"Yeah, that's a good point," he says. "The intent has to be magic. You'll find all these different pieces that are used in other things, but the pieces used in magic are used to create that particular whole."

A magician tends to be protective of his vocation, which is only natural when your livelihood relies on obfuscation. "The audience is often led to the mistaken conclusion that the only thing that separates a magician from a nonmagician is that a magician has a secret," he says. "This is utterly wrong. But it's very difficult to disabuse people of that notion because we are secretive about our methods."

I tell him about Marques Haynes and the Fabulous Magicians, and how their entire gambit relied on regular schmucks believing they could sniff out a trick in real time.

"Huh, I guess there's something to that," he says. "There's a certain amount of spontaneity with the audience in some kinds of magic. Certainly card magic. There's an element of physical skill, and there's an element of deception." He pauses. "But basketball is not magic!"

He may insist that only magic can be magic, but that hasn't stopped Swiss from enjoying basketball. (The same can't be said for all sports. "I don't give a flying fuck about football," he exclaims, unprompted, early in our conversation.)

"I told my son I was talking to you, and he showed me some videos of famous streetballers." Here Swiss makes a sound that I can only describe as a pleasurably resigned grunt. "Some of these guys are amazing. Just amazing."

"When I see someone make a phenomenal play," he continues, "I have this kind of intuitive, non-verbalized sensation. That, there but for the slight difference in DNA, endowment, and environmental upbringing, go I. That guy and I are a lot more similar than we are different. We are the same species. And the fact that somebody can do that, there's a kind of heroism in that. There's a subtle element of that in magic. If you allow the audience to perceive that by themselves and for themselves, then the audience feels that this is truly wonderful."

Like those nineteenth century Yalies who invented dribbling, modern-day ball handlers often fudge the rules to perform acts of on-court deception. Rarely is a crossover totally legal, as there is bound to be some palming or carrying involved. In 2010, the NBA tested what it would be like to strictly adjudicate against these kinds of violations. Referees were ordered early in the season to punish players who palmed or carried the ball during their dribbles. The result was disastrous, and the edict was scrapped after just two months of relentless whistle blowing. According to Shawn Klein, our sports ethicist, the league shouldn't have cared in the first place. The move is not a disqualifying ethical breach, and his reasoning sounds similar to Swiss's realization that magic and basketball share a sense of heroism.

"The aesthetic element of basketball is not just for the players," Klein tells me. "It is for the sake of the game. For the fans' overall experience. That's the nature of basketball. Not just that you're entertaining, but that you are creating something magical."

• • •

WHILE HANGING OUT at Misdirections Magic Shop, I keep pressing Pon about ballhandling magic, and he opines on what makes a dribbler decent and what makes one a borderline illusionist.

"It's not just about the technique," Pon says. "It's about the presentation. The performance. It depends on your style, your character."

Unlike Swiss, Pon grants there are a good number of similarities between basketball and sleight-of-hand. "You have to know your technique in magic," he says. "It's just like dribbling. You have to know how to dribble in an empty gym before you can apply it in an actual game." This is why magicians flock to his store. "I'm a coach," he says. "You can practice all day long by yourself, but when it actually comes to competition, you'll need to be able to act when the time presents itself. In magic, you need to read an audience, and you have to know when to apply the misdirection. It's exactly the same concept."

This line of thinking is echoed in the story of how God Shammgod invented his famous technique. "I did it by mistake," he admitted in an interview. "I watched the move on film and thought, 'Hey, this could work.' I then went to the gym and practiced it over and over again. I had to practice it thousands of times before I could do it in the middle of a game."

When a young novice comes into Misdirections and says he wants to be a magician, Pon's first question is, "Do you like to practice?" If he says yes, Pon gives him a beginner-level trick to work on by himself. If he says no, Pon sells him a joke book. "They'll get a similar reaction, but one takes less work."

Marques Haynes gave a version of this advice to the readers of *Boys' Life* who wanted to improve their dribbling. "I used to work at it for hours in a gym without taking a shot," he said. "You've got to practice, practice, practice."

In the corner by the books, the Silicon Valley Magician balances a coin on the back of his index finger and mouths what I assume is some accompanying, mystical narration.

"He's a professional," Pon says, "But he still comes in here for help. He works on his routine every single day. That's why he's so good."

"That reminds me," the Silicon Valley Magician says. "I wanted to invite you and your family to my next show as a way of saying thanks. My treat."

"My family isn't going to want to do that," Pon says. "They see enough magic."

As I head out of the store, the Silicon Valley Magician grabs hold of my arm. "You like that Yo-Yo Dribble? Check this out." He then produces a rubber band from his briefcase and wraps it around his wrist in a deliberate pattern. With a snap of his fingers the band flies from his hand and towards the open door, stopping right before the threshold. It then reverses its momentum and rolls across the carpet and back into his cupped hands.

I gasp. "That's a hell of a trick."

"Technique," Pon corrects me.

I'm too easy of an audience.

COUNTING DOWN THE SECONDS

Saving a sport in the nick of time

BY MOST ACCOUNTS, the worst game in professional basketball history was played between the Fort Wayne Pistons and Minneapolis Lakers on November 22, 1950, during the NBA's second season. It didn't want for star power, what with bespectacled scoring machine George Mikan playing center for the reigning-champion Lakers. The Pistons' entire game plan revolved around keeping the ball away from the six-foot-ten behemoth for as long as possible, and their guards dribbled around the perimeter for minutes at a time, passing up easy layups in favor of continuing their own personal game of keep-away. The strategy could fairly be described as "anti-basketball," but it worked. The teams only made eight field goals combined, and Fort Wayne won the lowest-scoring game in NBA history, 19–18.

As Lakers guard Slater Martin told journalist Terry Pluto for his book *Tall Tales: The Glory Years of the NBA*, "The fans hated it. They booed for a while. Then they gave up and started reading newspapers." When they finished reading, they crumpled up the papers and threw them onto the court. "They really bombarded our coach," Pistons forward Fred Schaus recalled.

James Naismith had feared this day would come. His biggest worry about his sport was that fans would lose interest, and he suspected that time-wasting would play a part. While he wasn't alive in the 1950s to see the NBA's early struggles, he witnessed stalling epidemics that plagued college and Amateur Athletic Union games in the 1920s and 1930s, back when defenses crowded the interior and waited for their opponents to make mistakes rather than initiate the action themselves. Naismith loathed the strategy, writing that "a great many people did not care to pay to see two teams at opposite ends of the floor looking at each other."

In 1932, a group of college coaches met to resolve the stalling problem. They did not invite the sport's inventor to join, but Naismith nevertheless sent along three suggestions of his own. One of his ideas was a penalty for defenses that sat back for more than thirty seconds without making an attempt to steal the ball. It was a version of the modern-day shot clock, but in reverse.

Recall that people didn't really listen to Naismith back then, so the committee dismissed his suggestions outright. They instead introduced a rule that forced teams to bring the ball past the halfway line in under ten seconds. Because players could take as much time as they wanted once they crossed to the other side of the court, stalling never went away—it just metastasized into strategy.

Weeks after that infamous Pistons-Lakers affair, the Rochester Royals and Indianapolis Olympians played a game that made a staring contest look like the Battle of Stalingrad. It went to overtime, and the team that grabbed possession of the ball at the beginning of each extra period held on to it and waited for the clock to wind down before attempting a desperate, last-second heave. As a strategy, it was both ineffective and boring. There wound up being six overtimes, meaning that, in thirty minutes of action, the teams combined to take only six total shots.

The NBA was officially in a crisis. The league tried a mishmash of rule changes that were too ineffective and too stupid to warrant mention here. OK, fine—I'll give you one: A new rule stated there would be a jump ball after each and every foul shot during the final two minutes of a contest. The intention was to curb fouling, but it instead made the games take even longer. What's more, the jump ball occurred between the person who was fouled and the person who committed the foul. All it did was incentivize big guys to violently hack the smallest opponents they could find.

What the league failed to realize was that fouling was a symptom of stalling, not the cause. A 1953 playoff game between the Syracuse Nationals and Boston Celtics featured 128 free throws. Bob Cousy, Boston's talented ball handler, took thirty-two attempts from the line (and scored thirty of them). The fouling became so egregious that a fight broke out between two players. When Boston police stormed the court to break it up, Syracuse guard Billy "the Bullet" Gabor took offense and started brawling with the cops. To be fair, that part of the game was actually pretty exciting, but it didn't make up for all the fouls and delays.

• • •

THE NBA WASN'T a world-renowned juggernaut worth billions of dollars in the 1950s. Many teams were owned by workaday businessmen looking for a hobby and a quick buck. Syracuse Nationals owner Danny Biasone is a good example. His day job was running and managing a ten-lane bowling alley in upstate New York. Putting on basketball games was a side hustle.

A short, smartly-dressed chain-smoker from Italy, Biasone said he "didn't know a thing about the game" when he paid the $1,000 entrance fee for the Syracuse Nationals to join the NBA. Still, he knew enough to understand that dreary affairs like the one between the Pistons and Lakers were hurting his secondary income.

"The game had become a stalling game," Biasone recalled shortly before his death in 1992. "A team would get ahead, even in the first half, and it would go into a stall. The other team would keep fouling, and it got to be a constant parade to the foul line. Boy, was it dull." Fans agreed, and attendance plummeted around the league.

Biasone's idea for a fix was a Matryoshka doll of timekeeping: a clock that runs concurrently and inside the existing game clock. "I started talking about a time limit on possessions around 1951, after the 19–18 game," he recalled. "No one would listen to me. I said forget all these different rules about fouling, what we need is a time limit."

The league had fiddled with basketball's temporal boundaries before. Naismith's original rules called for two fifteen-minute halves, but the college game featured two twenty-minute halves. NBA team owners, meanwhile, wanted paying fans to feel like they were getting some extra basketball for their buck, so they opted for a forty-eight-minute game split into four twelve-minute quarters. Despite a proven willingness to change, the shot clock was still deemed to be too radical. But Biasone was a gadfly, and gadflies don't give up.

In 1954, he enlisted the help of Nationals general manager Leo Ferris to figure out how to make his invention work. The biggest question (the only one, really), was how much time teams should be granted for each possession. The men brainstormed at the bar of Biasone's bowling alley and scribbled some ingeniously simple math onto a cocktail napkin. "I looked at the box scores from the games I enjoyed, games where they didn't screw around and stall," Biasone explained. "I noticed each team took about 60 shots. That meant 120 shots per game. So I took 2,880 seconds [48 minutes] and divided that by 120 shots. The result was 24 seconds per shot."

Biasone had a knack for coming up with clever fixes. Occasionally, these were for problems of his own creation. He was famous for screaming at the referees, and due to this behavior, the NBA banned owners from sitting on their team's benches during games. In response, Biasone made himself an assistant coach. He didn't do any coaching; he just sat there and continued to smoke his cigarettes and scream at the officials. The shot clock was an extension of this kind of thinking. He knew how to reverse-engineer a system to get what he wanted, be it a more entertaining sport or the freedom to heckle the shit out of the refs. He also knew how to sell his ideas. Biasone insisted on hosting the league's owners' meetings in Syracuse during the summer of 1954, and with all the bigwigs in town, he put on an exhibition game featuring the twenty-four-second clock to prove its effectiveness. It worked. "After they tried about everything else, they were willing to look at my idea," he said.

The shot clock's effects were immediate and dramatic. Scoring increased by an average of 13.4 points per game during its first season in use. In three years' time, every NBA team averaged more than a hundred points a contest. Fans responded to this faster, more dynamic experience, and attendance improved by 40 percent. "It gave us the kind of game we wanted for years," said Haskell Cohen, the league's publicity director at the time. "No endless stalling and fouling."

Nearly every major professional league around the world sets its shot clocks to the period of time that Biasone and Ferris came up with on a napkin. A glaring, non-professional holdout is the NCAA, though it can be considered "amateur" for no reason beyond the fact that the players aren't paid. Its first shot clock gave teams a laborious forty seconds with which to work. That was cut down to thirty-five seconds, but low scores and slow games inspired the NCAA to make the switch to a thirty-second limit in 2015. If your profits depend on maintaining an entertaining product, the closer to twenty-four seconds, the better.

Now, I'm not comparing a chain-smoking Italian guy doing some light math in a bowling alley bar to the birth of Jesus Christ, but Biasone's invention effectively cleaved professional basketball into two distinct epochs. To the sport's historians and statisticians, "the shot clock era" is analogous with modernity, while the decades predating it were a muddy swamp of anomalous performances and bizarre scorelines. Former league president Maurice Podoloff called the introduction of the shot clock "the most important event in the NBA," and legendary Celtics head coach Red Auerbach considered it "the single most important rule change in the last fifty years."

"There is something about twenty-four seconds that is just right for pro basketball," Hall-of-Famer Dolph Schayes said. Schayes participated in

Biasone's test game in the summer of '54 and immediately recognized that the cranky little bowling alley owner was onto something. "We saw the inherent genius in Danny's twenty-four seconds," he said. "You could work the ball around for a good shot."

What makes twenty-four seconds such a beautifully proportioned chunk of time? A 1967 scientific study published by G. J. Steinfeld in *Psychological Review* regarding the ways verbal cues affect visual cognition may provide a hint. Subjects were asked to identify a fragmented image of a ship, and the members of a control group that received no contextual information took an average of twenty-four seconds to realize they were looking at a picture of a boat. This seems to suggest that the human brain requires twenty-four seconds to conceptualize a jumbled piece of visual information. Could that mean that basketball possessions, with their inter-weaving passes and probing dribble-drives, require from us the same amount of processing time in order to be fully understood? I have no idea! I simply searched a database of scientific journals for "24 seconds" and then picked the most relevant information for this section of the book. You may call this cherry-picking, but I prefer to think of it as inductive reasoning. You know, the kind of thing Biasone and Ferris did at the bowling alley in order to invent the shot clock.

That story of simple napkin math is a sterling endorsement for the genius of working backward. *Teams attempted this many shots in games that were fun. If we force teams to shoot that many times during every game, then all the games will be fun.* It's pretty damned elegant, if you ask me.

Had a coach been tasked with picking a time limit for possessions, he likely would have tallied the amount of shots taken in the games his team won and then engineered the shot clock around that. But Biasone, like Naismith, cared more about entertaining fans than winning games. When the Fort Wayne Pistons won 19–18, he didn't think, "That's how the Nationals are going to beat George Mikan." He thought, "This sucks." Biasone approached the dilemma from the perspective of someone in the stands. Fans may not be geniuses, but we know a good game when we see one.

"Most people forget that Danny Biasone was the Wilbur Wright of basketball," Dolph Schayes said. "Because he invented the twenty-four-second clock, the game took off. Yet, he was a man who never played the game."

Exactly. If the Wright brothers were birds, they wouldn't have thought to attach wings to a heap of bicycle parts.

• • •

IMAGINE IF THE Fort Wayne Pistons' team bus had run through an intersection and T-boned a delivery truck on the way to their infamous game against the Lakers. A grim hypothetical, sure, but to further explore the genesis of Biasone's invention it will help to sift through this imagined wreckage of concussed ballplayers and pulverized pineapples. (I happen to picture the team bus colliding with a pineapple truck, but your macabre fantasy may involve different produce. It's all a matter of preference.) Such an accident would have prevented that 19–18 contest from ever happening. If that were the case, would Biasone have felt the need to invent the shot clock? The league's other games were slow, but that specific affair crystalized the stalling problem like no other and inspired a change. It was so unwatchable, it helped save the sport.

"That squeaky wheel is often what triggers action," Dr. Benjamin Coifman tells me. Coifman doesn't know much about the Fort Wayne Pistons, but he knows everything about intersections. He's a civil engineer and traffic expert who teaches at The Ohio State University. The squeaky wheel he mentions is a bad intersection, but it could just as easily refer to the snooze-fest in Minneapolis. "If there is a big accident, that gets the attention of city council members," he says. Or, in the case of 1950s basketball, it gets the attention of a bowling alley owner in Syracuse.

"With a shot clock, you're trying to have a certain amount of shots in a span of time," says Coifman. "Choosing the span of time for the shot is similar to what you do with a traffic signal."

American streets were not prepared for automobile traffic when Henry Ford's moving assembly line began mass-producing Model Ts in 1913. Whereas buggies moved slowly and the horses that pulled them were perceptive enough to avoid collisions, personal automobiles could reach speeds of forty miles per hour and were driven by sherry-drunk novices who didn't have the good sense to look both ways as they sped to pick up their cocaine prescriptions from the pharmacy. Car crashes killed more than 4,200 people that year, and this burgeoning public health emergency inspired an engineer in Cleveland by the name of James Hoge to get to work on a patent for a traffic signal.

Sixty-three years passed between the advent of basketball and the introduction of the shot clock, but motorists didn't have to wait nearly as long for the traffic signal to arrive. Hoge unveiled his invention in 1914, at the intersection of Euclid Avenue at 105th Street in Cleveland. The device tapped into the electricity from the overhanging trolley lines and was operated by a nearby police officer who could control automobile flow with the flip of a switch. It was an immediate success, though some motorists issued displeasure at the coldness of it all. While dangerous, early driving was a more social affair than what we're used to, and at intersections drivers would cheerily interact with each other to hash out who had the right of way. The proliferation of the traffic signal removed that human touch, as noted by a Michigan policeman who in 1930 complained that people were "becoming more and more critical and will not tolerate sitting under red lights."

There are no winners in traffic engineering, just a minimized amount of losing. Success is defined by a truly equitable outcome wherein each car waits at a red light for the shortest possible amount of time. Intersecting streets will rarely have identical traffic patterns, and automatic signals (invented in 1922) can allocate longer or shorter greens and reds to account for these incongruities.

Coifman asserts that a shot clock is only comparable to the simplest of all intersections. "Two one-way streets, single lanes, no turning." In real life, this scenario is too basic to warrant a traffic signal, but we're giving it one for the sake of this experiment. More complicated exchanges (turns, multiple lanes, etc.) require more complicated mathematics, and I have made it abundantly clear that I am capable of handling only the simplest of equations. Let this serve as yet another reminder that I am no genius; I am but an adult man who never learned his times tables and requires the help of a calculator to determine how much to tip on a twenty-dollar lunch bill.

Blessedly, Coifman is kind and patiently explains the similarities between a modern traffic signal—one that is timed to accommodate traffic flow—and Biasone's clock. "In basketball, they wanted to have 120 shots per game. For a green light, we don't pick the number of cars we serve. Instead, the demand dictates the time you will have," he says. "It's basically taking the same equation and going backward. If I told you, $a=b/c$, maybe that's your shot clock. But if I wanted to know c, I would just do $c=b/a$. You're taking the equation and doing some simple algebra."

Coifman points out another key difference between hoops and traffic science. A rebound both resets the shot clock and determines possession, but there is no way to box out your fellow motorists and physically grab a green light. You just have to wait your turn. "A little bit of running into each other is normal for basketball, but for traffic that's not good at all," he says.

Traffic engineers gather data via "traffic counts," which are like box scores for intersections. In the old days, this involved someone sitting at the side of the road tallying each and every car that passes. Some transportation departments still use this method, but the most common modern strategy involves laying out pneumatic tubes to record traffic density.

Coifman tells me a story about a peer who saw conflicting results when they stretched two sets of tubing across a street for a study. One set recorded extremely heavy automobile traffic, while the other, laid further down the street, did not. When Coifman arrived to observe the scene in person, he noticed something odd. "There was this car that kept driving around and around and around the block," he recalls. Unaware that there was another traffic-counting device on the other side of the intersection, this person drove in circles to give the illusion that there was more traffic than usual on that street. It was his attempt to trick the city into making that one light stay green longer than it should.

"That was gaming the system," Coifman says. "A traffic signal is ultimately taking time from one group of people and giving it to another. Why would you want to slow the game down and not let your opponents get the ball? So that they can't shoot." On a normal commute, that driver would have driven through the intersection once; by going in circles, they were scheming the system for their own personal benefit. In other words, they were stalling. The Fort Wayne Pistons would be proud.

• • •

A TIME LIMIT can mess with your head. The very first players to play with a shot clock had to be reminded to slow down. "We thought we had to take quick shots," Dolph Schayes recalled about Biasone's exhibition game in the summer of 1954. "A pass and a shot was it—maybe eight to ten seconds." Unused to the frenzied tempo, Schayes and company committed "dumb shots and turnovers," and Biasone offered some advice: "Twenty-four seconds is a long time," he told them. "Take your time."

Biasone knew the NBA's pros would be able to adjust to this new time limit because he had done the math. Twenty-four seconds wasn't just good—it was ideal. With this uniform boundary in place, the league's quality of play improved immediately and across the board.

"It is so important for creative people to have rules," John Emmerling tells me. "You don't want to hand them a blank sheet of paper." Emmerling is an advertising veteran who cut his teeth on Madison Avenue at Young & Rubicam in the 1960s, during the industry's *Mad Men*-era heyday. Back then, the standard length for a television commercial was one minute, a time span Emmerling thought was ideal. "The sixty was where it's at," he says. "Give me sixty seconds and I'll give you a hell of a commercial."

Early in Emmerling's career, companies began requesting a new format—the thirty-second ad. While the NBA implemented its twenty-four-second time limit as an effort to increase entertainment value, the change on Madison Avenue was all about increased exposure. "Thirties were more efficient for the client," he says. "We hated them."

Rather than approach this new framework with a totally fresh perspective, agency creatives tended to stick with what they knew. "Everybody was focused on the sixty. All the love got lavished on that," Emmerling says. "The thirties were really an afterthought. I can remember walking out of editing sessions where we'd been there for five hours and we finally got it right. As we're going out the door, I'd say to a junior producer, 'Hey, take that stuff and cut a thirty out of it, will you?'"

But thirty-second ads weren't going anywhere. Clients loved the efficient messaging and increased exposure, and it grew to be the dominant format. With more practice, agency creatives began to feel comfortable within this new restriction, and it showed in their work. "Mikey Likes It" only makes sense as a thirty-second spot. So does the 1980 American Tourister ad where a gorilla goes berserk on some luggage. If Wendy's famous "Where's the Beef?" commercial went on for a full minute, it'd cease being cute and instead paint a haunting portrait of an elderly woman in the clutches of dementia. Less isn't necessarily more, but it sure is snappy.

"Thirty seconds is the sweet spot for a conversation with a fun payoff at the end," Eric Kallman tells me. Kallman is a founder and the chief creative officer of Erich & Kallman, an ad agency based in San Francisco. He's one of the most successful ad executives in the country, and he earned that reputation thirty seconds at a time. "I've done a lot of humor-based advertising, and thirties seem to be better for humor and for comedy. How a joke plays out, you usually only need thirty seconds. You get to a point to where you're thinking in thirties, like coaches drawing up a play."

Rhythm is a hard thing to break. "It's just a matter of being used to what you know," says Kallman. "Like how basketball players have had a twenty-four-second clock since they were born. It's the parameters. A paradigm."

Remember those frenetic Old Spice ads where the handsome shirtless dude tells viewers they could smell like him if they used the company's bodywash? That was a Kallman idea. Same goes for many of the so-weird-they're-endearing Skittles commercials, like the one where a guy's ZZ Top beard plucks candies from a bowl during a job interview. There's a controlled, manic energy to his work. It always leads to a payoff, though, like in the Reese's Puffs spot where a DMV worker extracts deep psychological confessions from a teenager before she gives him what he "really really really wants": a bowl of his favorite cereal.

Erich & Kallman won a Clio Award for that Reese's commercial in 2019, which is like the Oscars of the advertising industry. The cereal company had originally hired the firm to do fifteen-second spots for their product, but Kallman fought for a longer shot clock. "We had to push back and make them realize that it's only maybe 15 percent as good in a fifteen-second format," he says. "The idea is made for thirty." Longer commercials cost more money, and Kallman says it's "virtually impossible" to convince a buyer to pony up more cash. He somehow managed to do it with Reese's, and the company got an award-winning commercial in return.

Online advertising has sparked yet another paradigm change. There is no industry standard for those ads, and companies will occasionally provide agencies a maximum time with which to work. For a series of tequila ads, Kallman was told he had to keep the spots under forty-five seconds. "The ideas never played out that long," he says. "There were a lot of twenty-seven-second videos." He instinctively went back to his bread and butter. He's attuned to his shot clock.

That kind of freedom is becoming rare, and, in recent years, Kallman has been forced to play with a shorter shot clock more and more. "There's less money in advertising than there used to be. We've been doing so many fifteen-second ads. They're popular now because they're cheaper." I ask him if this is like modern-day basketball, where teams rarely use the full shot clock. "Exactly," he says. "You just want the math of how many threes you can attempt in forty-eight minutes."

Like the NBA adjusting to a faster pace in recent years, Kallman has learned how to make fifteen-second spots work. "I'm used to writing them now," he says. "It's a really succinct thing. Whatever you're communicating has to be super-duper quick and to the point. Like, Little Caesars: It's a five-dollar pizza, so you will set up a joke, pay it off, and then hammer it home with delicious pizza footage and the price." Versatility is a valuable skill, but Kallman has his limits. "What's really big now with TV are six-second ads, which are terrible. It's like a video billboard, essentially. It limits your creativity." The same goes for basketball. While the "Seven Seconds or Less" Phoenix Suns team of 2005–06 inspired the fast-paced play we see today, their nickname was something of an exaggeration: 55 percent of their possessions lasted more than ten seconds.

Kallman was a talented high school player, though that's where his basketball career ended. (His Division III college team "took things too seriously," he tells me.) His grandfather Bernard "Ben" Schadler actually played in the early NBA. He was in the league both before and after the introduction of the shot clock, and he sounds like a player who was ahead of his time. "He was known for a shot in what was called the coffin corner—by the sideline and almost behind the hoop," Kallman says. "I would ask him why they let him shoot from there when it wasn't even worth three points back then. Why be difficult?"

Kallman's soft spot for basketball goes beyond family ties. "I think it's more exciting than football," he says. "Definitely compared to baseball, just because of that predetermined pace of play." A basketball game naturally gets broken down into twenty-four-second chunks and, like a commercial break, that dependable fragmentation holds your attention. In my experience, watching the two flow together has a metronomic effect that can be downright hypnotic.

John Emmerling still prefers the luxury and scope of a full-minute commercial, but the ad man concedes there is something special about how thirty-second spots work in the context of a basketball game. "You're watching around thirty-second possessions, then there's a time out and you cut to the commercials and you're seeing thirty-second possessions by Budweiser beer. The team has to accomplish, strategically, what they need to accomplish within their twenty-four seconds, and Buick or Budweiser needs to accomplish what they need to accomplish in their thirty seconds," he says. "It's got a nice feel to it."

Creativity is a finicky child. It dithers when you refuse to set boundaries and withers if you set them too tight. Therein lies the simple brilliance of the shot clock. Basketball teams are free to experiment and find their own rhythm thanks to its Goldilocks-approved parameters. Biasone deserves credit not only for getting it right with twenty-four seconds, but for doing so on his first try. These kinds of things usually take time.

• • •

WITH THE EXCEPTION of Naismith's decision to hang the baskets at a height of ten feet, few things have had a stronger or more lasting influence on the general look and feel of the game than Biasone's invention. It gives basketball its pleasing, seesaw flow, makes it watchable, and has helped prevent an untold number of fights between Boston police officers and ornery point guards.

Why didn't anyone think of it sooner?

"James Naismith was right when he laid out his original rules of the game in 1891," Nick Elam says. "He was right to govern basketball by time." Like Naismith, Elam is a teacher. He's an educational leadership professor at Ball State University, and he's spent the last decade trying to fix the worst part of basketball.

Back in March 2007, Elam and some friends were watching North Carolina State upset Virginia Tech in the ACC Tournament semifinal. The game ground to a halt in the final minutes as desperate Virginia Tech players intentionally fouled their opponents. This last-ditch effort to buy time is a form of stalling that the shot clock is powerless to stop. "Dick Vitale was the broadcaster, and I remember even he wanted to get the game over with," Elam tells me. "You have this highly intense and highly competitive game with so much life, and then you get to the final stretch and all of the air goes out of the stadium." It's a common strategy, but that doesn't make it any less dreadful.

Elam was teaching high school math at the time, and he gave himself some homework. "I was trying to dig deep and lay out sports by category to figure out why some rely on a game clock and why others do not," he says. "Volleyball, tennis, and baseball—why don't they need a clock? The answer is because they've got little mini accomplishments in the game that are accumulated so rapidly that they can be used instead." In volleyball, first to twenty-five wins. Because points are scored at a reliable clip, the game governs itself in this regard. Tennis scorekeeping is far more idiosyncratic, but the general idea is the same.

Points aren't the only units that serve as stand-ins for time progression. "In baseball and softball, outs are accumulated rapidly enough that you can use them in place of a clock," Elam explains.

That leaves the timed sports. "Football, soccer, ice hockey, field hockey, water polo, rugby, and lacrosse all have a very low scoring rate," says Elam. "They don't have any other accomplishment that could be used in place of a clock."

Here, he argues, is where Naismith made a good decision. "Basketball was the same way when it was first invented. He was right to govern basketball by time because then, in the sport's early days, it had that same common characteristic as all these other sports that had a similarly low scoring rate." Recall that the first ever game in Springfield ended 1–0. If they had been following volleyball's first-to-twenty-five rule, those incorrigibles would have played until they died, either by natural causes or mutually assured destruction.

As the sport progressed, players began making baskets at a rate Naismith never could have predicted. The talent boom made basketball flow like volleyball or tennis with its constant scoring, but the running clock remained. This incongruity begat stalling, as teams could use time against their opponents. Danny Biasone solved a good chunk of the problem by adding another clock— fighting fire with fire—but it wasn't a wholesale fix. At the end of game, when stakes are at their highest, a trailing team will have no qualms about racking up intentional fouls. This dark art literally stops time. Why expect them to do anything else?

"I feel like basketball is the only sport that can have the best of both timed and untimed worlds. But, at the ends of games, the presence of a clock was the problem," Elam says. "It's a situation where a team's only recourse to stay in the game is to deliberately and overtly violate the rules of the game. To me, that in and of itself is enough of a fundamental flaw to address."

His solution was radical: At the ends of games, remove time completely.

Elam speaks calmly, but, like an air traffic controller guiding a novice pilot through a storm, there is a palpable pragmatism and urgency when he explains the mechanics of the game. As an educational leadership scholar, his research focus is on teacher evaluations, but back in 2007 he turned his analytical eye to the game of basketball. He recorded nearly 3,000 games and studied their endings to better understand the causes and effects of intentional fouling.

Because basketball has similar characteristics to those untimed sports, Elam figured it should embrace governance by points accumulation—at least at the end of games. Rather than playing to a final whistle, teams would aim for a target score. "The four-minute mark is a good time to shut off the clock because that's around the time that you would see a team with a medium-size lead slow down and play very consciously and try to manipulate the clock," he explains. In the Virginia Tech–North Carolina State semifinal that sparked Elam's epiphany, the teams combined to shoot twenty-one free throws in the final four minutes. That is nearly the same number of foul shots that were taken during the first thirty-six minutes of the game (twenty-six).

Let's pretend Elam's ending was in play during that Virginia Tech–North Carolina State game. With four minutes remaining, the clock would have been shut off with NC State ahead, 54–48. To get the target score, seven points would be added to the leading team's total. After that, it's simple: First to 61 wins.

Why seven points? "If we're going to cut out four minutes of a forty-minute game, we're cutting out ten percent of the game and we need to find some way to add ten percent of it back. And ten percent of seventy is seven. Seventy represents about an average score in college basketball, so you add ten percent, and that's where the plus-seven comes from," Elam says. This format is for forty-minute college games. Other leagues would have different target scores to fit their individual profiles.

With no clock to stop, teams don't have a reason to commit intentional fouls. The benefits disappear, and all it does is give the opponent an easy chance to build toward that final target score.

Elam is a card-carrying Mensa member who can explain his rule in the plainest possible terms, but it's still difficult to comprehend such a stark departure from the norm. You really need to see it for yourself, but for years that was impossible because high school math teachers don't hold much decision-making power at the upper-reaches of the multibillion dollar sports-industrial complex.

Elam was undeterred. He had a good idea, and that was enough of a reason to push on. He typed up his research and sent emails and letters to nearly every basketball-affiliated person he could think of.

Now, imagine you are a league executive or college athletic director and you get an email from a teacher who says you need to get rid of the clock in order to save basketball. At best, you'd think he was a clever and passionate fan with a quirky idea. At worst, you'd assume that an insane person had found your email address. There were some polite responses, but Elam was no closer to making his idea a reality.

Elam went to grad school, got his doctorate, and kept teaching, but he never stopped refining his invention. "I don't think I ever got overly discouraged," he says. "I think part of that was because my livelihood never depended on the success of this format. It's not my full-time job. It's not even my part-time job. It's like an independent project. I never got into a situation when I felt ridiculous for pursuing it." He kept shooting off emails and, in 2016, he sent a sixty-seven-page explanatory PowerPoint to the general inquiries email address for The Basketball Tournament (TBT), a streetball-style event broadcast by ESPN during the NBA off-season.

The PowerPoint was forwarded to TBT CEO Jonathan Mugar, who thought it was "meticulously punctuated and well-written." Mugar also saw the logic in Elam's carefully plotted ending. TBT was a young upstart, so it was open to trying out radical ideas. For example, the winner of the tournament received a $2 million prize in the form of a giant Publishers Clearing House–like check. Mugar contacted Elam, and they worked on incorporating his ending into the play-in games for TBT's 2017 season.

The test cases were a smashing success, and TBT began using the "Elam Ending," as it is officially called, in all its games. "I've now seen 146 games with the Elam ending in play," the titular Elam says, "and the pace of the late game with the Elam Ending is much closer to what we would normally see over the course of the game compared to the late stages of the regular format, when it is so choppy and kind of a crawl to the finish. It's interesting that in that specific part of the game, taking out the clock is what is necessary to keep up a palatable pace."

Elam wasn't the only one who took note of the effectiveness of his fix. Oklahoma City Thunder point guard Chris Paul sponsors a TBT team, and he saw how this odd ending produced more entertaining games. Paul, a member of the NBA's competition committee, suggested to commissioner Adam Silver that the Elam Ending be used in the 2020 All-Star Game. Amazingly, he said yes.

For this high-profile exhibition game, adjustments had to be made to the ending's "settings," as Elam calls them. The clock was to be shut off for the entire fourth quarter, and twenty-four points would be added to the leading team's score in honor of Kobe Bryant, who died in a tragic helicopter crash the month before All-Star Weekend. "I thought that was a very touching tribute, but logistically I thought there's no way we're going to get a full quarter's worth of basketball in an All-Star game with just a twenty-four-point setting," Elam says, noting that the All-Star Game's original target score was supposed to be a thirty-five-point increase. "I was wrong. It worked out. We actually got more than a quarter's worth [of action]. I think it was fifteen-plus minutes of game time in that final quarter with just the twenty-four-point setting."

All-Star games are infamous for sleepwalking offenses and lackadaisical defending, but, thanks to Nick Elam, the players actually played hard during the 2020 event. With the target score locked in place, they played each possession like the game depended on it. The result was the most memorable All-Star Game in decades.

The East squad was winning 133–124 at the start of the fourth quarter, so whoever reached 157 points first would be crowned the victor. The West managed to mount a frenetic, floor-burn-covered comeback and won, 157–155. It was legitimately thrilling, and by the end of the evening, "Elam Ending" was trending on Twitter. The overwhelming majority of mentions were positive, marking the first and last time that has ever happened on the internet.

I'll admit I was skeptical of this new ending. But that's the catch with Elam's invention. You need to see it to appreciate it.

"None of us knew what to expect," LeBron James said afterward, "but throughout the whole fourth quarter and at the end of the game, everybody was like, 'That was pretty damn fun.' "

Anthony Davis, James's Lakers teammate, agreed. "It brings competition back, especially during the fourth quarter—it's about getting stops. You have to get stops to win the game. It was great. We all loved it."

The Elam Ending has other benefits, too. "Because of basketball's game clock, there's no guarantee that the game is going to end with any sort of accomplishment," Elam says. A target score ensures there will always be a game-winning basket. It's the basketball equivalent of leaving a party immediately after you get a big laugh. Excitement and pressure are unavoidable.

At the 2020 All-Star Game, Anthony Davis was at the free throw line when his team needed just one point to seal the win. When he missed the first attempt, gasps and shrieks filled the stadium. But Davis steadied himself and sank the second foul shot, and the basket sent the 20,000-plus fans in attendance home satisfied.

Nick Elam was one of those people. The NBA invited him to Chicago to watch the world's greatest athletes embrace an idea he had hatched while watching TV with friends in 2007. I called him for an interview as he drove back to Indianapolis the next day, and even his measured and analytical brain struggled to come to grips with such a surreal night. "It was beyond even what I had expected. It was just wonderful," he said. "Just the atmosphere in the arena, people on their feet for so much of that final stretch. I think the concept spoke for itself pretty well."

Elam is coy but hints that he's had discussions with the NBA regarding the continued use of his ending at future All-Star Weekends. Who knows, maybe one day the league will use it to decide the winners of all its games. Good ideas tend to stick around. Just ask Danny Biasone.

• • •

A GREAT INVENTION makes it nearly impossible to imagine the world without it. The shot clock seems obvious now, but basketball existed for over half a century before Biasone convinced his fellow owners to give it a whirl. "Other sports had limits," said our dapper Italian friend. "In baseball you get three outs to score, in football you must make ten yards in four downs or you lose the ball. But in basketball, if you had the lead and a good ball handler, you could play around all night." That thought process is almost identical to the one that helped Nick Elam shape his ending. Interestingly, Biasone didn't mention bowling, the sport he likely knew better than any other.

Danny Biasone and Leo Ferris are long dead, but the conditions under which they invented the twenty-four-second clock are still at play in bowling alleys all over the country. The closest one to me is in Albany, California. It's bigger than Biasone's ten-laner was, and it undoubtedly plays more Cardi B, but the space must carry some of the same subliminal triggers and psychic energies that were present at their basketball-saving brainstorm in the 1950s. To re-create this special environment, all one needs to do is grab a seat at the bar. (It also helps to have a little cash for nachos.)

Bowling alleys are loud and distracting places, so no one seems to notice me timing them with my phone's stopwatch app. A young couple on what looks to be a first date chats nervously about music. Not a specific genre or artist, but the general idea of using instruments and voices to produce sound. ("I like it," is the young man's verdict.) He's been holding his bowling ball for nearly a minute, and he waits for there to be a lull in their enchanting conversation before rolling it down the lane and knocking over five pins.

The ball return works fast, and it takes less than fifteen seconds for his bright orange fourteen-pounder to spin back into the rack. He doesn't notice. He's telling his date that his friend sounds just like Drake, and oh dear, he's doing an impersonation of that impression right now. He gets through two mumbled verses of "Hotline Bling" before his date politely gestures to the remaining pins. All told, it takes him three minutes and twelve seconds to get through the frame. (He bowls a six.)

Thanks be to Saint Biasone, not everybody at the alley is as slow as that young man. Two lanes down is a family, and they look serious. The mother and son remove balls from a monogrammed leather bag while Dad enters their information into the digital scoring screen with the confidence of a space shuttle commander switching to manual control. The boy takes three smooth strides (no stutter-step) and rolls a clattering strike. Mom is ready before the pins reset, and she bowls a tidy spare in under thirty seconds. There is no talking among the family members. There are definitely no Drake impressions.

These are considerate bowlers. They work fast not for the bowling alley, which has about a dozen open lanes at the moment, nor for me, the guy lurking behind them with a timer in his hand. By taking it seriously, the family gets to enjoy an optimized version of the sport.

A game of bowling progresses inexorably through ten frames. Everyone gets an equal opportunity to score as many pins as possible. A slow-moving bowler is not using the structure of the game to his advantage in any tangible way. When he stalls, he's just being selfish.

Professional bowling has slow play guidelines, though they are for the purposes of courtesy and not competitiveness. Rule 17.6.2.b in the Professional Bowlers Association rulebook states that, "[w]hen moving to the left lane or shooting a spare, a competitor will have twenty-five (25) seconds to start their delivery from the time his or her bowling ball comes back to the ball return." Twenty-five seconds, huh? That's a pretty tidy chunk of time.

Biasone would have spent countless hours in this kind of environment. If the bowlers at Syracuse's Eastwood Recreation Center were serious about their hobby—and my assumptions about mid-century upstate New Yorkers tell me they were—then they'd instinctively enjoy the sport at a respectable pace. The games would have proceeded in nicely-sized bursts roughly the size of an ideal basketball possession.

I don't know if this rhythm influenced Biasone while he was coming up with his shot clock. While this bowling alley doesn't explicitly prohibit séances, I figure it'd be too loud to hear his response even if I could ask him about it. All that's left to do is bowl. I'm careful to get through the frames swiftly. It's the courteous thing to do.

At the shoe-return desk, I ask the attendant whether the alley has a shot clock for slow bowlers. It's hard to hear over the din of clattering pins and screaming kids, so I ask again: "What happens if people take too long on the lanes? Do you have a shot clock?"

"Naw," the man says as he hands over my sneakers. "People stall all the time, but it's essentially the honor system. It sucks. I wish we had a shot clock."

YOU'VE GOT TO DRAW THE LINE SOMEWHERE

The delayed insurgency of the three-pointer

WHEN SUPERMAN DEBUTED in 1938, his creators gifted him with immense strength right off the bat. He was completely impervious to knives, batons, machine gun rounds, and pretty much any other device intended to inflict harm or pain. Within the next two years, the Man of Steel was revealed to have X-ray vision, super-hearing, super-breath, and the ability to fly (he had been merely leaping over buildings up to that point). For all intents and purposes, Superman was a god, and he used his powers to kick the shit out of every pickpocket and vandal unlucky enough to call Metropolis home. Those godlike powers went totally unchecked until 1943, when someone finally came up with the idea for kryptonite.

George Mikan was no god. As a lanky high school freshman, he was cut from the basketball team for reasons of fashion. "You just can't play basketball with glasses on," his coach told him. "You better turn in your uniform." He eventually made the squad, but the six-foot-ten center went overlooked by nearly every top college program in the country. DePaul University head coach Ray Meyer saw promise, however, and devised a few strategies to help the clumsy teen develop as a player. "When we had dances at school, he would tell me to dance with the shortest and smallest girls," said Mikan. "He figured that would force me to improve my footwork. Otherwise, I'd step on them and hurt them."

The young center learned to control his power like Clark Kent, but unlike the *Daily Planet*'s star reporter, Mikan kept his glasses on when it came time to dish out pain. On offense, he tore DePaul's opponents to shreds with a flurry of deft hook and flip shots. On defense, the bespectacled giant used his innate athleticism and some of that newfound grace to rise high above the rim and swat away goal-bound shots with ease. Whereas Superman was permitted to maraud around Metropolis without having to worry about kryptonite for five full years, Mikan only got two seasons at DePaul before the powers-that-be conspired to rein him in. The NCAA introduced the goaltending rule in 1944 to make the game easier for everyone not named George Mikan. Nonetheless, Mikan still managed to win Player of the Year honors in his final two college seasons with the rule in place.

The NCAA introducing goaltending to knock Mikan down a peg is in line with a familiar hero narrative in Western traditions, one where the seemingly invincible conqueror is given a glaring weakness in the name of fairness. It makes for a more compelling narrative, and we can trace the trope to Achilles, whose bum heel gave the Trojans a fighting chance. The Greeks sacked Troy anyway, but like the NCAA's goaltending rule, Achilles's podiatric ailment at least made things somewhat interesting for everybody else. The invention of kryptonite, meanwhile, is an entirely different tale, and it makes Superman something of an outlier to the Achilles-Mikan tradition.

Kryptonite did not make its debut in the Superman comics, but on the wildly popular *Adventures of Superman* radio program, in 1943. While the comic book had a relatively leisurely production calendar, the live radio show aired three times a week, and the frenzied schedule left Superman voice actor Bud Collyer exhausted. As the story goes, the producers had to devise a way to placate their star, and they came up with the radical idea to give his character a weakness: kryptonite. The show's writers could then craft multi-episode arcs where side characters worked to free the weakened Man of Steel from a hunk of glowing rock. Collyer would use this time to take a vacation while a fill-in actor provided Superman's frustrated grunts and groans in his stead.

You see, George Mikan was not Superman. If anything, he was even more impressive. They made the goaltending rule because the guy was too dominant, not because he needed a week off in Palm Beach.

Much of professional basketball's early history can be described as one protracted attempt to make things tougher for George Mikan. Recall that he inspired Danny Biasone's twenty-four-second shot clock, for his presence on the court scared the Fort Wayne Pistons so much that they conspired to starve him of opportunities. The Minneapolis Lakers built a foolproof strategy around his ability to set up shop right next to the basket, so the NBA doubled the width of the restricted area in 1951, from six feet to twelve feet, in order to push him farther away from the hoop. The change was dubbed the "Mikan Rule."

Basketball's anti-big man crusade continued after Mikan retired in 1956. As Wilt Chamberlain was wreaking havoc on the low post in the 1960s, the NBA introduced offensive goaltending and widened the paint even more, to sixteen feet, to keep him at bay. Efforts to hinder the supremacy of dominant centers weren't limited to the offensive end of the floor, and the league introduced the defensive three-second violation in 2001, just as Shaquille O'Neal was enjoying the prime of his career.

These repeated and escalating attacks on centers were made in the name of "fairness," but they did little to knock basketball's giants from the top of the sport's food chain. When the NBA established its Most Valuable Player Award in 1955, twenty of the first twenty-five recipients were centers. The Era of the Big Man would have been made eternal were it not for one specific change that was made in the 1970s but lay dormant for decades. Like a time-delayed sedative, the three-point line slowly drained the center position of its power and outsize influence.

The game has spread to the perimeter, and the traditional center that once ruled the court is on the verge of extinction. A feathery jumper—long the tool of smaller players unable to survive down low—is now an essential skill for big men if they want to keep themselves out of the scrap heap in the age of the three-point line. That two-inch-thick stripe might as well be made of kryptonite as far as any would-be Mikans or Chamberlains are concerned, and in a plot twist straight out of a comic book, Mikan himself is largely responsible for the three-pointer's existence in the NBA.

Superman, how could you?

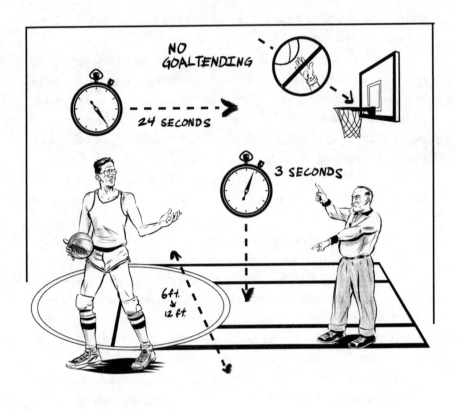

TO UNDERSTAND MODERN basketball, it helps to know about the American Basketball Association. Established in 1967, the ABA was marketed as a hipper, more exciting alternative to the old fuddy-duddies of the NBA. And it was! The ABA gave us the Dunk Contest, which helped turn the league's brightest star, Julius Erving, into a household name, and its famous red-white-and-blue ball really popped on people's cathode-ray tube television sets. It also made use of a three-point line that would, in the words of ABA Commissioner George Mikan, "give smaller players a chance to score and open up the defense to make the game more enjoyable for the fans."

Mikan was the ABA's first commissioner, and he knew that he had to offer people a more exciting product if the league was to pry any eyeballs away from its far more established competition. The three-point line was an overt signal that things were different—you could see it right there on your

TV!—and it became an intriguing wrinkle for the league. "We called it the home run, because the three-pointer was exactly that. It brought the fans out of their seats," Mikan told Terry Pluto in *Loose Balls*, Pluto's entertaining book about the ABA.

To be clear, George Mikan didn't actually invent the three-point line. That honor goes to Howard Hobson, who was head coach of the Oregon Ducks team that won the first-ever NCAA tournament in 1939. Hobson left Oregon shortly after that triumph to get his doctorate at Columbia, and his thesis was a broad analysis on basketball that he later turned into a book. "The long field goal," he wrote in chapter ten, "is the most spectacular play in basketball." To encourage more exciting action from downtown and a more open game, Hobson proposed awarding players an additional point for baskets made from twenty-one feet out or farther.

Hobson had watched dozens of college games at Madison Square Garden and recorded the location of every make and miss (he also tallied whether the players used one or both hands). Shooters converted 39 percent of their attempts from inside an imaginary arc he set twenty-one feet from the basket. Behind it, they only hit 18 percent of their shots, and he reasoned that an additional point would serve as an appropriate reward given the increased difficulty.

To test out his hypothesis, Columbia played Fordham on February 7, 1945, in the first-ever game with a three-point line. Columbia won the exhibition, 73–58, and the teams combined to hit twenty triples—a respectable tally even by today's inflated standards. Afterward, Hobson polled fans in attendance for their thoughts on the new wrinkle: 148 people liked it, 105 did not. Some members of the press, meanwhile, were firmly against the three-point line. "The experiment . . . was far from a howling success," wrote *New York Times* sportswriter Louis Effrat, and he predicted that Hobson's invention would "be permitted to die a natural death."

Hobson held a post as an athletics consultant for the army at the time. When an AP correspondent caught wind of his three-point experiment, they expressed concern for the troops and wrote, "Uncle Sam's soldiers have been guinea pigs for just about everything in the world. Now, they're going to do it for the improvement of basketball." Apparently, the United States Armed Forces had nothing else to worry about in February of 1945.

"Now don't get me wrong," Hobson explained to the AP reporter, "I know we have a good game, and I would be the first to oppose any radical changes in it. But I do think we can help the sport and create more spectator interest. . . . Experimentation will answer our questions, and that's where the army will come in handy. The general idea is there and, after the soldiers play a few games, statistics will prove the point. . . . I know many baseball fans would rather see a home run than a pitchers' battle. Many basketball rooters want to see the game opened up. They thrill to those long shots. If the army shows a way to make them pay off, we'll all benefit."

It's unclear whether the army ever actually proceeded with Hobson's experiment. If they did, it didn't move the needle, as the three-point line completely disappeared from the sport for nearly two decades. In fact, Mikan didn't even credit Hobson for inventing it.

"It was first used by Abe Saperstein in the old ABL and we adopted the rule and their distances," Mikan told Pluto. The ABL, or American Basketball League, was a financial disaster that lasted only one season (1961–62), but its three-point line caught Mikan's eye and he incorporated it into the ABA.

When the NBA merged with the ABA in 1976, the league absorbed four of its franchises (the New York Nets, Denver Nuggets, Indiana Pacers, and San Antonio Spurs). It also took the three-point shot, albeit with a slight delay. The NBA introduced the line in 1979 and painted it exactly where the ABA (and, thus, the ABL) had placed it: twenty-five feet from the backboard, which is four feet farther out than Hobson's arc.

Before starting the ABL, Saperstein had gained immense fame as the Harlem Globetrotters' promoter, marketing guru, and head coach. In 1948, he and Minneapolis Lakers general manager Max Winter agreed to put on an exhibition between the two squads. While the Globetrotters entered the contest on a 102-game winning streak (and, unlike the Washington Generals, their opponents actually tried back then), they were still considered under-dogs due to ugly stereotypes regarding black players' supposed inability to work as a team. Those stereotypes were egregiously stupid because, as anyone who watched them play could tell you, the Globetrotters were a stunning phil-harmonic of cohesive artistry. The Lakers, meanwhile, were totally reliant on George Mikan. They were the reigning champions of the NBL, a segregated, all-white precursor to the NBA, which itself wasn't integrated until 1950.

For decades, basketball progressed on parallel sets of tracks separated by anti-Black racism, and this exhibition provided an all-too-rare opportunity for the two to meet.

The event was held at Chicago Stadium, and it drew more fans than any other basketball game in the city's history up to that point. Mikan played well and led the Lakers to an early lead, but the Globetrotters double-teamed him in the second half and mounted a comeback. With the game tied at 49 points, Marques Haynes, that famous dribbling magician, used his ball-handling trickery to run ninety seconds off the clock. (He stalled, albeit with style.) With time set to expire, Haynes passed to Ermer Robinson, who swished a one-handed buzzer-beater from thirty feet out. Had there been a three-point line it would have counted for an extra point, but two were plenty. The Globetrotters won, 51–49, and earned the right to call themselves the greatest team on earth.

While the Harlem Globetrotters were internationally famous and played to packed houses wherever they went, Saperstein understood the upstart ABL's stiffs would be a tougher sell. When the league's team owners met to plan its first season, Saperstein insisted on installing a new gimmick. The three-point line, he urged, would be their "weapon" to compete with the NBA.

Unlike Hobson, who obsessed over data, Saperstein and his friend Ray Meyer (the DePaul coach who gave George Mikan dance tips) drew the ABL's arc twenty-five feet from the backboard because it just looked right to them. As the *Wall Street Journal's* Ben Cohen discovered via archival research, Saperstein's fellow team owners weren't convinced. They believed the line was too far out and voted 4–3 to approve a shorter, twenty-two-foot line. (It would be "impossible" to shoot from twenty-five feet, said one owner.)

But Saperstein held a trump card. To help gin up excitement for the inchoate league, ABL games were to be booked as double-headers with Harlem Globetrotters exhibitions. By controlling the superstar Globetrotters' schedule, Saperstein effectively had dictatorial power over his fellow ABL owners. He pretended their vote never even happened and drew the line according to his original specifications: twenty-five feet from the backboard (which means twenty-three feet nine inches from the very center of the hoop). In the corners, the arc's bend was interrupted by two straight lines that jut from the baseline to give shooters room. The ABL wouldn't even make it through two seasons, but the shape and dimensions of its three-point line were incorporated into the ABA by Mikan. That's the arc that eventually made its way to the NBA, where it is still painted to Saperstein's exact specifications.

Why is it important to know so much about the origins of the three-point line? Well, to be perfectly honest, it isn't *that* important, at least not in the grand scheme of things. You could have checked your voter status online or cleared your dryer's lint tray in the time it took you to read about Howard Hobson's and Abe Saperstein's adventures in line drawing. But assuming you've taken care of all those matters, it's worth spending a moment to acknowledge what the three-point line hath wrought. Its rather trivial history only elides the extent to which it has completely changed basketball.

• • •

THE HOOP ACTS as a drain of sorts, and basketball's natural gravity pulls action toward this vortex. While rules like the three-second violation and goaltending serve to punish those who loiter by or above the rim, the three-point arc is an incentive to lure players away from the paint. Or, at least that was the original intention. Mikan's ABA adopted the rule to drum up attention and excitement for the league, but the long-range shot never became an integral strategy for any of its teams. Over the ABA's nine-season existence, teams averaged 4.9 triples a game and only converted 1.4 of those attempts. The shot actually lost popularity over time, with teams averaging 3.7 and 3.9 three-point attempts during the league's final two seasons (1974–75 and 1975–76, respectively).

After the NBA merged with the ABA, its decision to incorporate the three-point arc in 1979 was an act of desperation. The league was yet again in a bad place. It suffered from low ratings, poor attendance, and sloppy, stilted play. There were also a good number of fights, and Howard Hobson spent some of his retirement writing letters to the NBA commissioner encouraging him to adopt the three-point line as a way to fix basketball's myriad afflictions. "Players are bigger now and when ten of them get into such a small area, body contact leading to violence is bound to occur," Hobson told a UPI reporter in 1978. "It's like putting two heavyweight boxers in a telephone booth and telling them not to clinch. The three-point plan would tend to draw the defense out, decrease the use of zone, relieve congestion near the basket, add a spectacular play for the fans, and would give the team behind a better chance to catch up."

Hobson had grand expectations for the three-point line, but, to be fair, everyone thinks their kids are special. The idea that an ABA gimmick would automatically fix all that was ailing professional basketball warranted skepticism. "The NBA's response to its sagging popularity is like applying a Band-Aid to a gaping wound," *Battle Creek Enquirer* sports columnist John Wilhelm wrote before the 1978–79 season. "Clearly, the three-point basket will not open up the game, as NBA officials hope it will."

He wasn't wrong, exactly. Teams averaged 2.8 attempts per game and 0.8 makes from behind the arc during that first season, and the shot accounted for just 3 percent of the league's total field goal attempts. The following year saw even less three-point enthusiasm, with teams averaging only two long-range shots per contest. The Atlanta Hawks, for example, made ten three-pointers *all season*.

Compare those statistics to the 2018–19 NBA season, when teams averaged thirty-two long-range attempts per game, and 36 percent of all shots were taken from behind the arc. Players combined to make 27,955 three-pointers that year, which eclipses the total number of threes made during the 1980s. As in the entire decade.

What the hell happened?

• • •

WHEN MIKE CAMPBELL is asked how he went bankrupt in *The Sun Also Rises*, he says that it happened two ways: "Gradually and then suddenly." I actually had no idea this was a Hemingway quote (I always figured Mark Twain had said it about drinking too much or growing a mustache), but it's a good way to describe how the three-pointer took hold of basketball.

Kirk Goldsberry was teaching geography at Harvard University when he first noticed that something odd was afoot. As a cartographer he specializes in data visualization—making the invisible visible—and he's used his skills to do things like map internet traffic in real time. He also loves basketball, and in 2011 he managed to get his hands on a prize he had long been searching for: the location data for every shot taken in the NBA.

Nowadays, the league collects location information with sophisticated tracking cameras, but the NBA's methods were a tad rustic when it first began compiling these data during the 1996–97 season. Scorekeepers were asked to mark by hand on a paper map of the court where all the attempts occurred during each game. (It was essentially the same technology Howard Hobson used to tally shooting percentages by distance at Madison Square Garden in the 1930s.) The information gleaned from the NBA's early shot charts is a little iffy, but the league got into the habit of expanding its box scores beyond simple statistics.

"I don't think they were trying to do anything else except help media outlets put individual game shot charts together," Goldsberry tells me. "Nobody would have thought that they were building something that, in aggregate, would have been a more powerful tool to understand how players, during the course of a career or a season, use space to thrive."

When he was a kid developing his jump shot, Goldsberry noticed that, no matter how much he practiced, he was always better from the right side of the floor than from the left. Likewise, NBA stars have their own preferred areas on the court. "I knew with my training, if the data were out there, I could quickly expose the hot spots and characterize the differences between these great players in meaningful new ways."

All that information was hidden in plain sight. While teaching at Harvard in 2011, Goldsberry noticed that ESPN.com was publishing rudimentary shot charts for every NBA game, and so he scraped the website and collected a veritable treasure trove of data.

Using that information he made "heat maps," beautiful charts full of color-coded hexagons that convey where an NBA player tends to make or miss his field goals and the frequencies at which they are attempted. For example, Miami Heat guard Dwyane Wade's heat map featured a flurry of big red hexes around the hoop because he was so effective and prolific from that area. Outside the three-point line, however, was a sparse, wintery mix of small blue polygons.

"Geography is a very powerful discipline in part because we can uncover hot spots," Goldsberry says. "*Hot spots* is a term that is generally associated with epidemiology and public health and disease outbreak, but to be sure those folks and those scientists know that maps and spatial analyses are the tools that can perfectly and congruently capture the spatial nature of a situation."

Goldsberry, meanwhile, had everything he needed to paint a fuller picture of basketball's trends thanks to all that valuable data he borrowed from ESPN.com. NBA players attempt around 200,000 field goals in a given season (in 2018–19, there were 219,404 field goal attempts during the regular season), and he now knew exactly where each one was taken. "I got millions of shots spatially referenced, and with my training as a geographer I needed to understand where the league as a whole was shooting and how efficient they were," he says. "I needed to establish a baseline."

That baseline helped explain which players were above or below average shooters from various locations, but it also revealed a shocking truth about basketball's geography. Goldsberry crammed multiple seasons' worth of shooting data through a "smoothing algorithm" to construct a map that displayed the estimated average point values for shots taken all over the floor. He found that, overall, an average field goal attempted in the NBA can be expected to yield 1.02 points. However, in the zones between the lane and three-point line, the crowded mid-range area where games coalesced for decades, Goldsberry discovered that shots taken there were only expected to yield 0.85 points per attempt. That's a pretty rotten return on an investment.

The real value, Goldsberry learned, came from behind the three-point arc. There, shots could be expected to yield more than 1.05 points per attempt. Jumpers from the two corners, where Abe Saperstein's arc collapses into a straight line, were even better. These areas produced an average of 1.10 to 1.20 points per shot. "I knew there would be a difference in efficiency behind the three-point line and in the mid-range," Goldsberry says. "I was not prepared for how stark that difference was. It definitely changed how I watched basketball."

While it is harder to make long-range buckets, Goldsberry's points-per-shot map revealed that basketball goes overboard in appraising these shots at a 33-percent premium. "That's what really stuck out at me," he says, "The magnitude that they subsidized the three-point shot, that subsidy creates such a major incentive from an efficiency standpoint to shoot more threes than twos."

The three-point line may have been introduced to the NBA in the 1970s, but it took decades before there was the collective realization that, if the league offers you an extra point for a shot, you should probably take them up on it. But it wasn't just blithe ignorance that accounted for the delay. In those early years, players were objectively worse at making long-range buckets. Every shot was worth two points for most of their basketball-playing lives; why would they have bothered practicing twenty-five-footers?

When the NBA was teasing the idea of adding a three-point arc in the 1970s, Howard Hobson foresaw a problem. He argued that the ABA's twenty-five-foot line was "too great a distance" and "will not draw the defense out as the percentage will be too small." Always the diligent note-taker, Hobson charted eight Portland Trail Blazers games in 1978 for evidence. "Only two shots, both unsuccessful, were taken beyond twenty-four feet in 1,340 attempts by both teams," he explained to a reporter. "Fifty-three shots were taken beyond twenty-one feet with fifteen made for a 28.3 percentage. Inside of twenty-one feet, 581 of 1,287 attempts were made for a 45.1 percentage." The sweet spot, according to his evaluations, was twenty-three feet—far enough to ease congestion by the hoop but close enough to entice people to shoot.

The NBA didn't listen to the old man. It stuck with Abe Saperstein's original dimensions and the three-pointer languished, unused and ignored, for years. It took ten seasons before teams averaged more than two three-point makes per game. The 1980s saw an influx of talented marksmen, but they largely ignored the free points offered to them behind the line and instead set up shop at mid-range. Larry Bird, one of the best shooters of all time, averaged only 1.9 three-point attempts per game during his career.

Hobson was correct in his assumption that the line was too far away to be a tempting incentive. Proof for this would come in 1994, when the NBA experimented with a three-point arc placed closer to the hoop. It was moved in nineteen inches, and the results were immediate. Team three-point attempts jumped from 9.9 per game to 15.3 per game in just one year with the adjusted arc. This upward trend continued for two more seasons until 1997, when the NBA moved the line back to its original location. During the period with a shrunken arc, three-point shots made up 21 percent of all field goal attempts in the league.

The three-point shot slightly declined in popularity when the arc was moved back to its original location, but players and coaches got a taste of its rich rewards and began to see the three-point line not as a gimmick but as a way to hack the game for more points. This realization accelerated young players' training in the long-distance arts, and kids began practicing threes as soon as they could muster the strength to throw balls twenty-five feet through the air. Those two factors—the knowledge that three-pointers are important and the increased shooting skill of players—collided in the middle of the 2010s and helped turn the NBA into a three-point free-for-all.

Like a geologist monitoring spikes on a seismometer, Goldsberry saw this shift coming. His heat maps had made him a celebrated figure in the basketball analytics world, and by 2014 he was contributing articles about the sport's geographical properties to *Grantland*. It was in this capacity as a writer that he called for a revolution: It was time for the NBA to move the three-point line farther away from the basket.

Three-pointers accounted for 26 percent of all shot attempts in the NBA during that 2013–14 season. Players made 36 percent of them, which was only a hair worse than the overall two-point field goal average (39 percent). Not only were players better at hitting their triples, teams were smarter at devising ways to spring them free for open attempts. The shot was simply too easy to make to be worth so many points.

Goldsberry continued to chart this untethered migration beyond the three-point line, and in 2018 he put his findings into a book, *Sprawlball*. In it, he expands his theory that the arc should be moved back, suggesting that it be changed each year in accordance with the league's shooting averages. For example, he examined the data from the 2017–18 season and found that NBA players made 33.33 percent of their attempts from a distance of about two feet behind the existing line. Set the arc there, he argues, and the points subsidy would actually be appropriate. "What are the chances that where the three-point line was placed in 1979, Magic Johnson's rookie season, would be the same place for Steph Curry's prime?" he asks. "What are the chances that that line should be in the exact same place? That's pretty ridiculous in my opinion."

Goldsberry thought the game was enjoying an aesthetic peak when he first called for change. "What I say is my favorite version of the sport doesn't matter," he tells me, "but the 2013 and 2014 Finals where the Heat and the Spurs played each other back-to-back years was incredible." San Antonio won that second series with gorgeous ball movement, and their aesthetically pleasing style was achieved due to spacing, which, in turn, was made possible by the three-pointer. But Goldsberry looked at his maps and saw a grim future, one where analytically-driven teams conspire to take advantage of that over-subsidized area on the court.

"I was starting to see that this was going to get out of control if something's not done," Goldsberry says before adding, with a laugh, "And then it did get out of control."

• • •

WHEN PEOPLE TALK about advanced analytics in basketball, the first name that inevitably comes up is Daryl Morey, the general manager of the Houston Rockets. Morey's background was, for a while, unusual for an NBA executive. He had never played or coached the game at the pro or even collegiate level. With a degree from MIT and a background in computer science and statistics, you'd sooner expect Morey to work with actual rockets than the Houston varietal.

After putting in time as a consultant at Ernst & Young, Morey worked his way up through NBA front offices and landed the Rockets' top job in 2007. Under his guidance, Houston has accumulated the second-most wins in the entire NBA during that period of time.

Morey did this, in part, by molding his team to exploit efficiency gaps that exist in basketball. Just as Goldsberry started to notice the geographic disparities on his points-per-shot heat maps, Morey reconstructed his team to better facilitate a style of play that encouraged players to attempt only the most valuable field goals available: layups, dunks, and three-pointers. The stuff in between—those mid-range shots that defined the NBA for most of its history—were to be treated like an axe behind glass: used only in case of emergency. As Mike D'Antoni, the coach tasked with implementing this vision in 2016, put it: "If we take a three every shot, so be it."

When *Sports Illustrated* writer Chris Ballard visited the Rockets' locker room in 2009, he took note of two monitors that cycled through "various esoteric stats" including one that ranked the team's players by the percentage of "high-quality" shots they took. These were three-pointers, free throws, and attempts right near the basket. Given Morey's background in management consulting, it's unsurprising to learn that Houston relied on passive-aggressive PowerPoint presentations to remind its employees to hit their target metrics. Tracy McGrady was the team's star at the time, and the Rockets' number crunchers calculated that only 63 percent of his attempts could be defined as "high-quality"—far below what the organization aimed for. Houston traded him to the New York Knicks the following season.

The Rockets' current star, James Harden, is a zealot for those "high-quality" shots. Thirty-nine percent of his attempts were from inside ten feet during the 2018–19 season and 54 percent came from behind the three-point line. He also made 754 free throws that year, the seventh-most in league history.

To fully embrace this new style of play, the Rockets surround Harden with at least three three-point shooters at all times. (When a center graces the court, he is mostly there on clean-up duty, scrapping for rebounds and tip-ins.) In 2018, Houston became the first team in NBA history to take more three-point field goals than two-pointers (3,470 to 3,436). They effectively flipped the game inside-out.

Daryl Morey is often credited for coming up with this dramatically different style of play, but basketball's most famous analytics genius was about thirty years late to the party. The three-point revolution was cooked up in a tiny Iowa gym hundreds of miles from the nearest NBA front office, and it sprouted from the mind of a guy who couldn't seem to catch a break.

"There's no genius here," David Arseneault Sr. says to me over the phone. He's taking a short break from looking after his grandkids to chat about his days as a basketball revolutionary, though he'd never call himself that. "Let's get real. I had no idea what I was doing."

Grinnell College could never be accused of being an athletics power-house. The small yet prestigious liberal arts school has produced more *Village Voice* jazz columnists than NBA players, and when Arseneault took the head coaching job in 1989, the men's basketball team hadn't enjoyed a winning season in twenty-five years.

The Pioneers were the dregs of Division III's Midwest Conference, which is kind of like being named "worst dressed" at the White House Correspondents' Dinner. When he took the job, Arseneault was a self-proclaimed "Bobby Knight disciple." "I think I even threw a chair across the floor before he did," he laughs. The no-nonsense taskmaster aimed to whip the program into shape through hard-nosed, traditional basketball. It was a total failure. During his first two seasons in charge, Grinnell went 5–23.

"Basically, there was no joy in the program," he says. "I wasn't having fun, and I only exacerbated the problem by being consistently negative." Arseneault was in a funk, and he did something few coaches would ever consider: change.

"We lacked physical toughness from our bigger players, which meant that it was difficult for us to score close to the basket," he tells me. "The only true positive that we had was that we had a collection of players who could shoot the ball reasonably well from the perimeter." The timing was excellent. The NCAA had adopted a three-point arc (set nineteen feet, nine inches away from the basket) two years before Arseneault arrived at Grinnell. It would be their advantage, and they'd use it to death. Then, they'd use it some more.

In his playing days at Colby College in the 1970s, Arseneault had a nice jumper but says that it went completely to waste. "Had I been able to use [the three-pointer], it would have made the game a lot more satisfying," he tells me. "We had talented inside players, and without a shot clock and without a three-point line, it really made no sense for me to take outside shots that I would make, at best, 40 percent of the time when those post players could make 60 to 65 percent of their shots. I think my claim to fame my junior year was that I played six games, all 240 minutes, and was a combined 0-for-0 from the floor. We won all six games! There was just no sense in my shooting."

As a coach, Arseneault had always considered winning to be his first and most important priority. But with a miserable and unmotivated squad, the notion of win-loss records felt trite. "The players were lacking in self-esteem," he tells me. In *The Road to 138*, a book about the Grinnell program by former player Ross Preston, Arseneault says this moment coincided with the realization that he had been suffering from depression and his decision to get help. "I was suffering from a chemical imbalance," he said. "Prozac literally saved my career."

Arseneault committed to nurturing his players' strengths, even if it meant throwing everything he had learned as a coach into the garbage. "Rather than force them to be something they weren't, we turned to find something a little bit different." Considering what would happen next, this is like describing King Henry VIII's approach to matrimony as "a little bit different."

"I went to my athletic director, Dee Fairchild, and asked if I could do an experiment," Arseneault recalls. "I told her it didn't make sense for us to try to practice what everyone else was practicing on a daily basis. In fact, I thought that our best chance of turning around the fortunes of the program rested on our ability to be better at something totally different from the norm." This experiment grew into a style of play that was unlike anything anyone had ever seen before. On campus, it came to be called, simply, "The System." The name stuck, but Arseneault preferred to describe it with a different term: "Organized Chaos."

It is tremendously difficult to convey the System with words. While it may seem like I'm forfeiting my duties as a writer, you really would be better served by searching for Grinnell highlights on YouTube and seeing it for yourself. The first thing you're likely to notice is the pressing. Multiple defenders immediately pick up the opposing ball handler and hound him for the entire length of the floor. The key to this strategy is "platooning," a strategy where groups of players are subbed in and out of the game in waves as a way to keep their legs fresh and energy levels high. Whereas most basketball coaches will only play their eight or nine best players, Arseneault called upon every single member of his squad, and seventeen different Pioneers could see action during a game. This frenetic defending almost always resulted in either a turnover or an easy bucket—either one was fine. All the Pioneers wanted was to get the ball as quickly as possible so they could unleash a monsoon of three-pointers.

The driving principle of the System was that at least 50 percent of the Pioneers' shots had to be taken from three-point land. Keep in mind this was the early 1990s, nearly three decades before the Houston Rockets turned the game inside out. It was practically unheard of back then to take 20 percent of your shots from behind the arc, let alone half of them. In his book *The*

Running Game, Arseneault wrote that, early in the experiment, he found Grinnell was able to reach this goal by:

1. Always having at least three capable three-point shooters on the court at the same time.

2. Shooting three-point shots in transition even when we had a numbers advantage.

3. Allowing our wings in the press to quick release to the offensive end of the court whenever they sensed they would be more effective trading baskets than hustling back defensively.

4. Matching our shooters against our opponent's big men in our pressing alignment so they had an initial mismatch in transition.

5. Encouraging our post players to kick the ball out to a shooter after a post-entry pass.

6. Dribble penetrating at every chance with the thought of kicking the ball back to a shooter.

Other than the stuff about pressing, all those precepts are now important components of modern professional basketball. Just turn on an NBA game and see for yourself.

The System had the effect of an ambush. Opponents didn't know what to do with these insane liberal arts kids from Iowa jacking up twenty-five-footers with fully juiced shot clocks. "When we came up with the faster tempo and the usage of the three-point shot, it was foreign to the way [our opponents] liked to play," Arseneault says. "For a long time I really felt that we weren't winning games as much as the other teams were losing to us. They just weren't comfortable."

The System even managed to baffle its inventor. "Honest to goodness, I had no idea what was happening during games," Arseneault tells me. "I just kind of sat there and I watched. 'Shoot faster, go faster!' was about all I could say. It wasn't until after a game when I could analyze film to figure out what was working and what wasn't. Watching it live was just too fast for my eyes."

Arseneault asked a few Grinnell math students to help him track pertinent statistics over a three-season span beginning in 1993. It was an attempt to better understand how this organized chaos worked, and the results were converted into a "Formula for Success." In his book, Arseneault explains the variables and breaks down the formula in layperson's terms:

$$150tr + 94sh* + 33\%or + 32to = W$$
$$*94sh = 47 \times 2 + 47 \times 3$$

"Honestly, I have no idea how they came up with this formula," Arseneault says, but he soon incorporated it into his post-game analysis.

In his book, Arseneault breaks it down in layperson's terms:

1. Force our opponents to run up and down the court 150 times. (Note: one trip = the crossing of both hash marks.)

2. Shoot the ball ninety-four times, with one-half of those shots coming from behind the three-point arc.

3. Offensive rebound 33 percent of our missed attempts.

4. Make our opponents turn the ball over more than thirty-two times.

The math was indeed sound. "When we accomplished all five goals, we won at a 97-percent rate," Arseneault says.

Things could get ugly when the Pioneers failed to meet all the criteria, but Arseneault didn't mind the occasional fifty-point loss. It was all part of the experiment.

In 2011, Grinnell statistics professor Tom Moore and two of his students independently analyzed the Formula for Success to see if it held up. "Everything pretty consistently kept pointing to those variables," Moore tells me. By then, the Pioneers were a known commodity and famous for breaking box scores. There were only two seasons between 1993 and 2012 when they weren't the top-scoring team across all levels of college basketball, and it was all thanks to the three-pointer.

"I was both surprised and elated that three-point shots were so easy to manufacture in the early to mid-nineties," Arseneault says. Unused to the strategy, opponents tended to overload to the side of the court with the ball. This meant that an open shooter was always just one pass away. "I knew that we could create a good look from the arc at any point in the shot clock within five seconds." Make or miss, the jumpers kept on flying.

"We're playing games for those three runs a half," Arseneault says regarding periods when the Pioneers would go on a hot streak from behind the arc. "We know we're going to get outscored the rest of the time, but three runs a half is usually enough to get us over the top."

If you've ever rooted against the Houston Rockets, you know just how deflating it can be when they get in a groove from deep. It takes but a few flicks of the wrist from Harden and company to have you cursing the grave of Howard Hobson. These streaks are a hallmark of the modern, run-and-gun NBA, but Grinnell embraced this brand of psychological warfare all the way back in the early 1990s.

"I suppose, in theory, just being good at something different would be an advantage. But it sure seems to me, from a scoring standpoint, that three-pointers are the mental daggers you throw at people," says Arseneault. "One of our rules is that if you get an offensive rebound, it automatically gets kicked back out to the shooter for a second shot. Usually, if they get another chance within two to three seconds they can make the adjustments, and they make that second shot at about a 55-percent clip. We make those about six or seven times a game. The mental lift we get from those, you can just feel a sense of impending doom from the other sideline."

Tom Moore had a front-row seat to the Pioneers' rise under Arseneault. Moore is a statistics scholar and professor emeritus at Grinnell, and for years he put that brain to work as the Pioneers' official scorekeeper. "People ask me, 'Was keeping score hard?' I guess it was at first, and then later on I had the feeling that, when I was scoring a regular basketball game, which I did occasionally, it would feel so slow. I would say, 'Well, isn't there something else I should be doing here?'"

The System really came into its own during the 1995–96 season, when Grinnell won the Midwestern Conference Championship Tournament. "David had been playing his fifteen-player rotation the whole season," Moore recalls. "I saw him one day before this tournament and said, 'David, now that you actually have a chance, you're going to constrain that in and not play as many people, right?' And he said, 'No, I think I'm going to try and work in more guys.' He did, and one of the players made a really big play in the semifinal game. That's when I realized this is a lot about getting these kids involved who ordinarily wouldn't get involved. I was a big fan after that moment."

By the time David Arseneault retired in 2018, he had won four conference championships and his teams shattered just about every scoring record

STEP 1:
SHOOT A
3-POINTER

STEP 2:
SHOOT A
3-POINTER

STEP 3:
REPEAT
STEPS 1-2

imaginable, which had been his intent. "It was like Christmas morning every day," he tells me. "All we had to do was open up the NCAA record book, flip through the pages, stick your finger down and go, 'Let's break this record.'" He's really reminiscing now, and I find myself wishing I had a chance to play for the Pioneers. I'd be a scrub and huge liability, even in the Midwest Conference, but at least I'd be a scrub and huge liability in a system and not on my own. "We had so much fun with it. That was part of the driving force in all of this. We told the team, 'We're going to be different. We're going to do something that has never been done in sports.' And they'd be like, 'Let's do it!'"

The most famous and controversial of those records came on November 20, 2012, when Grinnell's Jack Taylor scored an NCAA record 138 points against Faith Baptist Bible College. His stat line for that contest looks like a cat crawled across the keyboard: 52-for-108 FGs; 27-for-71 3FGs; 7-for-10 FTs.

"That was Jack's third game in a Grinnell uniform," says Arseneault. Taylor, a transfer from the University of Wisconsin–La Crosse, had been struggling to integrate into his new team, so his coach decided to force matters. "I said, 'Jack, we're going to let you go for one hundred on Tuesday.' And he looked at us with these bug eyes, not knowing if we were serious or not. I said 'Jack, we're serious, this is how we're going to do it: If in the first ten minutes you can take fifteen shots and score twenty points, then we'll roll over the next ten minutes and continue. Teammates will be instructed to force-feed you the ball.'" Seventy-one three-point attempts later, a college basketball scoring legend was born.

Arseneault tells me that there were no hard feelings from the Faith Baptist bench. "I was just looking for a reaction, like, 'Hey, that's enough' or anything like that," he says. "I looked at [their coach], and he seemed more concerned with his kids scoring and getting closer to one hundred points than anything else." (They made it, barely. The score finished 179–104). "After the game I went right up to him and said, 'Coach, are you OK?' And he said, 'That was awesome. No problem." Arseneault does add that he tried to schedule Faith Baptist seven more times, but the school politely declined every invitation.

Grinnell's trap-heavy defense allowed someone other than Jack Taylor to enjoy the game of his life. David Larson, a Faith Baptist player who was, in Arseneault's words, "averaging like a point a game," managed to score seventy against the Pioneers. His teammates set back screens to counter Grinnell's full-court presses, and he repeatedly sprang free to catch long passes like a wide receiver against busted coverage. "There was a point in the game when our crowd was booing any time any kid other than that kid [Larson] shot the ball," Arseneault says. "They wanted to see how many points he could get." (As a purely statistical marvel, Larson's game was nearly as impressive as Taylor's. When is the next time somebody's going to score seventy points without making a single three-pointer?)

A five-foot-ten Division III transfer scoring 138 points in a game tends to make national news, and Jack Taylor and the System found themselves thrust into the spotlight. The responses alternated between awe, disbelief, and condemnation. Critics argued that Arseneault cherry-picked records and ran up the score against lowly opposition. (The Faith Baptist Bible College Eagles aren't in the NCAA; they are members of the NCCAA: the National Christian College Athletic Association.) *Deadspin* called the strategy "a complete bastardization of basketball," and ESPN's Stephen A. Smith said that the Faith Baptist players should have thrown Taylor to the ground. (Thessalonians 13:7: *And so sayeth the Lord, "Don't bring that weak shit in here."*)

What Arseneault's detractors didn't realize, though, is that the System wasn't for them. It wasn't even designed for winning. He developed it for the same reason James Naismith invented basketball: So his students could have some fun.

I should note that Arseneault vehemently opposes any comparisons to the game's inventor. "You must be joking," he scoffs. (I am not.)

"My first few years coaching, I completely alienated and screwed up some really good talent. Those players, by and large, they don't stay in touch with me. I feel bad that they caught me in that stage of my career before I learned to let go a little bit," Arseneault says. "From the System years, they all stay in touch. It was just a wonderful experience."

• • •

IT WAS A sign of where things were heading in the NBA when, in 2014, the Sacramento Kings hired David Arseneault's son, David Arseneault Jr., to be the head coach of their D-League affiliate team, the Reno Bighorns. "I didn't know what was going to happen with him, if he was going to go out there and fall flat on his face or not," the elder Arseneault recalls. "I was very pleasantly surprised that, within two years, he was able get his players offensively comfortable enough to win their league." (For the sake of clarification, the Bighorns had the best regular season record in 2015–16, but they lost in the first round of the playoffs.)

Arseneault Jr. coached the Bighorns to play a truncated version of the System, as platooning can't work in professional basketball where you are allowed a limited number of substitutions. But the team still shot more three-pointers (1,893) and scored more points (123.4 per game) than any other squad. Soon after that successful D-League sojourn, David Jr. left Reno and replaced his father as Grinnell's head coach.

How did an assistant running a gimmick offense with a Division III liberal arts school attract the attention of an NBA organization? "Dean Oliver was [Sacramento's] stats guy, an analytics guru, and they wanted to bring David on to experiment," Arseneault Sr. tells me. Oliver, like Morey, is one of the NBA's most prominent number-crunchers, and he saw something about the System in 2014 that warranted a closer look. Keep in mind, that's the same year Kirk Goldsberry sounded the alarm about the league's outward migration, and the cartographer is keen to mention that Oliver has a PhD in environmental engineering. "He has a real spatial element to his thinking as well," Goldsberry says. Clearly, they were both working with the same kinds of maps.

Comparing the System to the game plans of modern NBA teams is a fascinating study in cause-and-effect. Arseneault devised his strategy because Grinnell couldn't attract talented, imposing big men to the school—the kinds of players around whom the sport revolved at that time. Teams like the Houston Rockets, meanwhile, are approaching it in reverse. In 2020, they traded away their starting center in order to more fully embrace this fast-paced, three-point-dominant style of basketball. In a game against the Dallas Mavericks, the Rockets didn't feature a single player taller than six-foot-six. It was the first time since 1963 that an NBA team won a contest with such a Lilliputian lineup.

The Rockets may be the first pro team to commit so heavily to an inverted style of basketball, but someone was bound to do it sooner or later—those points-per-shot numbers were just too tempting. But while letting it rain from downtown helped Houston rack up wins, it also makes for a rather jarring viewing experience.

In the latter part of the decade, the Rockets routinely made fewer passes per game than any other NBA squad. Think of it like house shopping: When a normal team wants to get a shot, they search different neighborhoods, narrow down their options, and hope that they've made the best possible choice given their constraints. The Rockets, on the other hand, sprint full-speed at the first door they see, and if it's dead-bolted they'll just try next door.

Kirk Goldsberry doesn't much enjoy watching Houston ram itself into doors for forty-eight straight minutes. In his book, he writes that the Rockets are the first representatives of "a hoops era that will be remembered more for its obsession with efficiency than for its aesthetic."

Goldsberry may look at the court like a map, but he still watches the game as a fan, and it doesn't take smoothing algorithms or advanced data visualization to understand his gripe with the way the Rockets play basketball. "The thing about a three-pointer is that 65 percent of them miss," he tells me. "You sign up for a world with more three-pointers, what you're really signing up for is a world with more missed jump shots."

The 2018 NBA Western Conference Finals were a defining moment for this inverted style of basketball. The Rockets hosted the defending-champion Warriors on their home court in Texas for a do-or-die Game 7. No one could accuse the Warriors of shying away from the three-point line, but they were significantly more staid in their approach to it than Houston was. During the regular season, the Rockets shot 1,100 more three-pointers than Golden State, which amounts to nearly a third of the Warriors' total three-point attempts. The Rockets weren't fighting fire with fire—they were bringing napalm to a marshmallow roast. Or, at least that's how they thought it would go.

That Game 7 will go down as one of the most infamous contests in pro hoops history. With everything on the line, the Rockets went 7-for-44 from downtown. No team has ever missed as many three-pointers in a single playoff game. One could reasonably expect embarrassment alone would have been enough of a motivator to make them stop, but the Rockets stuck to their game plan, brick after brick. At one point, they missed twenty-seven straight shots from behind the arc. Twenty-seven! They turned basketball inside out, but the sport wound up caving in on them. The Rockets lost, 101–92, and were sent out of the playoffs by their own petard.

It's hard not to be reminded of that highly misattributed quote about insanity being defined as "doing the same thing over and over again and expecting a different result." It is not the real definition of insanity, but the Rockets did their best that evening to enter themselves as a case study in its favor. Albert Einstein often and erroneously gets credited for the quote, but if you hopped in a time machine and showed him a replay of that Game 7 loss, the man behind the Theory of Relativity would surely have come to the same conclusion as everyone else: "This shit is crazy."

"I remember watching it and just being like, this sucks!" Goldsberry tells me. According to his math, viewers of that Game 7 were treated to one clanked three-pointer every forty-eight seconds. It may have been ugly, but to those who are already sick of three-pointers, the game had a beautifully appropriate ending.

"The Daryl Morey experiment was very, *very* close to getting to the Finals," Goldsberry says. "It was the most poetic collapse of the decade."

The Rockets may have lost that round, but the effects of the three-point line will continue to warp how the game looks. It's no longer enough to dump the ball down low and have your big man go to work; the action takes place at a more distant orbital plane. The three-pointer, subsidized as it is, is simply too enticing, and players who aren't able to shoot (and defend) it at a respectable clip are exiled to Outmoded Island where they must watch Betamax tapes and wait for the fax machine to bring news from the mainland. (It's never good.) While big men won the overwhelming majority of MVP honors in the 1950s, 1960s, and 1970s, it has been a full twenty years since a true center earned the NBA's most prestigious individual trophy (Shaq, in 1999–00).

Roy Hibbert is a startling example of how fast the sport has changed. Standing seven feet two inches tall, he was an effective post scorer and elite rim defender for the Indiana Pacers during the early part of the 2010s. Hibbert was named to two All-Star teams, and in 2012, he signed a $58 million contract extension. It was the maximum amount of money the Pacers were allowed to offer him. For almost all of basketball's history, Hibbert's inability to shoot or defend twenty-five feet away from the hoop would have been irrelevant. He was the dictionary definition of what a center should be . . . until he wasn't. By 2018, Hibbert was out of the NBA completely. The retirement was an unceremonious one, to say the least. There was no official announcement, and the news broke when a TMZ videographer recognized Hibbert at the airport and asked if he wanted to play anymore. "I'm good," he responded. "It's time to move on, sometimes."

Hibbert's retirement came when he was theoretically still in his prime, thirty years old, but the NBA had crouched down, crawled between his legs, and left him behind.

It's this particular side effect of the three-point line that bums Goldsberry out more than any other. "I miss all five position groups having relatively egalitarian chances of thriving," he says. "I want all of those positions that organically emerged throughout the history of the sport to still be relevant. I like that there's different sizes and shapes of basketball greatness, that different teams win in very different ways. I like that kind of stylistic and aesthetic diversity."

The lesson of basketball has long been to embrace change, but at what point is it appropriate to cry foul?

Goldsberry can hardly hold in his disdain when I broach the idea of a four-point line, saying it would "further erode the general shape of basketball and kill the big man even more." A version of the idea has been put into practice in the BIG3, a three-on-three league founded by rapper Ice Cube that features a mix of amateurs and former professional players. That league doesn't use a literal line, but rather three circles designated as "four-point zones" painted thirty feet from the basket. It's a gimmick, sure, but so was the three-pointer when it made its ABA debut.

While the NBA hasn't made any official overtures toward the four-point horizon, the idea does occasionally get bounced around when the league is discussing rule changes. In 2014, NBA president of basketball operations Rod Thorn said it is "something that's come up," though he didn't indicate whether or not they treated the notion seriously.

"I would say that, if there's a four-point line, put it inside the three-point line, down by the blocks," Goldsberry tells me. "Where Michael Jordan and Dirk Nowitzki hit their hardest fadeaways." According to the cartographer's heat maps, this is the toughest shot there is. "It's like, *I've got my back to the*

basket, I've got a six-foot-ten athlete guarding me, and I'm going to score any-
way. That shot is gone, but it is the most beautiful shot in the game."

How was George Mikan supposed to know that the gimmick he had promoted with the ABA would one day doom anyone who dared to play like George Mikan? For all his amazing powers, Superman couldn't see that far into the future. Those glasses didn't help much, either.

SECTION TWO
PUTTING THE BALL IN THE BASKET

TOPICS DISCUSSED IN THIS SECTION:

Launch angles
Karl Malone
Grandmothers
Soil conservation
Free throws
Myelin
Loneliness
The United States Postal
  Service
Noodle-pulling
Jump shots

Elena Delle Donne
The Nutcracker
Edna St. Vincent Millay
Lucille Ball
Hedge funds
The lockstitch sewing
  machine
William Randolph Hearst
The space shuttle
Awe

TOPICS NOT DISCUSSED IN THIS SECTION:

Papal succession
Eels
Papier-mâché combat
  decoys
Los Alamos National
  Laboratory
Linen care
Low-frequency harmonics
Gregor Mendel
Bosom Buddies
Fly-fishing
Livermore, California's
  Centennial Light Bulb

The Spanish Civil War
Pennies
Zinc toxicity
Escalators in Wyoming
Apollo 14's moon trees
Yaba College of
  Technology
Plinko
Folding methods for
  a fitted sheet
Jane Fonda

THE COST OF FREE THROWS
Loneliness at the line

I'VE BEEN THINKING about isolation. As I write this, the coronavirus outbreak has spread throughout the United States, forcing local and state governments to initiate shelter-at-home orders. Being stuck inside for months is never ideal, but my own personal situation during these frightening times is one of privilege. My wife and I have our dog to keep us company, and a little backyard provides fresh air and sunshine (weather permitting). Most important is that we are all healthy (knock on wood). Ours is a relatively peachy quarantine, but it is nonetheless enough to impress upon me the shape and weight of isolation. It itches after a while, and there's a heft to it—like wearing damp layers of wool.

Being cordoned off from the world gives you more time to think. This is not necessarily a good thing. Thoughts take up space, and the mind is an overpacker. Given the opportunity, it will add hundreds of soggy sweaters to the itchy woolen layers you're already wearing.

Early in the pandemic, I read an article on how to "make the most of" lockdown. It stressed the importance of sticking to a routine, which is a catch-all piece of advice you'll see given in response to pretty much any problem one may face. (It also happens to be a common strategy among dog trainers.) But, with the days and weeks bleeding together, I grew to appreciate any little interruption that managed to break into my established routine of visiting

COVID tracking websites and refreshing Twitter. Like that one afternoon when the internet at our house went down for a few hours. I look back at it fondly. All days are the same, except when they aren't.

When I want to give my mind something to keep itself busy, I usually watch basketball. That's what I was doing on March 11, 2020, when epidemiologists and infectious disease experts (but not the White House) were setting off alarm bells regarding an imminent public health catastrophe. That evening, I tuned in to a game between the Oklahoma City Thunder and Utah Jazz. The Thunder had been the season's surprise success story and were playing some pretty entertaining ball, but I'll admit I was mostly watching out of morbid curiosity. A few days prior, Jazz center Rudy Gobert took questions from reporters about the league's new coronavirus safety protocols and jokingly touched all of their microphones and recording devices before leaving the press gaggle. Flash forward to the Thunder game, and Gobert had been dropped from the starting lineup due to "illness." Was he suffering from that novel virus we'd all been hearing so much about? Would the commentators have news about his condition?

As the Thunder and Jazz—sans Gobert—prepared for tip-off, arena officials rushed onto the court and escorted the teams to their respective locker rooms. There would be no news for another half an hour. The local Oklahoma announcers, careful to avoid speculation, had almost nothing to contribute, and the broadcast alternated between the eerily quiet arena and a flummoxed studio crew. Eventually, the stadium public address man informed the crowd that the contest was cancelled "due to unforeseen circumstances." As confused fans shuffled for the exits, his voice boomed from the loudspeakers: "Everyone is safe."

That was the night everything changed. Gobert tested positive for COVID-19. Soon, his teammate Donovan Mitchell would, too. The NBA had no choice but to suspend the season. There were optimistic reports of a possible restart in the coming weeks, but the grim reality of the pandemic quickly set in. According to the COVID Tracking Project, there were 160,530 reported positive cases in the United States by the end of March. On June 4, the date the Finals were originally scheduled to begin, 1,843,315 people in the country had tested positive for the coronavirus, and there were more than 100,000 deaths.

In the long list of tragedies brought on by this pandemic, not having any sports to watch ranks somewhere between "can't get a haircut" and "my face mask itches." We can all manage. And, thanks to YouTube and NBA TV's cavalcade of classic games, my quarantine hoops diet has been surprisingly robust.

There's something both comforting and distressing about watching old games. Knowing the results takes away the suspense, and so the broadcasts take on the character of a lava lamp. It's easy to get lost in the glow of the action as it flows back and forth across the screen. That part's nice. The distress comes in the form of nostalgia, and the realization that the games you watched as a kid look fuzzy (literally, as there were no high-definition cameras) and out of sync with the rhythms of today's basketball. The pace is slow—sometimes frustratingly so—and the three-point line just sits there, unused, like Mr. Chekhov's firearm. The contests are still enjoyable; just different. If anything, you get to appreciate the things about the game that are impervious to change, like Hubie Brown and free throws.

The other day I rewatched Game 1 of the 1997 Finals between the Chicago Bulls and Utah Jazz. The teams were tied 82–82 with 9.2 seconds remaining in the fourth quarter (told you it was slow) when Dennis Rodman and Jazz power forward Karl Malone collided while trying to grab a loose ball. The officials whistled Rodman for a foul, gifting Malone two freebies and the chance to hand Utah a late lead. It's always embarrassing and impotent when a grown man yells at his television set during a game, but my moans of "weak call, ref—weak call!" while watching this twenty-three-year-old replay were particularly pathetic.

Malone was the league's MVP that year and one of the most reliable scorers on the planet. This dependability was reflected by his nickname, "The Mailman," an honorific that becomes all the more flattering whenever I see our mail carrier walking his route in a surgeon's mask and gloves. Not everyone can wait out a pandemic watching basketball reruns on the couch.

Malone finished his career second on the list of the NBA's all-time leading scorers, and a huge chunk of those points came at the line. He took the most free throws in league history (13,188) and made more foul shots than anybody else (9,787). Malone's nineteen-year career is as good of a sample size as you're going to get, and his 74.2-percent success rate at the free throw line is commensurate with the league-wide average.

NBA rules state that players have ten seconds to take each free throw, but Malone's pre-shot routine often lasted longer than this time limit. (The officials almost never called him for it, however.) Add it all together, and you'll find that he spent at least 37 total hours taking foul shots under real game conditions. By the end of his career, no one in history had spent more time shooting freebies than Karl Malone. He was prepared.

When Malone stepped to the line in Chicago, he did the same slow, protracted routine he performed before every attempt: He bounced the ball repeatedly (seven times, in this instance), spun it in his hands twice, and whispered a few words to himself. What he said before releasing his shot was a point of mystery and fascination in Utah, but Malone never divulged his secret phrase. That year, the *Salt Lake Tribune* hired two lip readers to analyze close-up footage of Malone at the line, and they determined that he used these moments of relative solitude to deliver a message to his son: "This is for Karl. Karl, my baby boy."

I know, I know: This is some pretty granular stuff. But free throws are, by definition, repetitive. The game literally stops for everyone but one person, and he can mutter a few secret words to his two-year-old child if he so chooses.

A foul shot can be intensely personal. It is the only time during a game when one's teammates and opponents are powerless to help or hinder their success. There may have been 21,000 screaming, largely drunk Chicagoans letting Karl Malone have it that Sunday afternoon at the United Center, but he was as alone as a basketball player can be. The island was familiar, even if the water surrounding him churned harder than ever before.

OK, I'll stop with the Jack London crap. You probably just want to hear what happens next (or, you already know): Malone misses both attempts, the Bulls get the rebound, and Michael Jordan hits a buzzer-beater over Bryon Russell for the win.

If it weren't for the Gary Glitter blasting over the United Center PA system, I'd argue that the game's ending has aged perfectly. The protagonists assumed their roles and provided two contrasting performances for the ages. Jordan, the all-conquering supernova around whom the sport gravitated, came up big with a devastating step-back jumper. Malone, his foil, lived down to his reputation as a shrinking scoring giant who couldn't hit a few free throws in the clutch. A coronation and condemnation, all in under ten seconds.

Adding insult to Malone's agony was Scottie Pippen. After the game, the Chicago forward told reporters that he had whispered something in Malone's ear, interrupting the Jazz star's routine as he prepared to take the first of those two fateful free throws. Pippen's trash talk is now legendary: "The mailman doesn't deliver on Sunday."

It's a great line, and for decades, I thought I had seen Pippen deliver it with my own two eyes. However, upon rewatching the game, I know this to be a false memory. The cameras didn't capture him issuing his *bon mot*—all viewers got to see was Malone's long, lonely routine, the ball rimming out of the hoop, and the agonized wince of a Mailman who failed to deliver.

There was another aspect of the game's ending that I had pushed to the far recesses of my mind. Right before Rodman's foul on Malone, Jordan had a chance to give the Bulls the lead from the foul line. He made the first attempt but clanked the second, which is why the score was knotted at 82. But, as if out of some cosmic arrangement, Jordan's stumble set into motion a sequence of events that resulted in yet another highlight-reel moment of greatness. All foul shots are the same, except when they aren't.

• • •

WANT TO LEARN something weird about free throws? For pretty much the entire history of modern competitive basketball, players haven't gotten any better or any worse at the game's most practicable shot.

Since the middle of the century, men's and women's college players have made roughly 69 percent of their attempts. In the pros, the average always hovers around 75 percent. Two- and three-point averages have steadily improved over time and across leagues and associations, but free throws have remained bafflingly consistent.

Since 1960, the NBA's league-wide season average has never climbed higher than 77.2 percent or fallen below 71.4 percent. Just take a look at this three-decade cross-section: Teams shot 75.2 percent from the line in 1978, 76.8 percent in 1988, and 76.7 percent in 2018. The athletes, equipment, and training regimens have all changed, but foul shooting has remained stagnant. It's truly bizarre.

"There's almost no change," Larry Silverberg tells me. Silverberg is a professor of mechanical and aerospace engineering at North Carolina State University. When I reach him over the phone at his house in North Carolina, he is struggling to come to grips with the loss of March Madness. "I can't believe they just cancelled it," he moans. "We're all at home and would appreciate the chance to watch sports." Keep in mind that Silverberg is a mechanical engineer, not an epidemiologist or immunologist. Specifically, he is a dynamist, meaning he studies the motion of things. He's designed radar programs to track objects' movements in space and developed control systems that have been used on multiple space shuttle missions. He's also absolutely obsessed with free throws.

To some, foul shots are a frustrating interruption to a fluid sport. To Silverberg, they're must-see TV. "When it's a really good shooter, say a 90-percent shooter, then I really look at it and notice how he's shooting," he tells me. "I'm always annoyed because, during free throws, the commentators will go off to something else. They're yapping so much, it kind of irritates me."

There are infinite permutations for putting a ball in a hoop, but some things never change. "The thing about a free throw, which is different from when you're playing, is that the conditions are like a beautiful experiment," he says. "It's a repeatable experiment." The lane is always clear, the line is always fifteen feet from the backboard, and time is always stopped.

In the late 1990s, Silverberg and his NC State mechanical engineering colleague Chau Tran had the idea to use advanced computer modeling to track all the ways a basketball moves through the air and how it interacts with the backboard and hoop. The free throw, with its immutable standards and structure, was the perfect subject for this study. The two scientists spent years honing their modeling, and in 2003 they released a paper titled "Numerical Analysis of the Basketball Shot" in the *Journal of Dynamic Systems, Measurement, and Control*. Silverberg and Tran kept expanding upon their pet project and put out more papers, like 2008's "Optimal Release Conditions for the Free Throw in Men's Basketball," published in the *Journal of Sports Sciences*.

"As we've gotten older, we've found that it's less painful to write journal articles about basketball than to actually find yourself down low on the court getting bruised up all the time," Silverberg says. "At our age, this is actually a lot of fun."

Tran shares Silverberg's pain regarding the perils of H.W.A. (Hooping While Aged). "This old body doesn't allow it anymore," he jokes. Like his colleague, he's finding the pandemic to be a slog. Teaching classes over Zoom, it turns out, isn't much fun for anyone. "You almost go through the motions, really." He likens it to watching basketball on television when you're used to attending games in person. "To hear the crowd and to hear the players live, it's better."

In Tran's mind, the fact that their free throw papers appeared in prestigious journals was as important as the actual information they were trying to convey. "The engineering community does a lot of stuff where the topic is pure science," he says. "The names of studies sound good. Like, 'Airplane Aircraft Automobile Control System,' and stuff like that." (Note: this is not a real paper, sadly.) He continues, "I think it's refreshing that we used an example of basketball. Engineers then say, 'Hey, wait a minute now, everything we use in engineering can apply to other things in life.'"

The two scientists approached the foul shot like a dynamics problem. "I was the first to curate computer codes where the ball can hit the rim and the backboard and spin," Silverberg says. His program simulates millions upon millions of different types of free throws—ones with high arc, low arc, fast rotation, no rotation, etc.—and provides accurate projections regarding which shots go in and why. "You don't get paid for doing this sort of thing," he says. "We're just dynamicists who like basketball."

Silverberg and Tran came up with the ideal geometry and dynamics for a foul shot. In other words, they solved the free throw:

Launch Angle: It changes based on height, but if a shooter's release point is higher than seven feet above the ground—which is the case for most NBA players—then the ideal launch angle is 52 degrees.

Low release speed: It behooves players to use as little forward force as possible. A "softer" shot will have a dampened, more friendly bounce should it hit the rim. The parabola achieved by the above launch angle ensures the ball will get to the hoop with a minimal amount of speed.

Rotation: Their computer modeling showed that 3 hertz of backspin is ideal. The ball takes about one second to reach the basket, meaning it should spin three times in the air.

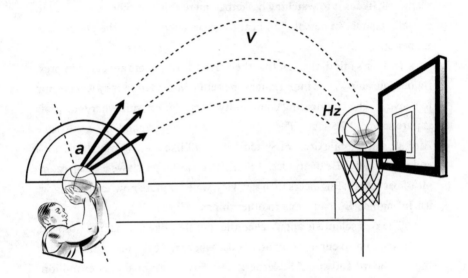

That's a lot to consider at the line, and Tran implores players not to treat these metrics as strict edicts. "If you think of too many things, it might counteract what you're trying to do," he says. Hertz, for example, is a unit of frequency most often used when talking about waves. In this application, it refers to the ball's rotation, but Tran advises you not to think too much about it. "Hertz is just a number. But you gotta have some spin. If the best you can do is 2 hertz while being comfortable, then go for that. If you can go to 2.5, that's good, but don't try to go up to 3 hertz if it makes your shot totally out of whack."

We may know the dynamics of a perfect free throw, but the biggest variable remains that nervous clump of gray cells and electricity inside of our heads. It has to contend with concepts like pressure and embarrassment, things that elude even the most advanced computer modeling. "Those of us who know the free throw are all saying the same kinds of things, really," Silverberg tells me. "You have to practice. *A lot.* Until you just don't think about it. When I have my mind together, I can shoot it at about 90 percent. But that's not with a stadium of people. That's just me shooting by myself."

Stepping to the line during a game is a totally different kind of isolation than shooting in an empty gym. It's why Shaquille O'Neal made around 80 percent of his foul shots at practice but only converted 53 percent of his attempts when it counted. "When I'm by myself I shoot like Steve Kerr," O'Neal has said. "But it's just something about when I'm in a game, there's pressure, I just tighten up." Wilt Chamberlain (51.1 percent career free throw average) more or less experienced the same exact thing. "I know the problem is in my head," he wrote, "because I shot well in practice."

Shaq takes full responsibility for his struggles at the line. Just kidding, he blames God. "Because the way I played, the way I made everyone else around me better, all of the publicity I was doing—imagine if I was doing that and had shot 90 percent from the free throw line," he told *USA Today* after his retirement. "I would have been arrogant. I'd probably be so arrogant. So it was just His way of saying, 'Hey, buddy, you're just like everybody else.' " Thank God he's not arrogant.

Shaq does make an interesting point. What would happen if everyone shot 90 percent from the line? Would you even need to go through the motions of taking a free throw if the points were practically guaranteed? Really, the only reason we watch free throws is in case they don't go in.

When James Naismith invented basketball, each team had one dedicated person take all the free throws. "This player soon became so expert that he could throw the ball into the basket a large percentage of the time," he wrote. "This meant that a foul was practically as good as a goal." In 1923, the rule was updated to make it so the person who gets fouled has to earn the points at the line themselves.

Naismith called the change "excellent," because "each member of the team developed skill in this part of the game." But we have reams of data to show that this is not at all what happened. Only a handful of players shoot 90 percent from the line. Everybody else drags the average down to around 75 percent, and they've been doing this for decades.

"Free-throw shooting should be easy," Hot Rod Hundley told the *Los Angeles Times* in 1996. Hundley played in the NBA in the 1950s and 1960s before becoming the Jazz's longtime radio announcer. He got his nickname from his dribbling antics and not his shooting ability, a fact made evident by his blasé lifetime free throw average of 72.1 percent. (It should be mentioned that Hundley was one of the last true Weird Free Throw Guys—he was known to shoot some as hook shots.) Even so, he felt confident in his assumptions. "You walk up there and you're fifteen feet away from the basket and you don't have anybody bothering you. If you're a shooter, you're going to make them. We've really got some terrible shooters, compared to past years."

That wasn't true, of course. In 1963, Hundley's last year in the NBA, players averaged 72.7 percent from the line. In 1996, the year plagued by "terrible shooters," the average was 74 percent.

Hundley made a more controversial claim while announcing a particularly ugly Jazz game against the Miami Heat in 1996, a contest where our chum Karl Malone took a career-high twenty-eight free throws but only made fifteen. Even worse, the game was on a Monday, so the Mailman had no excuse. "I did a terrible job," he told reporters afterward. "Just terrible."

As bad as Malone's shooting was that night, it wasn't nearly as embarrassing as Hundley's performance in the booth. During the broadcast, he told his listeners, "Women could shoot free throws better." The comment sparked a brief controversy for Hundley, and as a bombastic sports radio personality, he tried to capitalize on it by hosting a promotional free throw contest against a group of women. (He lost.)

I bring up a decades-old radio controversy not to shame Hundley, who died in 2015, or to further humiliate Karl Malone. (OK, maybe I want to needle Malone a little bit more.) It's just that Hot Rod's comment is a convenient excuse to explore Silverberg and Tran's most recent foray into the world of free throw science. They had intended to send their newest study to various sports media personalities for coverage, but as Silverberg aches to me through the phone, "The season got cancelled!"

While Silverberg's field of research is motion, the unrelenting steadiness of free throw averages caught his eye. "Men. Women. NBA. WNBA. NCAA. It's all the same. For forty years. Across gender. Consistent. If you have a little sense of humor you go, 'So, who's better? Are the men better, or are the women better?' "

Silverberg analyzed the numbers over decades of college games, where the yearly free throw average always hovers around 69 percent. One could assume that there would be no difference in skill because both men and women make and miss foul shots at a nearly identical rate, but there are a few minute variables to take into account. "We spent four years doing this because the data is so close," Silverberg tells me. "At first, we assumed men were better because they play with a slightly larger ball. The circumference of a women's basketball is about one inch smaller, which means it has one additional inch of wiggle room when passing through the hoop." But this is science; there is no reason to make assumptions when you have state-of-the-art computer modeling at your fingertips.

"A women's basketball is pumped up to the same pressure as a men's ball so it bounces more," Silverberg explains. "According to NCAA rules, it bounces higher. If a regulation women's basketball just touches the rim, it's more likely to bounce out. So on the one hand you have a 2- to 4-percent difference in size, but you also have a 2- to 4-percent difference in, not to be technical, but we'll say 'bounciness.'"

The next variable they studied was height. The average women's college player is shorter than the average men's player. One of the things Silverberg and Tran learned while computing millions of free throw simulations was that it's easier to make free throws when you have a higher release point. That, they discovered, was the most influential factor in free throw success between the subject groups.

Because they shoot from a less advantageous angle and use a bouncier ball, free throws are harder for women's NCAA players. Nevertheless, they shoot them with the same accuracy. "The criteria we used is consistency," Silverberg says. "And we found that women were about 3 percent better than the men."

See, I wasn't trying to shame Hundley. I merely wanted to prove that he was right all along: Not only could women shoot free throws better, they *do* shoot them better, and now there's a peer-reviewed research study to prove it.

• • •

ELENA DELLE DONNE is the best free throw shooter in the history of professional basketball. She plays for the WNBA's Washington Mystics, and in her seven years in the league, she has missed sixty-two free throws. Total.

Delle Donne's career average is 93.8 percent, a rate that comfortably tops Steve Nash, the NBA's all-time free throw leader who shot his freebies at a rate of 90.43 percent. Watch her at the line and you'll see a smooth, brisk motion. It'd be relatively unremarkable were it not for the fact that the ball is almost guaranteed to go in every single time. She is as close to automation as flesh and blood can get.

On the other end of the spectrum is Andre Drummond. The two-time NBA All-Star is one of the most physically intimidating players in the league, and he also happens to be its very worst foul shooter. Against the Houston Rockets in 2016, Drummond set the NBA record for most misses from the line in a single game with twenty-three. Astonishingly, he shot better that night (13–36; 36 percent) than he had in the months leading up to it (35 percent). The worst free throw performance in history actually *raised* his average for the season.

In his first five years in the league, Drummond's free throw average never topped 39 percent. It wasn't for lack of trying. The Pistons hired experts to work with the center on his form, and he frequently stayed after practices and games to take hundreds of extra attempts. As is the case with most professional players, he made the majority of those practice shots. (One reporter who stayed to watch him shoot after a particularly poor performance noted that Drummond hit 80 percent of his attempts in the empty arena.) Still, when it mattered the most, Drummond couldn't put it together. Things got so desperate that he even tried wearing a virtual reality helmet to re-create the high-stress experience of being at the line. It didn't work.

All told, Andre Drummond likely worked on free throws more than anyone else in professional basketball. But while Delle Donne's shot almost always produces the perfect arc, speed, and rotation, Drummond's is all over the place. How can it be that two people who have spent their entire lives playing the same sport have such divergent experiences taking an open shot fifteen feet away from the basket?

Some will argue that bigger and taller players have more trouble making foul shots, but the game is replete with giants who had or have little trouble from the line. The seven-foot-six-inch Yao Ming shot 83.3 percent over his career. Kristaps Porzingis, the Dallas Mavericks' seven-foot-three center, hits them at an 81-percent clip.

"When I'm studying all of this, I look at best practices," Silverberg tells me. "I find out what are the things you really have to focus on. What are the variables?"

When preparing to take a foul shot, the first variable is aim—getting the ball directed at the hoop so you don't miss to the left or to the right. "You can see if you're not lined up," he says. You can't see all the vital things that haven't happened yet, however, like the speed, arc, and rotation of the ball after it leaves your hand. "Those involve your entire body. There are many different movements that can get to that trajectory. Body motion is a coordinated event that gets built up from the time you're a little kid. You end up having lots of different kinds of movements that will lead to the same result."

Because everybody's body is different, there can be no such thing as perfect free throw motion. Perfection only exists after-the-fact, when the ball has detached itself from our flawed human forms. Bending my elbow at a right angle could help me achieve the desired trajectory, but the tendons in your arm might not want to play that game. Silverberg says the key is teaching your body to perform an easily repeatable sequence of movements that will produce a desired result. "Getting a nice smooth body motion, that's the most complicated of all the variables," he says. "It's kinematic."

This, Silverberg argues, could be the secret behind the always controversial "granny shot," wherein a player tosses a free throw from between their legs. "They would not approve of you calling it the 'granny shot,'" he warns. "They would call it an 'underhand shot.'"

The "they" in question here are the proponents of this method, most notably Rick Barry. The NBA Hall-of-Famer was one of the best free throw shooters in history (89.3 percent), and he took them all underhand. Despite Barry's success, almost no one in professional basketball has adopted his style since he retired in 1980. A twenty-first century exception is former Houston Rockets reserve center Chinanu Onuaku. He only played six games in the NBA, but he was perfect from the line: four-for-four.

According to Silverberg's analysis, the granny—excuse me, *underhand*—method is not inherently better than a traditional shot. It just happens to be easier to repeat. "It has a pro and a con," he says. "The bad news is that you're releasing the ball lower, and that means that you need to be more consistent. The pro is that the body motion is a single motion. It's like a pendulum;

it's a smooth motion to commit to memory, kinesthetically. Getting that velocity and angle committed to memory is actually very easy with a lot of practice."

Barry is an underhand evangelist, and he's spent decades unsuccessfully trying to convert the league's more helpless foul shooters. "I really truly can't comprehend the aversion people have to trying something that could be very effective for them," he told NPR. The biggest impediment has always been pride. Apparently, millionaire athletes are absolutely petrified of being associated with grannies.

When Wilt Chamberlain switched to the underhand free throw style for a brief spell during the 1961–62 season, he made 61 percent of his attempts, the best mark of his career. Chamberlain was a seven-foot superhuman who incessantly bragged about his romantic pursuits and carried himself as the most confident dude on the planet, but he quickly ditched the method because he said it made him look "like a sissy."

Shaquille O'Neal, the heir to Chamberlain's brand of he-man dominance and swagger, also inherited Wilt's terrible foul shooting. He was a logical target for Barry's conversion efforts, but the big man wouldn't budge. "I told Rick Barry I'd rather shoot zero percent than shoot underhand. I'm too cool for that," he said.

In 2016, when Drummond was mired in the worst free throw funk of his life, his coach indicated that drastic steps would have to be taken. "As far as shooting underhand or anything else," Stan Van Gundy told reporters, "Everything is on the table." The announcement countered something Drummond had tweeted as a rookie: "Let me make this clear. . . . I'm not shooting free throws underhand. . #Relax."

Silverberg argues that the biggest advantage of the underhand shot is that it forces players to try something different. "If you've got a really bad free throw shooter, and he really wants to be better, it's very possible that telling him to do the granny shot will be the best thing for him. Because the granny shot is so different, he's going to break his habits with it." Notice how he fails to catch himself saying "granny shot." Like it or not, the term sticks.

This stigma may have prevented Drummond from faithfully mimicking Rick Barry, but he did find some success with a totally new form. Drummond reunited with an old trainer during the 2017 off-season and the two tore down his free-throw motion and started from scratch. Originally, Drummond held the ball in front of his face with his elbow bent—the picture of proper form. The problem was that he literally freeze-framed in this position just before his release. The effect was a mighty hitch, one that hijacked any of the smoothness one would hope to see in a shooter's motion.

For his new-and-improved shot, Drummond bends his knees and keeps his arms straight while pointing the ball at the floor. He then levers smoothly upward, like a wall in an Amish barn raising, and finishes the move with a wrist-snap. If you squint, it almost looks like an enhanced and inverted granny shot. No one would mistake it for perfect form, but the awkward motion is far smoother than his old hiccup of a shot.

Drummond started the following season by going 30-for-40 from the line. After failing to shoot above 40 percent for five straight years, his per-season average never again dipped below 50 percent. By his ninth year in the league, he managed to raise his lifetime average to 46.1 percent. In a vacuum, this is still awful. But in the peculiarly consistent world of foul shooting, his improvement represents a monumental achievement.

It's an uphill climb to go from terrible to bad, and it's essentially impossible to go from bad to great. Drummond would have to make 22,300 free throws in a row in order to match Elena Delle Donne's career average. Daunting, sure, but it's never too late to start trying.

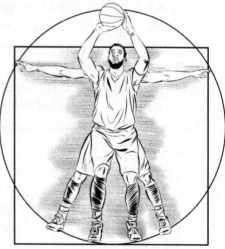

• • •

A LOT GOES into setting a Guinness World Record. "You've got to have two official witnesses, you need a referee, you need two timekeepers. Why you need *two* time keepers, I have no idea," Bob Fisher tells me over the phone from Centralia, Kansas. Fisher, a soil-conservation technician, is prepped and ready to set the record for most foul shots made in one hour while blindfolded. He's confident he'll crush it, but the ongoing pandemic means he'll have to wait. "You've got to have it videoed, you've got to have a photographer taking still photos, you've got to have two people counting." In a town of 512 people, that counts as a pretty big gathering. "We're not locked down here but it's definitely factored in," he says. "Schools are closed. It would be difficult to get everybody together."

Fisher already holds Guinness World Records in fourteen different free throw categories. He has made more foul shots in thirty seconds (33) than anyone else on the planet. He's also made the most free throws in a minute (52), two minutes (92), ten minutes (448), an hour (2,371), one minute while blindfolded (22), two minutes while blindfolded (37), and one minute while standing on one leg (49). The most prolific foul shooter on God's green earth was not born this way. In fact, making baskets from fifteen feet out only became an obsession as he neared retirement.

Fisher speaks with a calming, high plains intonation (think Hank Hill). He designs soil conservation systems for the government, a job he humbly describes as "civil engineering, to a certain extent." He definitely thinks like an engineer, and in 2008 he became enamored with John J. Fontanella's book *The Physics of Basketball,* which lays out the geometry and math of the game, much like Silverberg and Tran's research. Fisher coached high school basketball in northeast Kansas, and he had long searched for a reliable method to teach people how to shoot. "Using science to come up with an answer really appealed to me," he says.

Inspired by Fontanella's take on launch angles, Fisher built a giant wooden protractor to help guide the release points of his players. It soon became clear to him that there was no such thing as a correct shooting motion—what matters most is that very last moment, when the ball rolls off the fingertips. This blossomed into an ethos for shooting, one that focuses on experimentation and feedback rather than a dogmatic adherence to mechanics.

Fisher met with a marketing team about manufacturing and selling his giant protractor, but they convinced him to film an instructional DVD instead. "The video came out with a thundering silence," he says. Fisher hated the jokes their writer-for-hire included ("corny," he calls them), but he attributes the flop to his lack of name recognition. "When you're a high school coach there's really no claim to fame."

Even that claim to non-fame was fleeting. In his third year as a head coach, Fisher tried to re-create David Arseneault's record-breaking experiment in Iowa, but the System failed to get the desired results. While pragmatic and cerebral, he did not turn to the System because he was impressed by the analytics behind Grinnell's Formula for Success. "I had gotten so sick of the kids turning the ball over," he says. "I was like, 'Just shoot the damn ball.'" The team finished the season .500 and Fisher was let go from his position.

It was a rough period, and Fisher couldn't help but be reminded of a tidbit of conventional (albeit inaccurate) wisdom he had heard many times as a child. "You picked up on the fact that, when you get to the age of eighteen, your brain just kind of stops growing," he says.

The year after his failed instructional DVD, Fisher read *The Talent Code: Greatness Isn't Born. It's Grown,* a self-help book by author Daniel Coyle. In it, Coyle discusses myelin, a substance that insulates axons of the brain's nerve cells. Fisher could build myelin, he learned, just by practicing something, and the prospect of changing his brain chemistry proved to be irresistible.

Coyle's book led Fisher to other works and studies concerning self-improvement, and he rattles off the luminaries responsible for these texts with the familiarity of someone listing the neighbors they had spotted at the grocery store that morning. There's Canadian kinesiology professor Dr. Joan Vickers, economist Geoffrey Colvin, Dutch sports scientist Dr. Raoul R. D. Oudejans, and K. Anders Ericsson, to name but a few of the gurus and thought leaders Fisher has curated into his own personal salon.

Ericsson is a Swedish psychologist whose research on "deliberate practice" was particularly inspiring to Fisher. Deliberate practice describes a laser-focused approach to training where repetition is buttressed by incessant fine-tuning. Personally, as someone who's never really striven for greatness, deliberate practice isn't my bag. But it clicked for Fisher, and he reached out to Ericsson to learn more. Much to his surprise and delight, the Swedish psychologist wrote back, and the two began corresponding over email. "That's the great thing about this day and age," Fisher says. "You're able to make contact with people."

Fisher filled his bookshelves to critical mass, and the overflow turned his basement into a rolling field of texts. It is undoubtedly the most impressive self-help library in all of Centralia. "They were all saying basically the same thing," he tells me. "All it takes to be good is knowledge, practice, and time. Once I learned that, I applied it. Knowledge practice time. Knowledge practice time. *KPT,* I always say."

Fisher had already tried and failed to be a shooting instructor, but that was before he unearthed the secrets of myelin and KPT. There were no longer any limits to his self-improvement. And so, at the age of fifty-two, he set out on his quest to change his brain and become the greatest free throw shooter on earth.

Superlative foul shooters, the ones who set implausible records and break impossible streaks, don't tend to be professional basketball players. The pros need to focus on all facets of the game, and free throws are often an afterthought. But the consistent nature of the foul shot makes it a perfect focus for obsessives with tons of time on their hands. Take Tom Amberry, a retired podiatrist who at the age of seventy-one sank 2,750 free throws in a row without missing a single attempt (a Guinness World Record at the time). The person who topped that mark was Ted St. Martin, a sixty-one-year-old dairy farmer who in 1996 made 5,221 consecutive foul shots. Amberry and St. Martin have both since passed away, leaving the sixty-four-year-old Fisher, who knew both of them, as the heir to the throne.

"Why is it that all the great foul shooters start so, uh—" I stammer for the words.

"Late in life?" he finishes my sentence with a chuckle. "For Dr. Tom, he retired at sixty-nine and he was bored. It was something for him to do. The first time he went to the gym after retirement he tried to play. He said, 'They almost killed me!' After that he just stepped up to the foul line and got into a routine where he shot five hundred free throws every morning.

"Ted St. Martin is a different story," Fisher adds. "He just had a knack for it, so to speak. As far as studying it, I don't believe he did. He just went out and did it and intuitively learned how to do it."

With his fealty to KPT, Fisher is obviously entrenched in the Amberry camp of free throw mastery. "Dr. Tom was very proud of his practice," he says. "He was a foot doctor. He did time and motion studies, and he broke things down and reduced the amount of time it took to do certain surgeries. He had that same approach when he went after free throw shooting." In a 1998 story about Amberry published in *Orange Coast* magazine, a podiatrist colleague describes Amberry's obsession with these so-called "time-and-motion studies": "Everything from the way you pick up the instruments to where you make the incision . . . Don't waste time. Don't talk. If you have to use a certain type of blade, you use it for everything you need it to do before you put it down."

Fisher is not a doctor, but he studied shooting like a Harvard Med valedictorian. He read esoteric medical texts in his spare time and mined every relevant source he could find for information on biomechanics. Leonardo da Vinci famously dissected cadavers in order to better understand how face muscles controlled the Mona Lisa's smirk, and I have no doubt that Fisher would do the same in the service of free throws had he access to a morgue. When his wife, Connie, slipped on a patch of ice and broke her leg, he used her appointments to pepper the orthopedists with questions about wrist movement and the angles at which a person's elbow naturally bends. One of her doctors gave him his medical textbooks so he could consult them directly himself.

Fisher didn't set out on his quest with the goal of becoming the king of blindfolded and one-legged free throws; he just wanted to build as much new myelin as possible and teach folks how to shoot better. "The records were just something that were available for me to do," he says. "It was more of a validation of the fact that I had something to share which was of value to people."

When he rewatched his instructional video (the one with the corny jokes), Fisher saw an incomplete document. "It was early in the process," he says. By 2016 he had broken more than a dozen world records and decided to put his evolved philosophy onto the page. The result is *Straight Shooter,* a fascinating book that's both an instructional text and a peek into Fisher's ceaselessly percolating mind. Within the first two pages you'll find wisdom from Johann Wolfgang von Goethe and Dr. Joyce Brothers. Needless to say, I loved it.

"In shooting, there is so much misinformation," Fisher says. "It really can, and it does, lead kids astray. I hate that."

High on Fisher's shit list are broadcasters who share their own takes on what constitutes a perfect free throw. When he heard an announcer critique the form of University of Kansas center Udoka Azubuike, Fisher almost blew a gasket. "He said, 'He'll never have success [making free throws] until he gets his elbow under the ball.' You've got to be kidding me!" Fisher didn't spend years researching the "bucket-carrying angle," which is a term used for the natural bend in a person's arm, to hear someone say such things on national television. (From Fisher's book: "In a study by the National Center for Biotechnology Information, the carrying angle in females was more significant than the angle in males ($16.2° +/- 3.2°$ versus $13.6° +/- 3.0°$). . . . For most players, keeping the forearm perfectly vertical when shooting is biomechanically awkward and therefore ineffective.")

At a high school shooting clinic hosted by Fisher, one boy refused to square his feet at the free throw line. "Let me ask you a question," Fisher told him, "Did you happen to watch that game where Bobby Knight said to stagger your feet back like that?" When the student replied in the affirmative, Fisher shot back, "What the heck does Bobby Knight know about shooting? He was a defensive specialist!" The rejoinder worked, and his young charge agreed to try out a new stance.

To be clear, Fisher doesn't champion one specific elbow angle or foot position. Not even close. His entire philosophy revolves around feedback, listening to your body, and making adjustments. He certainly practices what he preaches. When training for an hour-long free throw record, Fisher noticed that his fingers went numb after about ten minutes of shooting. He hypothesized his release point was too high for his heart to pump blood to the extremities, and he responded by concocting a new, lower release for his shot. (The podiatrist Amberry displayed similar adaptability. He was a southpaw, and when he blew out a tendon in his left elbow he simply switched hands and practiced until he could break records as a righty.)

Fisher's full philosophy can be found in his book, and despite all the references to biomechanics, much of the actual instruction is refreshingly straightforward. "Players do not want to know how the engine works; they just want to learn how to drive it," he says. "It has to be simple." Young players seeking to improve their foul shooting needn't engage in ongoing correspondences with Swedish psychologists—Fisher's done that grunt work already.

Take his "centerline" method, which is a strategy for shooting the ball straight and with high efficiency, even if your wrist snaps at an angle. While he provides the physics and biomechanics behind his theory, the actionable instructions are succinct enough to be printed inside a fortune cookie. "Go out, balance the ball in one hand, and snap your wrist," he says. "The ball is going to go straight."

The seeds of that theory were actually planted in soil conservation. "In surveying, I was familiar with the term *centerline*," he says. "You go from point A to point B when you set up the instrument." It's an early step, one where an engineer begins to establish the geometric parameters of the land upon which he or she is working. "You kind of lock back in on certain points. That reference occurred to me when I first noticed that I could make shots with my hand going at an angle to the basket."

It's all about making a reference vector, which is precisely what Fisher gets his shooting protégés to do when he asks them to balance the ball and snap their wrists. They're creating a centerline around which the rest of the shot will be built.

Fisher's quest to become a free throw guru impacted his day job as well. "All it takes to become good is KPT. Did I apply that to my work? Yes. I became very, very good at my work. I retired at the end of August, after thirty-two years, but now I am sidelining that because people are paying me to come out of retirement."

Fisher believes his philosophy, and not the Guinness World Records, will be what he is remembered for. "I came up with a new and better way to teach shooting," he tells me. "That is going to be my legacy."

When Fisher read about Silverberg's work with computer modeling, the ever-curious soil conservation technician reached out to the mechanical engineering professor to discuss free throws. The two formed a bond, and

Silverberg contributed a chapter to Fisher's book about the physics of a foul shot.

"A lot of the coaches spend too much time telling you where you put your elbow," Silverberg tells me. "[Fisher] tends to focus on the feedback stuff a lot."

Silverberg, like Fisher, finds that tweaking your form after missing a shot is the "most important form of correction." It's kinesthetics—how the body learns to develop a repeatable motion. When a motion can reliably produce the arc, speed, and backspin endorsed by those computer models, you're in luck. "After that, it's just practice," Silverberg says. "I tell a person, if they know the principles and if they're willing to practice every day for around an hour, they can get it in about three months or so. They'll be a 90-percent shooter."

His claim only applies in no-pressure, empty gym situations, and while I'd love to put it to the test, all the basketball hoops in my neighborhood have either been boarded up or removed completely in order to promote social distancing. The closest I come to practicing my free throw motion is in the form of cliché, and I am pleased to report that this uncoordinated writer is now tossing crumpled papers into his waste bin with Elena Delle Donne-like accuracy.

• • •

LET'S GO BACK to those missed free throws by Karl Malone. No, not the ones against the Miami Heat that inspired Hot Rod Hundley's impetuous correlation between gender and the ability to shoot a ball from fifteen feet out. I'm talking about the following year, when Malone wasn't able to seize his opportunity against the Chicago Bulls.

Slow-motion replays reveal just how close those attempts were. On his first shot, the ball dips inside the rim and then spins out, leaving Malone a victim of centrifugal force. If you tracked the free throw in Larry Silverberg's computer software, you might see that the arc wasn't soft enough to engender a friendly roll. Or, perhaps there was too much hertz on the backspin and his release speed was too high. Either way, he blew it.

Karl Malone is not a pitiable figure. (Seriously, Google him.) Other players have missed hugely consequential free throws, and they don't have his long résumé to fall back on. Some were never able to recover.

Two years before Malone's big misses, Orlando Magic guard Nick Anderson found himself in a similar position to the Mailman. It was Game 1 of the 1995 NBA Finals, which, conveniently, is available in full on YouTube. Watching it is a decent way to pass two hours during a months-long pandemic, though the ending is tough to sit through. With the Magic up three points in the waning moments, Houston fouled Anderson and sent him to the line. A single free throw would have effectively sealed the win, but it wasn't Anderson's night. He missed them both.

After a scramble for the rebound, the ball ended up in the last place Anderson wanted it: his own hands, again. He desperately tried to pass it away, but the Rockets fouled him once more and granted a second chance (or, more accurately, a third and fourth chance) to redeem himself. What followed was one of the most famous collapses in NBA Finals history. He missed both attempts and Houston hit a miracle three-pointer to send the contest into overtime. Had the Magic won in that extra period, Game 1 of the 1995 NBA Finals would not be known as "The Nick Anderson Game." But they didn't, and it is.

Before that night, no one would have accused Anderson of being a nervous dude. Just a few weeks prior, he and the Magic knocked the Chicago Bulls out of the playoffs. Michael Jordan had returned mid-season from his baseball hiatus and was not yet in basketball shape, and the aggressive Anderson took advantage. In the opening game of those Eastern Conference Semifinals, he famously stole the ball from Jordan and gave the Magic a come-from-behind victory in the final seconds.

"No. 45 is not No. 23," Anderson told reporters after that game, referring to Jordan's post-baseball squad number. The comment made Jordan un-retire his old jersey mid-series. Anderson managed to rip Superman's cape off his back and sent the mighty Bulls packing. Who could have foreseen that, in a few weeks, a quartet of free throws would leave him completely unraveled?

In his book *The Art of a Beautiful Game: The Thinking Fan's Tour of the NBA*, writer Chris Ballard spoke with Anderson, and the retired guard told him that those misses were "like a song that got in my head, playing over and over." Anderson was at the airport shortly after those Finals when he looked up in horror at the televisions hanging at the gate. They were playing the worst moment of his basketball life. "And I'm sitting there, right, and people are looking, looking at the game," he said. "And I'm like, 'Oh, God.' One would look, then another, then the whole damn airport, saying, 'That's Nick Anderson, sitting there!' " Once again, Anderson found himself totally surrounded but also completely alone.

Before those Finals, Anderson's career free throw average hovered around 70 percent. It plummeted to 40 percent the following season. He was haunted. Things got so bad, his coach refused to play him in the fourth quarters of games.

Those missed free throws turned him into a different player. As an oversize guard he once bullied smaller opponents, but he had to abandon that strategy because initiating contact meant getting fouled, and getting fouled meant taking a trip to that lonely spot on the floor, a place where the weight of isolation is enough to bring you down.

Bob Fisher tells me that "shooting free throws can be meditative, and, at times, lonely." His wife stopped accompanying him during his practice sessions, and he now feels like "the Lone Ranger without Tonto." But his practices are low-stakes, and he's learned to use the solitude to "lock in on the most minute details" of his form. Without that repetitive work to anchor him down, he knows his mind would wander right out of the gym.

The scenario Nick Anderson faced cannot be re-created in a laboratory. Even a supernatural foul shooter like Fisher admits he'd get intimidated by those stakes. "Going for a Guinness World Record is totally different than end-of-game situations," he says. "I'm able to shoot more than once. I can get a rhythm going." While he is obsessed with developing his brain, Fisher knows that it can also prove to be a shooter's downfall. "At the end of a game, a player is stepping up the line and he's got time to think about it."

Like Fisher, Tom Amberry didn't waste time between free throws. By getting rid of the ball quickly, the foot doctor starved his mind of any opportunities to swaddle him in the itchy wool of thought. "Thinking is the worst thing you can do," he once wrote. "What's there to think about?"

Not everyone has the Zen calm of a retired podiatrist in Southern California. Professional basketball players have *a lot* to think about. The flow and pace of the game may be a good distraction, but what happens when there's a foul and everything grinds to a halt? You're isolated on the line with nothing to focus on but the hoop and a frozen clock. What's the mind supposed to do then?

Paula Kout saw first-hand just how difficult it can be for NBA players to slow down. Chicago Bulls head coach Phil Jackson hired her to teach the team some basic yoga principles before the 1997–98 season. "The players had no frame of reference for it," she tells me. "If you take a player today and tell them they are going to do yoga, well, everyone does yoga." Back then, however, the practice was practically unheard of, and the Bulls organization was so skeptical of its benefits that Jackson had to pay Kout with his own money.

"I was taking a bunch of guys who had spent their whole lives in one mindset, one method of training their bodies," she says. Getting Michael Jordan and Scottie Pippen into downward-facing dog was a bit odd at first, but everyone on the team was open to the experience. "They were such good sports," she recalls. The biggest surprise, though, came during the quiet moments.

These were the only times in their professional lives, Kout believes, that someone told them to do nothing. "Don't succeed. Don't excel. Don't be aggressive." It may have been the strangest and most difficult experience the players faced during her classes. She loves to imitate Dennis Rodman doing shavasana, or "corpse pose," where you lie still on your back. "He would be lying on his mat with his eyes closed, drumming his fingertips on the floor." He had no idea how to not do anything. (Rodman's career free throw percentage: 58.4 percent.)

"That moment of doing nothing wasn't the prelude to something that was demanding pressure and stress," Kout says. "It was a total free space on the bingo card. Do nothing now, and do nothing afterward. That's the beauty of a yoga class. You're not thinking of anything else. You are in the moment. You are absorbed in this mind-body experience."

Karl Malone could have benefited from doing nothing after missing that first free throw against the (not yet yoga-limbered) Bulls in 1997. Watching the replay, it's obvious that the man's mind is racing. He saunters toward half-court with furrowed brow and grunts a word of frustration that likely upset Utah's finest lip-readers.

Andre Drummond would surely recognize Malone's march. The league's worst free throw shooter used to perform a similar frustrated stroll to center court in between his attempts. When he changed to his more effective shooting form, Drummond also stopped wandering from the line. Now, he stays put and takes a meditative inhalation. "It's just this brief yoga breath that I do before I shoot the shot," he told ESPN. "It relaxes my whole body and I feel great."

Karl Malone clearly didn't feel great, and his second attempt against the Bulls reflects this. The ball dips tantalizingly below the rim and then spins out and to the left—an identical reproduction of the first shot. He learned nothing. Those initial mistakes concerning arc or hertz or speed were copied and pasted into the fibers and sinew of Malone's kinesthetic machinery and they produced an agonizing sequel.

Malone's inability to process feedback, as preached by Fisher and scientifically backed up by Silverberg and Tran, proved to be his downfall. "I think both of them were right on line," Malone's teammate Jeff Hornacek said while doing some quick motion modeling in his head. "I think it was a case if it was a half-inch shorter, it would have hit the rim, bounced off the backboard and went in. If it was a half-inch farther, it would have been a swish. Both free throws were right there, but a half-inch here or there makes a difference."

Malone failed basketball's most repeatable experiment, but Chicago guard Steve Kerr credited the laboratory conditions for the Bulls' fortunate break. "That rim down there the last two months has been loose because of our mascot dunking [on it] all the time," he dished to a reporter after the game. Chicago was experimenting with a newer and more extreme mascot at the time named Da Bull. Unlike the charming and portly Benny the Bull, Da Bull was a buff daredevil who entertained the crowd with fierce, trampoline-assisted slams during breaks. According to Kerr, Da Bull's antics loosened the rim at one end of the court so severely that a maintenance crew had to come in and tighten its mechanism before Game 1 against the Jazz. "And thank God because both those free throws were right there," Kerr said. "They tightened them up just right."

Facetious or not, Kerr may have been onto something. According to Dr. Chau Tran, a free throw is at the mercy of "the vibration of the whole structure—the rims, the backboard and the bridge in the middle." He says a stiff rim is less forgiving and, under much tighter conditions, "We assume that the player has to make it with a swish."

Karl Malone made more foul shots than anybody else in NBA history, but he is remembered for two misses that may have rolled out because of an overzealous mascot.

All free throws are the same, except when they aren't.

JUMPING PAST CONCLUSIONS
Breaking the surly bonds of bad coaching

R EMEMBER THAT INDUSTRIOUS student at the YMCA who worked on his shot before a befuddled James Naismith? The guy who introduced the notion of practice to the game's inventor? I can say with utmost certainty that this young man's shooting motion was garbage. With feet planted firmly to the ground, he most likely thrust the ball forward from his chest with two hands, like a pass. Transplant him to a modern pickup court and he'd get each and every one of his attempts blocked back to the nineteenth century. Then, he'd see a plane flying overhead and faint from shock. It'd be a rough afternoon for our friend.

Everyone's shot is clumsy when they're new to basketball. Chau Tran, the professor who studies free throws (among other more complex mechanical engineering matters), says this is a by-product of a player being uncomfortable or unable to release a shot above his or her head. "Especially when someone plays basketball when they are young, to reach the height of ten feet they've got to push from their chest," he explains. "That form continues to be bad. When you or I watch basketball, we say, 'Oh man, he didn't shoot; he 'pushed' the shot. That's why he clanked off the rim.' "

For all the monumental changes basketball experienced throughout its adolescence, that eminently stuff-able heave practiced by Naismith's student remained the default shooting style for decades. The motion could be described as a "set shot," which applies to any attempt where one's feet are stuck to the ground, or a "push shot," as Tran explains. But, for the sake of colorful taxonomy, let's coin a different phrase for this maneuver. I vote for "creaky carry-on," because it looks like someone with arthritis shoving their bag into an airplane's overhead compartment.

Players refined the creaky carry-on over the years. Other variations included the one-handed duffel bag shove and an underhand toss that sadly doesn't lend itself to luggage pantomime. But, no matter the movement, jumping was not involved.

The jump shot seems obvious: By releasing the ball at the highest possible point you greatly reduce the chances of it getting blocked. It's a real no-brainer, but the move didn't appear in organized basketball until around the 1930s, nearly half a century after Naismith's class of incorrigibles took the floor, and it wouldn't become commonplace until the 1950s. It's a case of stunted evolution, and the people charged with growing and nurturing the game are the ones to blame for impeding the development of the jumper.

There was never a rule that said you couldn't jump while taking a shot, but early coaches drilled it into their players' heads that they must remain glued to the parquet in order for their shots to be effective. You could bring one leg up off the floor or drift laterally on layups, but those who had the nerve to add any real elevation to their mid- or long-range efforts would find their asses planted on the bench. Perhaps Naismith was right about those "evil" coaches after all.

This slow, deliberate shooting motion went hand-in-hand with the slow, deliberate offenses of the era. Without a shot clock to force the pace, players could exchange an endless series of passes until *someone* was open enough to attempt a creaky carry-on without it getting blocked.

These laborious instructions from *Scientific Basketball*, a 1922 book written by East Coast basketball legend Nat Holman, may read like a guide for free throws, but he's actually describing best practices for taking a shot in open play:

Just as soon as the player receives the ball, let him advance one full step forward with the right foot, bring the left up close to the right, actually clicking the heels, and extend both arms outward about waist high and parallel with the ground.

Place all the weight on the toes, and bend the trunk slightly forward. The ball is adjusted properly, through the sense of touch, and it is revolved quickly so that when it leaves the hand it will rotate with the stitches facing upward.... With eye on the basket during this act, the player should locate the center, measure his distance from the basket, and give the ball the proper elliptical arch.

Why stop with the heel-click? Surely there's time for the player to hold a quick Q&A with the crowd. (*Hi, yes, this is more of a comment than a question: You should probably shoot the damn ball.*)

Coaches demanded this exacting shooting form, and the creaky carry-on became codified within the sport. Any experimentation had to occur at the margins, meaning on ramshackle courts, driveways, or basically anywhere else inventive young players could throw a ball into a basket without incurring the wrath of unimaginative clipboard jockeys. The jump shot was contraband; it had to be smuggled in.

Many of the jump shot's pioneers have been identified. Glenn Roberts grew up playing on mud courts, and in the early 1930s he brought to Emory & Henry College a signature move where he caught a pass in midair and then released it toward the basket before landing. At around the same time, the University of Missouri's John Cooper peacocked with a shot that looked like an early version of the turnaround jumper. His coach benched him for his treasonous act, but he was eventually reinstated when it became obvious that Cooper was the team's most talented player. Cooper led Mizzou to a famous victory over rivals Kansas in 1932 thanks to what the Associated Press described as a "bewildering jump-turn shot."

Stanford's Hank Luisetti became the first nationally recognized jump shooter, and he rose to fame thanks to his performance against Long Island University at Madison Square Garden in 1936. The East Coast juggernaut had been riding a forty-three-game win streak, but Luisetti tore them apart with his signature running one-hander. Luisetti himself never claimed that his move was a true jump shot, but it was a preview of what could happen when players added some dynamism to their games.

Luisetti's flamboyance wasn't everyone's cup of tea. The head coach of Long Island University at that time was our pal Nat Holman, and the *Scientific*

Basketball author was appalled by the Stanford man's crude improvisation. "I'd quit coaching before I'd teach a one-hand shot to win a game," he sneered. If only Luisetti had clicked his heels.

Just as the 2010s have seen a mass awakening regarding the three-pointer, the 1940s and 1950s represented the dawn of the jump shot. Basketball was a popular diversion on American military bases during World War II, and players from around the country mingled and mixed playing styles. A San Diego team of U.S. Marines dominated the circuit and gained notoriety for its two star jump-shooters, Joe Fulks and Kenny Sailors. Fulks became the first NBA player to jump-shoot his way to the top of the scoring columns. Sailors, meanwhile, got the *LIFE* treatment, and in 1946 the magazine published a handsome photo of him soaring at the apex of his jumper.

Sailors's shot looks like something you'd see in today's NBA—soaring, straight-up elevation with his elbow tucked at a right angle. Fulks, meanwhile, had a famously pathetic vertical leap, one that compelled hometown fans in Kentucky to comment that "you could hardly slip a shingle under his feet on his jump shot." He nonetheless used it to become one of pro basketball's most prolific scorers during his time with the Philadelphia Warriors. Fulks was a gunner's gunner, and in March 1948, he set a record by missing forty-two field goals in a game against the Providence Steam Rollers. (He still scored thirty-five points, and his team won by thirty-one.)

Timing worked in Fulks's and Sailors's favor. Thanks to the new goaltending rule, giants like George Mikan were no longer allowed to swat away arcing attempts as they descended toward the hoop. Shooting from a distance was more viable than ever, and the jump shot allowed them to take advantage of the opportunity.

It's difficult to convey just how novel the move was in those days. I'll leave that to a December 8, 1957, issue of *Sports Illustrated*. The magazine had a recurring feature where a panel of celebrities and athletic luminaries were presented with sports-related questions. For that week's issue, basketball's newest craze was put up for debate: "Do you think that old-time, low-scoring basketball—before Hank Luisetti popularized the one-hand jump shot—was a better and more interesting game than it is today?"

The replies were a mixed bag. Ed Hickey, a former president of the National Association of Basketball Coaches, was strongly committed to the good ol' days and opposed the jump shot. "Yes. I favor more conservative offensive play," he answered. "Our offense is built on control and we are definitely opposed to a helter-skelter type of play."

The person on *Sports Illustrated*'s panel to most eagerly embrace basketball's jump-shooting revolution had seemingly nothing to do with the sport. The magazine asked Joan Crawford for her thoughts, and the *Mildred Pierce* actress argued that the jumper was the wave of the future. "From the spectator's point of view, today's game is much better, although much harder on the players. It particularly appeals to young boys the ages of my children. Any sport that appeals as strongly to spectators as basketball does today will be a success, but it must be full of action."

I wouldn't recommend taking parenting advice from Joan Crawford, but her basketball analysis was spot-on. Her take harkens back to Naismith's original intention for basketball to be an "attractive" game for fans. Unlike the creaky carry-on, the jump shot is dynamic and, in its own way, brash. To go *over* a defender is downright confrontational, and Crawford immediately recognized that putting offenses at an advantage made for a more exciting product. Here was an actress who, at least in this instance, understood the sport better than an entrenched member of the coaching establishment. I think this makes a wonderful amount of sense. Wouldn't a professional entertainer be well positioned to understand that the game was improving in this regard? Coaches, meanwhile, were tied up with the sport's quotidian particulars and less likely to understand the benefits of change.

The switch to the jump shot was jarring, even for those who managed to thrive during its emergence. "Kids today don't even think about playmaking. All they think about is getting off the jump shot," Celtics Legend Bob Cousy told reporters in 1963, about a month before he retired from the NBA. The Hall of Famer was a renowned dribbler and passer, but, for all his talent, he never had much of a jumper, and he exited the league cursing the move's existence. "I think the jump shot is the worst thing that has happened to basketball in ten years. Any time you can do something on the ground, it's better." For a Freudian reading of that statement, refer to the fact that Cousy's father worked for an airline.

Whom could traditionalists blame for creating the jumper? While the game itself can be traced to a single person, no one knows who invented basketball's most common scoring maneuver. The James Naismith of the jump shot remains a complete and total mystery.

Jump shot anthropology has become something of a cottage industry. There are multiple books dedicated to the subject, and many of them are quite good. For *The Origins of the Jump Shot*, journalist John Christgau embarked on a journey to discover the move's inventor and narrowed his findings down to eight possible candidates. Author Shawn Fury expounded and expanded upon that list for his own entertaining book, *Rise and Fire: The Origins, Science, and Evolution of the Jump Shot—and How It Transformed Basketball Forever*, and it was through his work that I learned about Joan Crawford's keen basketball analysis. Both authors searched far and wide, but the originator of the jump shot remains an elusive target. "The early shooters operated in isolation, independent of each other, mostly away from what little media existed," writes Fury.

When I reach Fury on the phone, he explains that it is impossible to find the identity of this basketball Prometheus. Even so, the quest can become addictive. "There's that natural curiosity, at least from the perspective of a fan," he says. "The jump shot holds a mystical appeal."

The first jump shooters bludgeoned conventional wisdom with every leap, and the move gradually bled into the game as their willingness to ignore their elders increased. Like the sport itself, this most important element evolved due to subversion. Like fire or the margarita, the jump shot is one of those massively influential things that cannot be traced to a single creator, and anyone who claims it can be is a misguided fool.

In related news, I believe I have found the person who invented the jump shot.

• • •

THE 1927 SILENT film *The Fair Co-Ed* is notable for a few reasons. It was funded by newspaper baron William Randolph Hearst and starred his mistress, Marion Davies, as a college student who joins the school's basketball team in order to cozy up to its hunky coach (played by former Crimson Tide football star Johnny Mack Brown). Hearst despised its director Sam Wood and called the movie a "cheap-looking comedy," but critical response was largely positive. A reviewer for the *Knoxville News-Sentinel* called it a "rol-licking good show with plenty of action," and noted that it marked "the first time we ever heard of basketball being featured as a major sport in collegiate movies." Not only that, but the film may also contain evidence of the first jump shooter in history.

The Fair Co-Ed's ending plays out in a similar fashion to pretty much every sports movie ever made. There's the big, climactic game, and the home team, Bingham College, finds themselves losing big to hated rivals Claxton. However, Davies's character was absent for the entire first half. (I won't belabor you with plot details, but know that her absence was due to some madcap shenanigans.) She returns at halftime, makes amends, and then leads her team to a last-second victory by hitting a game-winning, three-quarters' court toss as time expires. It's essentially *Teen Wolf* without all the body hair.

Despite the fact that this was the first basketball movie ever made, there was at least one critic who found the ending to be clichéd. "Someday we hope a movie director will get up one of these collegiate pieces in which the big game is won by 'our side' by something like 44 to 10 instead of by a lone point in the last few seconds of play," the *Knoxville News-Sentinel*'s writer drolly observed.

But *The Fair Co-Ed* is a worthwhile artifact no matter how it ends. Filmic evidence of basketball from that era is incredibly rare, and the movie offers a fascinating peek at the sport in its toddler-hood. The game is rough and physical. There are more steals than shots, and possessions are awarded via center-court tip-offs after every made basket. (In-bounding the ball from under the hoop wasn't made a rule until 1937.) It's not totally unrecognizable, however. There are at least two sights that would be familiar to modern fans, and they occur within thirty seconds of each other. Early in the game, a Claxton player catches a rebound and, with a hand in her face, hops up to shoot over the defender. A few moments later, that same player regains possession and drains an airborne, one-handed shot—a move that predates Hank Luisetti's headline-making runners against LIU by nine years. Could it be that the first jump shots in history have been hiding inside a pre-War rom-com for the better part of a century?

There are reasons to believe that *The Fair Co-Ed* presents a relatively accurate portrayal of a basketball game. The *San Francisco Examiner*'s

Louella O. Parsons wrote it was "so real that I forgot that I was seeing a movie." According to contemporaneous reports, players from the Pomona College team filled in as extras for the climactic basketball scene. The filmmakers also hired Lillian Copeland, a world-renowned track-and-field athlete, to work as an advisor. The *Daily Record* says she "trained a number of the girls for the basketball game in *The Fair Co-ed*, and played the role of a basketball player in the latter part of the picture." Could she have been that pioneering jump-shooter captured on film? Neither she nor that specific character are listed in the credits, but in photos Copeland cuts a similar figure to the movie's mysterious jump-shooter.

Copeland was a four-time national champion in the shot put. She also won the silver medal in discus at the 1928 Olympics and took home gold in 1932. The Southern California Jewish Sports Hall of Fame describes her as an "excellent" basketball player, though she wouldn't have played the sport in college. She attended USC, and the Trojans didn't have a women's team until 1976. She'd have been in law school while filming *The Fair Co-Ed*, meaning Copeland would have been many years removed from any official basketball coaching. I like to imagine that she was free to play as she wanted, and, if my assumptions about her role in the film are correct, this would have given her carte blanche to experiment with her game. Who better to tinker with basketball's established shooting motion than a versatile, world-class Thrower of Things like Lillian Copeland?

I sent footage from *The Fair Co-Ed* to Shawn Fury so he could judge this evidence for himself. His response featured the most wonderful words someone researching old crap can hear: "How in God's name did you find that thing?" I doubt Marion Davies and Bingham's big win will be on Netflix any time soon, but a quick Google search will direct you to a streamable bootleg should you desire to watch it for yourself. (At least until the Hearst estate reads this and demands its removal.)

"I don't know how I'd actually classify those two shots," Fury says of the baskets attempted by the woman I assume to be Copeland. "I kind of see both of them as being more like running one-footers where their feet do leave the floor, but maybe not what I'd think of as a jump shot. Not that that is the correct interpretation or anything. With both of them I see it more as little push shots where the feet might rise off the floor. It's not that straight vertical leap that I think of as being a jump shot." Before I can make my case, Fury offers a polite concession: "I also don't think it's wrong or anything to say that it is a sort-of jump shot."

This kind of murkiness is endemic to the Great Jump Shot Quest. I've dipped my toe into the waters, but Fury rafted 'round its banks and through its churn to conduct his research. When he got a tip that there may have been a guy from Springfield, Massachusetts, named Jimmy James who supposedly shot a jumper in 1928, Fury traveled to the town and scoured its archives in an attempt to crack the case. "I looked through literally every paper that existed from the time and that description was not listed anywhere," he says. "I spent two days in Springfield chasing down this paragraph. If you ever find it, let me know."

Fury warns me not to "fall down the rabbit hole" of searching for that first jump shooter. Granted, I've already spent a few hours of my life watching and rewatching blurry footage of a game between two made-up colleges. I know how tempting it can be.

"If you do write about early shooters, be prepared to be yelled at by people," he tells me. The country is filled with stories of would-be jump-shot pioneers, and Fury still gets emails from readers who are upset that he managed to ignore one local hero or another in his book.

As tempting as it is to harangue him further about Lillian Copeland, Fury is correct in saying that it's best to leave *The Fair Co-Ed*'s proto-jumpers open to interpretation. For one thing, I still can't figure out whether it's actually Copeland tossing in those shots for Claxton or if someone else deserves the credit. Whoever it is, we can add them to the list of early hoopers who were adventurous enough to try something new. That is what's really important.

"It's so odd. Why didn't everyone jump right away?" Fury sounds exasperated at the mere thought of this most basic question. "Why did it take sixty years? It's such a weird thing to think about."

Naismith contended that "each generation that has played basketball has passed on some new developments to the next," and that tracking and classifying each one of these changes would be "uninteresting and monotonous." And this is coming from a man who was so obsessed with rote record-keeping that he collected urine samples at a high school basketball tournament to chart the players' sugar and albumin levels.

Poring over each and every incremental change the jump shot has endured over the past ninety years would indeed be a tiring exercise. Watch the game today, though, and you'll find plenty of reasons to believe the move is nearing its evolutionary endpoint. There is no going back.

• • •

WE ARE IN a golden age of shooting. Well, not me, personally—my jumper is about as useful as a shower toaster oven—but professional basketball as a whole is enjoying a renaissance in this regard, and the Golden State Warriors' backcourt is the House of Medici where prized artists Steph Curry and Klay Thompson ply their trade. Their collective prowess from distance helped make the Warriors the defining team of the decade. But even while they were flambéing the league to the tune of sixty-seven wins during the 2014–15 regular season, hoops old-timers like Charles Barkley, Phil Jackson, and Byron Scott insisted that "jump-shooting teams don't win championships." That refrain was repeated right up until the moment when Golden State celebrated its first of three NBA titles and shut them up for good.

That season, Curry and Thompson hit 286 and 239 three-pointers respectively, putting to rest any doubts regarding their status as the greatest jump-shooting backcourt in history. While Curry's form has made him the most prolific, record-breaking long-range shooter the league has ever seen, his teammate's motion is considered to be the platonic ideal. Thompson is as efficient and concise as a line of computer code. "If I'm teaching someone how to shoot," Golden State assistant coach Bruce Fraser told *Sports Illustrated*, "Klay is the model."

Thompson's form never changes. He squares to the hoop and raises off his feet with the unwavering verticality of an Atlas rocket. There is no wasted motion. The ball gets to its release point in a hurry and departs his fingertips with equal impatience. From start to finish, he only needs a fraction of a second to get his shot off. It is a marvelous piece of engineering.

Thompson's efficiency is responsible for what I would argue are the two most mind-boggling statistics in NBA history:

1. On January 8, 2019, Thompson scored forty-three points against the New York Knicks. He only needed to take *four dribbles* to do so.

2. Thompson scored sixty points against the Indiana Pacers on December 5, 2016. His time of possession during that game was ninety seconds.

Thompson is able to turn a brief encounter with a basketball into a prolific scoring performance. Not since the *1812 Overture* have there been such impactful bursts of cannon fire.

CAN YOU SPOT THE DIFFERENCES?

Examine a thousand photos of Thompson at that point of release and try to spot the incongruities, *Highlights* magazine style. You'll note the differing jersey colors, shoes, and crowds, but his body shape and positioning? That doesn't change a bit.

While Thompson and Curry look similar at the peak of their jumpers, they take different routes to get there. Curry's buildup is an infinitely forking path of possibility. He'll be dribbling behind his back or ducking below an outstretched arm when, all of a sudden, his body uncorks skyward and the ball is pulled into position. Thompson, meanwhile, does not indulge in superfluity; the ball goes from point A to point B immediately.

"He gets it [up to his head] and once he gets it here, it's over," Curry told reporters in 2015. "I kind of am fluid from the time I bring it up to the shooting pocket and all the way through. Both work, obviously."

In 2017, data scientists Panna Felsen and Patrick Lucey used a high-tech camera system called SportVU to examine how the NBA's best shooters move their bodies while taking jumpers, and their findings revealed the fascinating juxtaposition that is the Warriors' backcourt. Thompson had the most balanced shooting form of all the players they evaluated—meaning he was always squared perfectly up to the hoop—while Curry took more off-balance shots than anyone else.

A few years ago, I had the privilege of seeing Thompson's and Curry's shooting forms up close. I attended a Golden State Warriors practice for a story (which never got written) at the organization's old training facility located inside a Marriott in downtown Oakland. I use the term "practice" generously; it was a relaxed session, the kind of easygoing shootaround reporters are allowed to watch. Because I got off at the wrong BART station and had to sprint to the gym, I wound up being the only person who broke a sweat all afternoon.

For NBA beat reporters, the purpose of visiting these practices is to grab quotes from players and coaches during an allotted scrum time after the shootaround. Watching the world's greatest basketball players is nothing new to them, and the gaggle of writers spent most of the session scrolling through their phones and talking among themselves. I must have looked terribly out of place, then, as I stared, slack-jawed, at the team tossing up routine jumpers.

Next time you get the chance to go to a professional basketball game, arrive at the arena early so you can watch the pregame warmups. The main thing you'll notice is that everyone—and I mean everyone—makes a majority of their jump shots. The last player off the bench, the clumsy-looking center, it doesn't matter. Each is in possession of an exquisite and enviable jumper. When unencumbered by defenders or pressure, they needn't make any adjustments or rush their releases, and so, under these ideal circumstances, misses are rare. What makes Thompson and Curry special is that their forms are as pure in Game 7 of the NBA Finals as they are during no-stakes, defense-free shootarounds.

Curry's pregame routines have become legendary. He doesn't take the kinds of shots you might see in a game. He uses an assistant coach as a prop and attempts acrobatic heaves around, above, and underneath this human impediment. He also tries (and often makes) shots from behind the backboard and in the tunnel leading to the locker room, forty feet from the hoop. The routine is anything but routine, as evidenced by the screaming crowds of people who show up early just to watch him warm up. What goes unseen, however, are all the normal jump shots he takes when no one is around. According to a 2014 *ESPN the Magazine* profile, this includes the nearly one thousand jumpers he shoots before practice even begins. As Curry told reporter David Fleming, "There's so much flying at you during the game, there's no time to think, *Oh, am I elbow in? Did I bend my knees enough?* You have to rely on the fact that you put the work in to create the muscle memory and then trust that it will kick in." To paraphrase what a wise soil-conservation technician once told me, "It's all about that KPT, baby."

Curry kept it simple at the practice I visited. You could even say he was a bit lackadaisical with the ball. Though, when it came to his jumpers, the form clicked into place at the moment of release each and every time. Thompson, on the other hand, was the picture of repetitious perfection. It was the stuff of optical illusions. His motion unfurled and repeated itself across the court like an assembly line's flowing pattern of pencils or toothpicks or Tootsie Rolls. Maybe some invisible giant was using the cut and paste shortcuts on her proportionally appropriate keyboard to transplant him from spot to spot around the gym. The results were downright hypnotizing. It was also a tad unnerving. Perfect repetition is for machines, not humans. We're supposed to err, damn it.

Upon leaving the practice facility that day, I noticed a small crowd gathered at the window of a nearby Chinatown restaurant. Inside, a man was throwing dough between his hands and pulling it into stringy noodles for the bustling lunch crowd. While his movements were unflinchingly consistent, he looked utterly relaxed as he tossed and yanked the puffy clumps. Were it not for the concentration in his eyes—a look shared by both Curry and Thompson, mid-jumper—there'd be little evidence to suggest he wasn't undergoing an out of body experience.

When I ask Shawn Fury if he had come across any analogous experiences to watching a jump shot while working on his book about the subject, he struggles to find an answer. "What has different moving parts to it that is both functional and pleasing to the eye? Nothing comes to mind." Before seeing those noodle makers, I would have agreed. But there's just something so artfully extraneous about going to such lengths to re-create the same thing over and over again.

The motions may be quick and minute but they are essential to manufacturing such a consistent product. A wad of dough is yanked and stretched repeatedly between the chef's two outstretched hands before it's flicked upward and slapped against the table like a jump rope. On the reverberant bounce, one end is twirled around the other and the momentum twists it into a droopy, noose-like loop. The chef then grabs the starchy coil and repeats the process until the gluten is uniformly aligned and ready to be pulled into stringy, boil-able noodles.

It's a flamboyant performance, one that manages to turn repetition into art. There's a reason restaurants put these chefs where everyone can see them.

It can take years to learn how to make hand-pulled noodles. Peter Song, the head chef at New York's KungFu Kitchen, had to make five hundred bowls of noodles a day in order to master the technique. Now, after ten years of practice, he can make 128 noodles in ten seconds.

"There are hundreds if not thousands of varieties of noodles that are much faster and easier to make," Thy Tran tells me. Tran is a Bay Area–based writer and chef who teaches classes on homemade noodle making. Whether you're flinging dough in the air by hand or rolling it with a machine, the end result depends on a specific set of conditions achieved at the molecular level. "You're trying to align the glutens in one direction," Tran says. This is what makes noodles noodles. "Unlike making bread where your gluten network and protein network is very complex, in noodle-making you're stretching it over and over again so that your gluten strands are longitudinally being stretched. That whole process is very symmetrical."

Tran has an omnivore's appreciation for cooking, and she urges me to expand my education beyond noodles. "Bagel rollers are incredibly fast and subtle and disciplined with their wrist flicks," she says. "It's a much overlooked skill, not nearly as sexy with all the attention noodle-makers get."

Emily Winston agrees. "It is not glamorous dough work," she says. Winston owns my favorite bagel place in the Bay Area, Boichik Bagels, and she was gracious enough to fill me in on what goes into making this sumptuous nosh. "It's really common for people who are hand-rolling bagels to develop wrist problems. Like, you *will* develop problems."

Leverage is key, and you really need to get on top of the dough in order to wrench it into place. "You're putting your body into it. It's the stiffest dough there is." Standing five feet tall, Winston says she is at a disadvantage when it comes to both playing basketball and shaping bagels. "I should have made myself a lower rolling surface," she reflects.

Winston didn't learn her technique at culinary school. In fact, she didn't even go to culinary school. She's a mechanical engineer, and her relationship with baking began because she wanted to reproduce the bagels she loved back home in New Jersey. It took her five years of experimentation, but she eventually produced a bagel she deemed satisfactory. "The whole thing has been an engineering project," she says.

Engineers make for good bakers (and vice versa, one presumes), and Winston's pragmatism resulted in Tri State–quality bagels three thousand miles from the Hudson River. "There's no truth to the stuff about the secret being in the water," she says, regarding the rumors that New York's municipal supply contains magical properties. "Temperature is a big deal. There are a lot of nitpicky things. The hardest part is the process. A real water bagel has to be boiled and then baked directly on stone. You can't get that ultimate New York bagel without those two things." There is one thing she doesn't find necessary, though: hand-rolling.

While experimenting with recipes, Winston rolled two-dozen bagels a day and gave them to friends and family for review. The routine took its toll. "I started getting carpal tunnel problems just from doing tiny batches." When she opened her restaurant, she finally gave her wrists a rest. "I found that the hand-rolling does not actually contribute anything to that, so I'm happy to use a machine here."

Without the help of this piece of mechanical engineering, Winston says, it would take three talented, tireless people working nonstop from before opening until way past closing to shape the two thousand bagels they sell every day (and three thousand on the weekends). Her team of bakers can instead use their time to focus on mixing, boiling, and cooking the bagels. As an added bonus, avoiding the hand-rolling means they're able to hold pencils without enduring excruciating bursts of carpal pain.

Robots are not allowed in the NBA (yet), but there are literal shooting machines that manage to score with impressive accuracy. Toyota designed one in 2019 called Cue 3, and it makes about 62.5 percent of its shots from downtown. It can't dribble or play defense, but neither can Winston's bagel machine, and that still manages to get the job done.

Nevertheless, Winston found all those years of hand-rolling invaluable. "There's intimacy with a dough that I think is the same with any craft," she says. "You know it by feel, by touch, by taste."

It may sound like a science, what with all that talk of longitudinal gluten alignment, but dough resists exactitude. Tran says that her most successful students are the ones who are confident with uncertainty. "I definitely am trying to wean my students away from the fear of exact ratios and the perfection of recipes and make it more intuitive and more responsive to all of their senses," she tells me. "What's the humidity today? What kind of flour am I using? What kind of surface am I using? Are my hands big or small? If my hands are big and I have higher body temperature, then my dough is going to behave differently. It's not because the recipe is wrong, it's because life is just like that. You need to adjust."

Shooters don't operate in a vacuum, either. When Chicago's United Center opened in 1994, many of the Bulls despised it. Michael Jordan complained about the shallow rows of seating behind the hoop, as the slow slope of fans eliminated the "background" he appreciated at the team's previous stadium. Steve Kerr had his own gripes. "In Miami, the ball kind of sticks to the glass, then comes off the way it is supposed to. Here, it slides. Maybe it's because of the ice under the floor," he said, alluding to the United Center's dual life as an NHL venue. "This is the worst gym I have ever shot at." Harsh words, but the climate didn't seem to hinder his success. He shot 52.4 percent from behind the arc during that first season in the United Center, the highest mark in NBA history.

As a player, Kerr had one of the best-looking jumpers in the league. As the head coach of the Golden State Warriors, he gets to appreciate Thompson's and Curry's forms on a daily basis. "I think Steph is more rhythm-based," he told reporters. "From a technical standpoint, I think Klay is as good as anybody I've ever seen." In other words, Curry pulls noodles in the window while Thompson cranks out bagels. If you're the Warriors, everybody gets to eat.

A jump shot is a compound movement, as Klay Thompson explains in an instructional video for the NBA: "You almost have to use every muscle in your body, and it starts with your toes." he says. "Imagine a reverse waterfall starting with your toes all the way to the end of your release. It's one fluid motion." Any tweaks to it can spark a butterfly effect that jostles the process out of whack.

This is what struck me as I watched the noodle-pullers in the window. Their smooth, subtle movements looked so consistent and repetitive that I didn't even notice the end product: they were making different-size noodles for different dishes. Like Curry calibrating his jumper from twenty-five to thirty-five feet on back-to-back possessions, the adjustments are invisible to the naked eye.

"It is astounding," Tran says. "I mean, there are noodle houses in Beijing where you can order your noodles by the millimeter and by the cross-section. You can ask for a flat shape, you can ask for a triangular, propeller shape, and the guy *just does it*. You can't really tell the difference visually because it's a split-second. I mean, it's literally a millimeter flick of the wrist." She continues, "I call it 'modern spectacle cooking.' It's about the theater of food and the theater of a restaurant."

When produced by capable hands, repetition is worth the price of admission. But what if you get sick of noodles?

• • •

WE'VE ALREADY DISCUSSED what happens when basketball prioritizes long-range shooting. You see a lot of jumpers, which, as cartographer Kirk Goldsberry points out, translates to a ton of misses. But a made jump shot can be a beautiful thing to behold.

Bob Fisher, our record-breaking, soil conserving, free throw shooting dynamo, knows from experience that jump shots require astounding levels of precision. "There are a thousand different ways you can make a free throw," he says. "It's more forgiving. What I've found is if you can take your time and get things lined up, you can make anything work. With a jump shot, you have to be more precise. You have more joints moving and more muscles moving. It's so much easier to lose control."

Curry is especially impressive in this regard. In 2015–16, the year he won his second NBA MVP award, he hit 51.6 percent of his attempts between twenty-eight feet out and the half-court line. (The rest of the league's average was 20.8 percent.) A big reason why he's so accurate at such far distances is that his form barely changes. It's not a grunting heave but a version of that same, smooth release you'd see just beyond the line. Fisher, a master from fifteen feet out, can't comprehend that kind of range. "That's the thing about him that's so amazing, he just . . ." He searches for the words, to no avail. "Yeesh."

After spending years analyzing the way a basketball moves through the air, Chau Tran likens the experience of witnessing Curry's jumper to watching a science-fiction movie as an engineer. "Sometimes it takes the fun out of it. I fall into the trap of saying, 'Wait, that can't happen.' " But with Curry, that disconnect brings joy. The key to his success is his ability to generate force with high efficiency. "In engineering we call those conditions the 'least effort,' " Tran says. But he doesn't like to use technical language when discussing jump shots. Instead, his voice hits a surprisingly sultry baritone: "Stephen Curry, man. That's *smooth*."

Personally, I could watch Steph Curry or Klay Thompson shoot for hours. But chilled-out, low-effort repetition isn't for everyone. In Oakland's Temescal neighborhood there is a massive, twenty-eight-foot-high mural of Kevin Durant throwing down a one-handed slam dunk. It's a stunning and awesome piece of work, but I always wondered why the artist chose Durant and not Curry, the Bay Area's favorite adopted son, as the subject.

"They definitely said do Curry. And I was like, 'Uh, can I not?' " JC Ro tells me. Don't get him wrong—Ro, the Los Angeles-based artist behind that Durant mural, has plenty of love for Curry. "I really respect Steph and his game," he says. His problem is with the jumper itself, the move that best represents Curry's game and defines his dominance on the court. "A three-point mural is just a portrait with armpits."

Ro toyed with the idea of painting an ode to Curry's handles, as dribbling presents more fertile ground for a work that conveys motion and excitement, but he decided to go in a different direction. "The dunk murals are really dynamic. Visually, they're poetry in motion. They're detached, they're pushing gravity," he says. "I found some cool overhead shots for Durant. The way he looks, he's long, he's lanky. He's visually unique and appealing. It looks like he's moving, whereas Curry taking a shot just looks like he's jumping up and down. Like he's jumping rope, you know?" (I should note that Durant has a feathery jumper on par with Curry and Thompson, which is patently unfair given the fact that he is nearly seven feet tall.)

Ro composes his murals completely out of triangles. From afar, the spray-painted works appear stylized and jagged, but the subjects are always unmistakable. Look closer, though, and you'll see that the work is a field of polygons, layered and shaded to convey depth, movement, and emotion. "I always thought it was kind of freeing," he says about this style. "It was simple, but it always represents something complex. If I can make a basketball out of triangles, it's like, how does that make sense? Can I make an inanimate object look like it's moving?"

Ro can make anything out of triangles, but that doesn't necessarily mean he wants to. "Trust me, I've tried to figure out how to romanticize and visually elevate someone taking a jump shot. It's kind of a dud assignment," he says.

The jump shot has evolved to become as efficient as possible. Whereas its first practitioners experimented with odd, janky motions, most kinks have been ironed out in the pursuit of perfection. Gone are players like Bill Cartwright, the center on the Bulls' first three-peat team who appeared to be suffering the effects of rigor mortis every time he lined up one of his rigid attempts. Modern players' forms tend to be subtle variations on the same theme, and it can take multiple up-close viewings to discern the aesthetic differences between shooters no matter the accuracy of their end products. To paraphrase *Anna Karenina*, perfect jump shots are alike; each ugly jumper is ugly in its own way.

"Everyone can shoot now, no matter what size they are or what level they play at," Shawn Fury tells me. "It seems right now that there isn't a lot holding back shooters. It's become the crucial skill." You'd think that a jump shot anthropologist like Fury would enjoy this new era of long-range bombs, but his favorite practitioners of the art were masters from a now-ignored area of the court. "Kobe Bryant or Michael Jordan, when they pulled up from mid-range, their form was just so great to look at. It was physically pleasing to the eye," he says.

Players can get away with more idiosyncratic releases from mid-range because being closer to the hoop reduces the margin for error. The farther away from the hoop you are, the smoother and more streamlined your shot has to be. "With the dominance of the three-pointer, you kind of need an ideal shooting form to be consistent from long range," Fury explains. "We're losing those quirky forms that we'd see back in the day."

He catches himself. "When I say that, I think about all those writers and coaches who hated the jump shot originally. Do I sound like those guys now? I need to reassess my grouchiness."

The problem with being an old-timer is that you don't realize it until it's too late. If only Joan Crawford were still around to give us her take.

DAWN OF FLIGHT
Dreaming about dunking

WRITING A BOOK is a rather self-involved endeavor. There's a reason authors expect our names to be printed on the front cover, down the spine, across the title page, and anywhere else the publisher can cram it. We even include a little picture of ourselves inside the jacket cover because we assume you want to know what we look like. (No need to check and risk losing your page: I'm squinty and somewhat pallid.) It's a whole production that screams, *Look at me! I did this!* While I'm tempted to compare it to a slam dunk in this regard, I must concede that publishing a book is nowhere near as cool as dunking. It's not even close. Nothing is more exciting than throwing down a monster jam on a regulation-size rim, even if the feeling wears off shortly after I wake up.

I started having the dreams as a teenager. I'm in my school's gym when somebody tosses me a ball, and with little hesitation, I spring upward, past the limits of my waking life's vertical leap, and soar above the rim. There is plenty of time to savor the view (the braided nylon net looks especially beautiful at eye-level) before I confidently slam the ball home with aplomb. The trip back down to earth is surprisingly easy on my knees, though I guess I am cushioned by a cloud of pure, ebullient joy. A group of impressed onlookers asks me to do it again. Who am I to deny them the pleasure? The only thing that can stop me is my alarm clock.

The feeling is not merely one of flight—it's flight with purpose and style. Sure, there's the unavoidable pangs of sorrow when I wake up and realize I cannot actually do this wonderful thing in real life, but I still have the ability to watch others dunk. That is a pretty nice consolation prize.

Dunks are audacious feats of grace and athleticism, but the first dunk in history was just plain audacious. Recall that, for a period in the early twentieth century, there were no out of bounds markings. Courts were instead enclosed inside cages, and it was this feature that allowed New York baller Jack Inglis to soar during a game in the 1910s. According to author Bill Gutman, Inglis "jumped up alongside the basket, grabbed the cage, and pulled himself up alongside the basket. While the defenders looked up at him helplessly, a teammate passed him the ball. Inglis caught it while hanging on to the cage with one hand and dropped it through the basket." According to Gutman's book, "It was a perfectly legal play, because no one had ever seen it done before."

Legal or not, that shouldn't count as the first dunk. Much like finding the identity of the jump shot's inventor, the provenance of the slam dunk is murky. Anyone with the ability to rise above the hoop should have been able to do it, but reports are surprisingly rare. "We all could jump high enough, but we never envisioned doing anything like dunking the ball," John Isaacs, a player on the all-Black traveling New York Renaissance (aka New York Rens) team in the 1930s, told a reporter in 2004. "All we wanted was the basket."

What's more, there wasn't even a word for the move until 1936. That's when *New York Times* writer Arthur J. Daley got to watch the U.S. Olympic team train at the West Side YMCA before the Berlin Games. There he saw Texan Joe Fortenberry, who stood either six feet seven inches or six feet eight inches tall (reports vary), and the six-foot-nine Willard Schmidt show off their athleticism. The men "did not use an ordinary curling toss," wrote Daley. "Not those giants. They left the floor, reached up and pitched the ball downward into the hoop, much like a cafeteria customer dunking a roll in coffee."

Fortenberry left his job with a Kansas oil refinery in order to captain his country's team that summer. It was a good decision. He scored eight of the United States' points during its 19–8 win over Canada in the gold medal game. James Naismith was in Berlin to watch in person, and the old man saw a peculiar version of his sport, one that was played on a muddy court in the driving rain. As Fortenberry told the *Amarillo Globe-News*, "Adolf Hitler said it was an outside game and that's where we were going to play it." History's greatest monster loved streetball, apparently.

Fortenberry was a precursor to Mikan and Chamberlain, a giant who managed to make the sport look so easy that his opponents protested his very existence. After the Olympics, a group of humiliated teams unsuccessfully lobbied basketball's international governing body to impose a height limit of six feet two inches for all competitions.

Height was an obvious advantage in basketball, but Fortenberry had the special combination of size, speed, and coordination that allowed him to dominate at both ends of the floor. He was the prototypical "athletic big man," and journalists treated him like a walking oxymoron. "[I]n spite of this height and his awkward, lumbering appearance, [he] is the best all-around athlete at West Texas State Teachers College," the Associated Press quipped in 1933. Fortenberry was the school's heavyweight boxing champion and a standout gridiron receiver, but his sui generis feats on the hardwood garnered national recognition. In the words of the Associated Press, he "slaps at a basketball much as a cub bear would at a bobbing apple." How terrifyingly charming.

Whether you think of the move as dunking a roll into coffee or an ursine apple-slap, Fortenberry's use of it represented an evolutionary leap in how the game was played. It's why that *New York Times* reporter dedicated a significant chunk of his article on the U.S. Olympic team to the soaring centers who "left observers simply flabbergasted" at practice. As writer Michael McKnight explained in a 2015 *Sports Illustrated* story, "[Fortenberry] may not have been the first man to dunk a basketball, but he was the first to do it in an aesthetically stirring way, and in front of the right people."

A dunk is a stunning thing to behold. When the Wright Brothers made history at Kitty Hawk on December 17, 1903, their aircraft ascended to an altitude of ten feet, and this achievement was deemed worthy of the term *flight*. Naismith, meanwhile, hung his peach baskets at that same lofty mark. He nailed them to a balcony, a structure that is out of reach by design. Humans really have no business meddling up there without the use of stairs or stepladders.

For a time, Graham Lustig shared the view of the *Fort Worth Star-Telegram* regarding athletic big men. "You don't typically think of large people as being so beautifully precise," he tells me. Lustig is the artistic director of the Oakland Ballet Company. He is accustomed to feats of transcendent grace, but he was unprepared for what he saw one December at a Golden State Warriors game.

The team had invited his company to perform a selection from *The Nutcracker* suite during halftime, and Lustig remembers standing with his dancers near the court as they waited for the cue to go on. "That gave me a unique vantage point," he says. "The first thing you notice is that these are huge guys. I have a ballet dancer in my company now who's six-foot-five, but that is really somewhat unusual in the world of ballet. Most male dancers are around six feet tall or six-foot-two or something. But these guys are incredibly tall."

Basketball players are tall may be an obvious observation, but it's one that's worth chewing on. The average NBA player is six-foot-seven, which would be head-turning in any context other than in their particular workplace, where they're made to stand next to their similarly gargantuan peers. See someone that big on the street and you'd expect their joints to produce an audible groan with every movement, like a cruise ship launching from its berth. But these aren't your average giants, not by any stretch. They float with the kind of effortless grace that leaves professional ballet dancers astonished.

Lustig trained at the Royal Ballet School in London and danced with the Dutch National Ballet before becoming a choreographer, and he spends a considerable chunk of his workday examining what makes certain leaps more beautiful and elegant than others. "Some people are gifted with a bendy, loose, long Achilles that really helps them," he says. "Some people have very short, tight Achilles; therefore, when they go to bend their knees, they don't move as far. They have less chance of elevation. Everybody's working against their own particular limitation and length of leg, whether your bones are straight or whether you have a slight bow to your legs. All of these things make a very minor difference, but those minor differences add up."

He notices some of the same movements in basketball, like when players root themselves to the ground—"what we would call 'deep into his plié' "—before takeoff. It's a moment of analysis, to find "where gravity is and how he's going to push from it. That's the skill that a dancer tries to use as well," Lustig says.

"The other aspect to jumping in ballet is landing in ballet," he continues. "When you go to ballet you don't want to just see them go up in the air and look elegant, you want to see them come down effortlessly. The ground is rubber, it just melts like a mattress beneath their feet. This is also what these players are able to do. It's just like as if they're on this incredible, enormous great trampoline. It not only supports their elevation into the air, but also helps them to rebound and to absorb the power of that jump before they make that next move."

But the thing about basketball that most enamors Lustig is what it doesn't have in common with his line of work. "What we do in the ballet is always rehearsed," he tells me. "There is no element of surprise. When you leave the ground, it's a jump that you've rehearsed thousands of times before. You know exactly what you are going to do. But these guys," he says, referring to the NBA players he and his troupe watched as they readied themselves to perform *The Nutcracker* before a Christmastime crowd in Oakland, "what they are doing is absolutely and incredibly spontaneous."

Lustig's company has become an annual holiday staple at Warriors halftimes, and he cherishes the ten minutes or so at the end of those second quarters when he gets to watch the players from up close. "It brings it home to you in a new way," he says. "What they do in the air, you can see their decision-making skills kicking in as they think through this scenario and that scenario and they're going higher and the ball is moved to this side of their body and then that side of their body. They may have had one in mind when they left the ground, or when they were leaving the ground, but it might have changed by the time they got to the top of their leap. So refined. The movement is so exact. It does happen in the splittest of seconds."

People tend to be protective of their craft, and I had expected Lustig to contrast the beauty of ballet to the sweaty intensity of basketball and find the latter wanting. He would have had every right, for ballet is a most incredible example of the human form traveling through space. There's a reason why anytime someone does something with a modicum of grace they are called "balletic." But Lustig frames dance in practical terms compared to the breathless reverence with which he speaks about basketball. "It's so compelling to watch," he says. "It fills me with wonder and admiration."

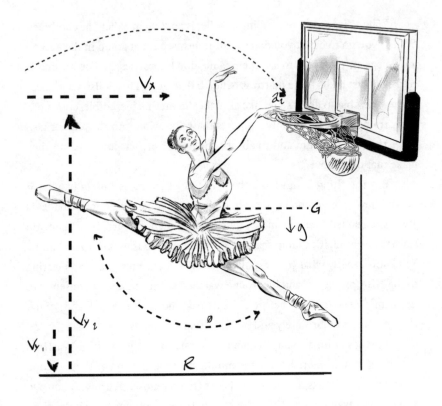

• • •

LIKE ME, MIKHAIL Baryshnikov also experienced recurring dreams. "It's very real," he told the *Los Angeles Times* in 1976. "I am on stage. And something goes wrong, but I cannot control that something. I do this step, and it is wrong. I fault my partner, or I fall down. Or I jump and I land in the orchestra or something terrible. And it is real . . . real ballet with real costumes, real makeup, real audience, everything real. And I cannot control it. A very terrible situation."

Much like my own dreams, Baryshnikov's nightmare will never come close to happening in real life. When he defected to America from the Soviet Union in 1974, he was already regarded as the greatest male ballet dancer of his generation. In those early years stateside, a considerable amount of newspaper acreage was dedicated to descriptions of his leaping ability. He's small for a dancer—about five feet six inches tall—but he managed to live up to the hype. "It was Baryshnikov flying through the air on the big stage, seeming to have found some secret way to hang suspended during his leaps, that gained the roars of the young audience," gushed the *Post-Star Falls* when he made his official debut for the New York City Ballet in Saratoga. "The press releases were all true, he really could fly." Basketball fans call it hang time, but ballet aficionados have a different word for that moment when someone appears to float in midair: *ballon*. (Pronounced *à la mode française*.)

Reporters hounded Baryshnikov in those first few years in the United States. He loathed the attention, but it was part of the deal: move to America, get your sex life broadcast in the New York tabloids. However, no one asked him the one question that really matters: Could he dunk?

I've spent an embarrassing amount of time thinking about this, but my attempts to figure it out have all come to dead ends. The Baryshnikov Arts Center in New York won't return my calls or emails.

Lustig thinks certain basketball players would do well on the ballet stage (he's convinced Steph Curry would be a star), and he doesn't hedge when I ask for his take on whether Baryshnikov could dunk. "Oh," he says with a sigh. "I think if Baryshnikov wanted to, he could probably do anything."

Nobel Prize–winning poet Joseph Brodsky wrote a poem about his friend Baryshnikov in full flight. It doesn't mention whether or not he could dunk, but that's the great thing about poetry—there's always meaning to be unearthed in the subtext:

How splendid late at night, Old Russia worlds apart,
to watch Baryshnikov, this talent still as forceful!
The effort of the calf, the quivering of the torso
rotating round its axis, start
a flight such as the soul has heard for from the fates

A dunk is a staggeringly beautiful event. Here is the part of the chapter where I should probably describe the experience of watching someone the size of a grandfather clock float through space like a cluster of soap bubbles, but I fear I can't do it justice. A nasty dunk short-circuits the language center of my brain. Usually, the most I can muster is a *gwwwwuuugh* or, if I'm lucky, an *Oh my ahwaaaaaghk*. A poet is better suited for this job. I'd choose Edna

St. Vincent Millay, who played on her Camden, Maine, high school basketball team in 1907, but alas, she never committed her thoughts on the tomahawk slam to paper (at least not in her published work). Thankfully, other capable bards have given it a shot.

Former Poet Laureate Donald Hall wrote some gorgeous prose about hoops. (He also won the Edna St. Vincent Millay Award in 1956, so we'll count that as an endorsement.) Enamored by basketball's physicality, Hall called it "the purest sport of bodies":

Professional basketball combines opposites—elegant gymnastics, ferocious ballet, gargantuan delicacy, colossal precision . . . It is a continuous violent dream of levitating hulks. It is twist and turn, leap and fly, turn and counter turn, flick and respond, confront and evade. It is monstrous, or it would be monstrous if it were not witty.

These athletes show wit in their bodies. Watching their abrupt speed, their instant reversals of direction, I think of minnows in the pond—how the small schools slide swiftly in one direction, then reverse-flip and flash the opposite way. NBA players are quick as minnows, and with an adjustment for size great whales drive down the road.

Much like Lustig, Hall appreciated that these incredible moments of grace are, improbably, spontaneous. "In all sport, nothing requires more of a body than NBA basketball, nothing so much uses—and celebrates—bodily improvisation, invention, and imagination."

He wrote that in 1984, which was a uniquely inspiring era for basketball fans. The NBA possessed a glut of charismatic and talented stars who seemed to be as committed to creating works of aesthetic import as they were to winning. It was a year of glorious generational overlap, when Julius Erving, Michael Jordan, Bernard King, Hakeem Olajuwon, Moses Malone, Dominique Wilkins, Kareem Abdul-Jabbar, George Gervin, Larry Bird, and Magic Johnson all shared a stage. (It is fair to point out that the final two players mentioned aren't exactly known for their dunking prowess. They sure did pass the ball to some great dunkers, though!)

The mid-1980s NBA revolution was televised . . . sort of. CBS was the NBA's main broadcast partner, and it infamously aired many playoff games on tape-delay so as to not disrupt its normal primetime programming. As such, viewers on the East Coast often had to wait until 11:30 P.M. for tip-offs. The league's audience surged once the network stopped this practice for good in 1986 and began carrying every postseason contest live. (Terrible as it was, it was still better than ABC's approach in the 1960s, when viewers were occasionally unable to watch full games because the network limited its NBA broadcasts to *Wide World of Sports* highlight packages.)

As basketball's television coverage increased, so did production values. In decades prior, broadcasts had to rely on a single camera for the majority of the game. Alternate angles were used sparingly, and the archaic technology made those "close-up" shots look as if they were being filmed through the scuzzy porthole of a World War I submarine. But by the 1980s multi-camera setups became the norm, and viewers were treated to instant replays of exciting and important in-game events.

Instant replay was invented in the 1960s, but it took a while for it to reach its full potential with basketball. In the early days, action intended for replay was recorded on a separate feed that had to be run through refrigerator-size tape decks. CBS director Tony Verna invented a strategy to expedite the process, and the first genuinely *instant* replay premiered during the fourth quarter of a 1963 Army-Navy football game. It would have made its debut earlier in the contest but for Lucille Ball's semi-translucent head. The production crew recorded its replay clips on a tape carrying an old *I Love Lucy* episode, and it took thirty recordings before Ms. Ball's visage disappeared from the footage. Despite those kinks, it was immediately apparent that this technology was no gimmick. "What you've done today is non-retractable," Lindsey Nelson, the announcer of that Navy-Army game, told Verna. "People are going to expect instant replays . . . it's never going to go away."

The philosopher and media theorist Marshall McLuhan took great interest in how instant replay impacts our relationship with sports. In a 1971 interview on public television, he said the technology fomented a "totally new form of audience participation in the dynamics of the game." Because the humble television viewer could now witness immediately and out of the flow of the game's action how certain events came to be, they learned to adapt the "attitude of every artist to every artistic production . . . the public now demands that the game be changed so that they can see the process by which the effects are attained."

Instant replay sparked a fundamental change in the public's perception of football, a game that progresses with orderly cadence. But basketball lacks the continuous context of yards and downs. It would be benefited by a more magical sort of manipulation.

Slow-motion videotape wasn't an immediate hit like instant replay was. The two were developed at around the same time, but slow-mo's production process was far too glacial and the footage was too choppy to be of much use during live broadcasts. It was a retrospective act, one ABC engineer and slow-mo pioneer Bob Trachinger likened to "smoking a cigarette after you've had sex and reflecting back on it. Was it good? How was it? That was slow-motion videotape." Apologies if this conjures up any unfortunate images of Y. A. Tittle in the throes of coitus.

Slow-motion footage may have been subjected to frustrating delays in those nascent days, but early examples revealed something new about the hitherto underappreciated game of basketball. ABC used an extremely rudimentary version of the technology during its coverage of the 1968 NBA Finals, but the stilted footage still left a mark. "Slow-motion replays showcase the unusual balance and delicate touch of these sports giants," gushed the *Boston Globe*. "[E]ven some who are not enthusiastic about basketball concede that the NBA may possess the finest athletes in the world."

Slow-motion technology steadily improved, and it seized its big break in 1984 during ABC's broadcasts of the Olympic Games in Los Angeles. Earlier that summer, CBS heavily incorporated it during its coverage of the NBA Finals between the Boston Celtics and Los Angeles Lakers. The network used what was considered at the time to be a surfeit of cameras—eight!—but, as *Philadelphia Inquirer* columnist Lee Winfrey noted, all those angles were "overshadowed by contributions from the network's five slow-motion replay machines."

It may have been George Orwell's nightmare year, but 1984 was pretty great for the NBA. The league was awash in athletic stars, and it embraced the spectacle of flight with its first-ever Slam Dunk Contest. A showcase of leapers attempting impressive and difficult maneuvers for no reason beyond manufacturing aesthetic beauty? If I didn't know any better, I'd call that ballet.

Slow-mo was essential for the event. Without it, fans wouldn't have been able to fully comprehend the superhuman elevation of winner Larry Nance. Roll the tape back and, yep, he really is just hanging there in midair, looking down at the rim.

The most important NBA moment of 1984 didn't happen on the court, however. That summer, the Chicago Bulls drafted Michael Jordan, and the league would never again be the same.

Jordan was ineligible to participate in that inaugural Slam Dunk Contest, but his performances in 1985, '87, and '88 helped make the event a must-see staple of the NBA calendar. If you can, please find the YouTube clip of the 1987 event in Seattle (Jordan's first win) and watch it with your eyes closed. That way, nothing can distract you from focusing on how the crowd reacts in waves after each of Jordan's dunks. There are screams, a pause, a chorus of astonished gasps, another pause, and then sustained cheering that turns into what can only be described as incredulous laughter. The sequence happens like that after each and every one of his attempts. You could track it with a tide calendar.

For his most memorable dunk that evening, Jordan approached the hoop with his back to the baseline, floated at a forty-five-degree angle, and, with legs splayed, windmilled the ball through the hoop. It's astonishing at regular speed, which accounts for the crowd's initial screams. But, as *Sacramento Bee* sportswriter S. L. Price wrote, "Only when it was shown on the screen again did those in attendance realize what they had seen: Michael Jordan drifting in slow-motion toward the basket, mouth open, eyes wide, leaning toward the basket like an apple picker on a ladder." Those replays are what sparked the rolling waves of gasps and laughter. Jordan's performance won over the hard-to-please celebrity judges, and they awarded him a fifty for his efforts. Yes, even Joe Piscopo gave him a perfect score.

"That was probably the best dunk I've ever seen," Terence Stansbury said. "He flies through the air, he literally flies." Stansbury wasn't a fan sitting in the crowd—he was a Seattle Supersonics guard who competed against Jordan in that very contest. But even ostensible rivals couldn't resist the allure of No. 23's supernatural grace. It also helped that Stansbury had a view of the stadium's Jumbotron. "The instant replay was so much better than real life," he said.

For Jordan, slow-motion replays worked as a multiplier of sorts. Like a ballet dancer, he already knew how to manipulate his body to make it look like he was floating. "When you look at the physics of jumping, there's really no such thing as hang time," he said in a 1993 interview. "There's just the perception of it, the appearance of hanging in the air. I use my legs, some arm movements, like flapping wings, but it's more illusion than anything."

Perhaps the best example of this is from the 1988 Dunk Contest, when Jordan famously soared from the foul line for an era-defining slam. He wasn't the first person to execute this type of dunk—Dr. J did it in the ABA's dunk contest in 1976, and Jordan himself did it in a previous event—but the '88 iteration was balletic perfection. Jordan cocked the ball back in one hand and simultaneously thrusted his legs akimbo while he sailed fifteen feet through the air as if aloft on some invisible current.

"He hit that fucking foul line, and everything seemed to slow down," Ron Harper, Jordan's future teammate, told *Sports Illustrated*. "He was going in slow motion." That fans in attendance immediately got to see it slowed down even further on the Jumbotron was almost unfair. There was no chance he was going to lose that contest. As NBA reporter John Schuhmann wrote, "Watching it in slow motion inspires everyone who ever played or watched the game of basketball. It was a beautiful sight."

Peter Brancazio was a Brooklyn College professor who explored the physics of sports, and he debunked the widely held belief that Michael Jordan defied gravity. "Most people swear he stays up there for two or two and a half seconds," he told the *South Florida Sun-Sentinel* in 1995. According to Brancazio, Jordan's hang time was actually only nine-tenths of a second. "For the record, Baryshnikov's hang time is also nine-tenths of a second," he added. It's fitting that those two athletes would have matching hang times (or *ballons*), for few have done more to inspire the collective imagination with feats of flight than they.

Brancazio didn't calculate whether or not Baryshnikov possessed enough bounce to dunk, however, leaving that mystery unsolved. (The physics professor died in 2020, before I could ask him directly.) He did provide some helpful context, though. Spud Webb is only about an inch taller than Baryshnikov, and the former Atlanta Hawks guard famously won the Slam Dunk Contest in 1986 with a series of mind-blowing jams. According to

Brancazio's measurements, Webb actually had superior hang time to both Jordan and the ballet dancer. "He can stay up there for almost a full second," he found. Whether or not Baryshnikov could have thrown it down, one thing is for certain: He would have been the underdog in the 1986 Slam Dunk Contest. As for Webb, it's a shame no one ever thought to put him in a leotard onstage at the Bolshoi.

• • •

HANG TIME IS largely about perception, but, in the sage words of my college weed dealer, "Perception is everything, man." Graham Lustig's description of watching basketball may sound familiar. "They're airborne seemingly for ten seconds at a time," he says. "Of course, it's a lot faster than that, but within that it seems like they have ten seconds' worth of time to consider what it is they are going to do with the ball as they leave the ground."

It is important not to confuse this with being "in the zone." For basketball players, "the zone" can manifest itself in many different ways—the hoop looks bigger, defenders slow down, passing lanes reveal themselves before they're even there—but the general idea is that the game becomes easier for them. Hungarian psychologist Mihaly Csikszentmihalyi dubbed the phenomenon "flow," but flow tends to be for doers, not watchers.

"When you have that perfect balance of ability and the challenge of the task at hand, in those situations you get a lot of time distortion," Melanie Rudd tells me. Rudd teaches marketing at the University of Houston and has done extensive research on time perception as it relates to consumer behavior. Consumers are not exactly nature's doers, and her work helps explain why even us watchers can experience the psychogenic effects of a nasty dunk.

"The brain is a strange thing when it comes to time," she says. "We see it in different ways." For a 2012 study, Rudd found that the feeling of awe actually altered one's subjective experience of time. Specifically, it gave people the sensation that they had more of it.

"In the overall literature of awe, in general people have reported some time distortion," she says. "In some cases you might have both senses of time being plentiful and time slowing down." These are two distinct feelings, though they are often entwined. "Separately or in combination, you might have a sense of time affluence, or a feeling that time is plentiful and you are rich in time."

For her study, titled, "Awe Expands People's Perception of Time, Alters Decision Making, and Enhances Well-Being," Rudd showed subjects videos that were intended to conjure up that specific feeling of awe. "Things like nature and art, or music, or other people's accomplishments seem to be more universal elicitors of awe," she tells me.

The videos varied in subject matter, but they all had one thing in common: none of them were filmed in slow motion. "We specifically made sure that there was no element of time distortion within the videos," she says. "Because then it could have been argued, 'It's not awe, it's just time distortion.'"

It turns out that slow-motion is something of a cheat code. "In order to experience awe, you need this perception of vastness. And that doesn't necessarily have to be in size, but it could be in complexity or ability or social bearing, like fame or power. Slow motion, or being able to see something broken down, could help people better grasp the vastness of the ability," Rudd explains. "The second key component is this need for accommodation. Your brain goes, *Whoa. Either I've never seen this before, or I don't fully understand it. This thing is making me think.* Slowing things down really helps highlight those elements that make something awe-inspiring."

I find it heartening, and even a little sweet, that awe is one of the least self-absorbed emotions one can experience. We are *inspired* by awe, and, in order to appreciate vastness, we ourselves must feel small. "When you ask people, 'What makes you feel awe?' they usually don't point to something they did themselves," Rudd says. "But other people's accomplishments? People often report it as a common awe-elicitor."

Even Michael Jordan couldn't make himself feel awed in the moment. His performance at the 1987 Dunk Contest sent waves of insanity rippling through the Seattle crowd, but Jordan himself was dumbfounded as to what the hell was going on. "I don't know what I'm doing," he said after his win. "It's hard to explain, but I felt really high. Higher than I've been in a while."

I pass this quote along to Melanie Rudd, and she understands why Jordan was at a loss for words. "In that moment he would have consciously had to have been thinking about the vastness of the ability and also have this mental accommodation process going on," she says. "Given how focused you would be on the actual mechanics of what you are doing, odds are you probably wouldn't experience a lot of awe in that moment. But, potentially, looking back on the event, if he's sitting there watching his highlight reel or something, then the full awe of the moment might then happen."

Jordan did, in fact, marvel at his own replays. In 1987, decades before you could pull up YouTube highlights on demand, he excitedly told a sports-writer, "I wish I could show you a film of a dunk I had in Milwaukee. It's in slow-motion, and it looks like I'm taking off, like somebody put wings on me. I get chills when I see it."

That feeling of retrospective self-awe wouldn't fade. In his 1998 book *For the Love of the Game*, Jordan described it thusly:

There are plays that stand out in your mind, things you did that when you see the replay almost seems like you're watching someone else in your body. I remember one dunk early in my career that I saw on video a couple of years ago. I don't remember what year it was but the replay was in slow motion. I looked like one of those Apollo blastoffs in slow motion. I just kept going up. I knew I was watching myself, but I still couldn't believe how it looked.

Slow motion escorts a moment out of time and into an entirely different reality. If instant replay makes fans artists, as Marshall McLuhan argued, then slow-motion turns us into choreographers. The spontaneous yet refined movements Graham Lustig appreciated from his *Nutcracker*'s-eye-view during those Warriors games happened at speeds beyond normal human comprehension. Our tiny lizard brains aren't always suited to processing the sight of someone weaving midair and through bodies en route to the hoop. Jordan knew this, which is why he contorted his limbs to enhance the experience in real-time. Watching his highlights in slow motion, then, is an act of gluttony, and his entire career amounted to a trans-dimensional feast.

The Slam Dunk Contest was a perfect venue for Jordan to show off his brand of temporal jiu-jitsu. Every camera in the arena had to be focused on him so no movement went unseen or unappreciated. But Jordan pulled off similarly incredible dunks in the flow of normal games, and networks changed their production strategies in order to keep up. "It was common [in the 1980s] to use a ground-level camera for reaction and close-up shots," Turner Sports executive Don McGuire told the *Boston Globe*. "The overhead shots would take care of live action. But we changed it with Michael to a [live] camera, placing it on him fifteen to twenty feet from the basket and following him as he drove."

When cost overruns forced CBS to reduce the number of cameras used at live sporting events in the mid-eighties, the producers decided to keep a lens pointed at Jordan anyway, even though it was at the expense of one of their wider broadcast angles that would have otherwise focused on the game as a whole. It was worth it to have a dedicated eye following Jordan. He defied belief so frequently, television directors had to obtain proof in the moment that he actually did what everyone thought they saw him do.

It wasn't enough to merely follow Jordan's movements on the court. The man bent time to his will, and so television networks invested in new technologies to enhance his supernatural abilities. In the 1993 Finals, NBC used a giant, state-of-the-art machine to process super-slow-mo footage of Jordan's moves as they happened. Crews wheeled the device to the Bulls' offensive side of the court each quarter like a group of indecisive ornithologists lugging their equipment back and forth between bird-watching camps.

"I thought no one could replace Dr. J," CBS director Sandy Grossman said, "but later I decided that while he had been perfect for slow-motion replay, Michael was for super-slow-mo."

Players haven't gotten any less athletic, and the technology has only improved. The modern NBA is full of superstars who are capable of pulling off gravity-defying dunks in the blink of an eye, and nary a movement goes unappreciated. It should be enough to see breathtaking feats of flight on a nightly basis; that we've come to expect the world to slow down after each one is a sign that we are truly spoiled.

All this talk about beauty and time is making me wistful. I should probably call on the services again of our Poet Laureate Donald Hall to help out with some nice words and whatnot:

This is a game you can study on television because it is small enough to fit in the box; and, through television's slow-motion replay, we study at our leisure the learned body's performances—as when Dr. J or George Gervin soars from the baseline, ball in the right hand, appears to shoot, pauses in midair, and, when a shot-blocker hovers beside him, transfers the ball to the left hand, twists the body, and stuffs the ball through the hoop.

No one *has* to dunk. It is a scoring maneuver in the way that ballet is a means to educate people about the Sugar Plum Fairy and the plight of the Mouse King. But physical beauty doesn't need an excuse to exist. "It is only two points," Hall wrote. "If this were gymnastics or diving from the high board at the Olympics, it would be *ten* points."

• • •

WHILE HALL LOVED the slam dunk, he alludes to a common rejoinder used by basketball grouches: *A dunk may look cool, but it is only worth two* *points*. It's tempting to dismiss these naysayers as ignorant cranks, but the sport's most amazing move has had its fair share of powerful and enlightened enemies.

Phog Allen, Naismith's protégé at Kansas and one of the most celebrated coaches basketball has ever produced, despised above-the-rim play. "Dunking does not display basketball skill—only height advantage," he wrote in his 1937 book *Better Basketball*. Allen advocated for decades to raise the rims to twelve feet, but his idea to take away the advantage taller players enjoyed was never widely accepted.

The NCAA infamously banned slam dunks from all competitions for nine full seasons, starting in 1967. Many believe the rule was enacted due to the dominance of UCLA center Kareem Abdul-Jabbar (then known as Lew Alcindor), who, like Fortenberry, made the game look easy. The rules committee explained (unconvincingly) that the ban was due to safety concerns, but their reasoning also included the claim that the dunk "was not a skillful shot."

John Wooden, Abdul-Jabbar's coach at UCLA, was on that committee, and while he denied the ban was passed explicitly to hamper his star, he never did hide his disdain for the move. "I hate the dunk," Wooden told the *Denver Post*. "I think it's showmanship and it hurts team play."

Wooden earned the right to be a curmudgeon. He won ten national championships, which is six more than any other coach in college basketball history. (The bulk of those titles came during an unprecedented stretch when UCLA won seven times in a row.) I obviously lack the credentials to say that he was an "out-of-touch geezer" or a "wrinkly old killjoy." Rather, I will respectfully describe the late Coach Wooden as a basketball ascetic. "People ask me if I'd permit fancy things, like dunks," he said. "Well, if they did dunk, it was with no fancy flair. No behind-the-back dribbles or passes unless necessary. If it was for show, you were on the bench."

Wooden approached the game as a problem of geometry that should be solved with Euclidean simplicity. "I say, if you work a good give-and-go, that ought to be worth five points," he told the *Los Angeles Times*. "And a dunk, I wouldn't give more than one for that."

Wooden may be a legend, but he never held the kind of juice to actually reduce the value of a slam dunk. As his fellow killjoys—sorry, *ascetics*—like to say, it still counts for two points.

But what if that weren't the case?

North Carolina State's David Thompson was one of the greatest dunkers of all time, but he played his entire college career during the NCAA's prohibition. "It was tough not to be able to dunk the ball when you are way over the rim," he recalled in an interview. "It would have been way easier to catch it and dunk it in one motion."

Thompson obeyed Wooden and company's edict until his last home game at NC State. Alone and on a breakaway, Thompson unloaded four years of frustration on the poor rim. "I got a technical foul and a standing ovation at the same time," he said. It was his final moment as a college player.

That's only worth two points?

Or, how about this hypothetical: It's late in the fourth quarter of a nail-biter. The teams exchange blows, but neither manages to pry itself free from the deadlock. Equilibrium reigns. There's a layup on one end, a jumper at the other, and a whole bunch of free throws scattered about like rose petals in a honeymoon suite. (In this shaky simile, everyone is desperate to score.) A small forward gets the ball at the top of the key and waves away a screen before cutting into the lane. The defender's rotation is late, but he gamely tries to block the effort anyway. Big mistake. It results in a thundering poster slam that sends the stadium into hysterics.

DUNKS   JUMPERS

Again . . . you're telling me that moment of divine detonation is only worth two points?

Momentum is a contentious subject in basketball. There's an entire area of study dedicated to the "hot hand," the assumption that a player who's made multiple shots in a row will be more likely to continue this streak. In the famous 1985 paper "The Hot Hand in Basketball: On the Misperception of Random Sequences," a trio of cognitive and mathematical psychologists argued this was more or less a fallacy, that the outcome is random even if it looks like the shooter is, in *NBA Jam* parlance, on fire. However, many subsequent studies have either been inconclusive or found evidence supporting the notion of streakiness. It's complicated.

"This idea of looking at past performance to identify ability is very natural, but it turns out that it has some issues," Brett Green tells me. Green is a financial economist and associate professor at Washington University who has spent a lot of time studying the notion of streakiness. "What I find fascinating when thinking about sports is how forces of equilibrium lead to different outcomes than they do in a world in which there aren't endogenous responses."

Endogenous is a good word. And, now that I've looked it up, I can tell you what it means: It refers to something that is produced within an organism or closed system. For example, when you see your favorite player dunk all over a hated opponent, your brain will produce peptides to make you feel good. These chemicals are called "endorphins," which is a combination of the words "endogenous" and "morphine." However, if you were to inject yourself with a similar compound, the effect would be *exogenous*. You're just doing drugs.

When Naismith wrote those thirteen original rules, he created an organism of sorts. You can track the end results of its endogenous occurrences using statistics, but you can also examine how the organism's various qualities manage to affect production within itself. "In basketball, you want to take the best shot that you can," Green explains. "That might mean your best player takes a shot. Or, it might mean that your most open player takes the shot. It's not necessarily the case that you want your best player to take every shot, because defenses are allocating their attention to your best player more heavily than they are to your worst player."

This, Green explains, is why a superstar like Steph Curry will have a similar career field goal percentage (47.6 percent) to a capable yet completely forgettable role player in the mold of, say, Otto Porter Jr. (48.2 percent). "Field goal percentage doesn't correlate very well with other measures of ability like salary or number of points scored per season or who's on an All-Star team," Green says. "There is this endogenous response, that better players take harder shots and they're guarded more heavily."

That's why the notion of the "hot hand" is difficult to pin down in basketball. Resources are constantly being shifted around to either harm or improve a given player's chances of scoring. The organism is complex.

While interesting in its own right, Green sought to extrapolate this thinking to the world of finance. "There's a similar argument that's been made for why we don't see persistent performance or we can't identify skill for hedge fund managers," he says. "That's because those who do very well and have high returns over a two or three year period are going to get inundated with funds. Investors are going to want to send their money to them. And when they go out to find their next best investment, they're going down the pecking order of their investments, and they are investing in lower and lower return projects to the point where they're going to look just like an average fund manager."

Oh dear, I fear we have wandered rather far afield of our original topic of conversation. Who cares whether a hedge fund manager is on a hot streak? You came here for in-your-face dunks, not to learn why one guy's yacht is bigger than his golfing buddy's yacht. But Green has dedicated his life to studying how fluid systems affect things like value. If anyone can tell us how much a dunk is worth, it's him.

"You've got me thinking about crowd effect," Green says when presented with that scenario of a thunderous slam breaking a game wide open. "Having an energized crowd may be valuable, but I don't know how valuable it is."

No one dunks by accident. There is intent there, and it goes beyond scoring. When it comes to a work of aesthetic import, any value is predicated on people experiencing and enjoying it. The Bolshoi Ballet charges to get in, but audiences convey their appreciation during the curtain call. "The kinds of analogies that I think about are, like, relational interactions where we use one act to motivate another," Green says. "This is a relational contract. It is not a formal contract and there are no prices. But it's an agreement that I have as a player with my fans that when I give more effort they're going to cheer louder. That's the story you're telling, that they're not really worth two points because they have this additional motivating effect on the crowd."

Green is a macroeconomist. He's analytical. Slow to make assumptions. He won't even commit to the suggestion that a nasty dunk gets people off their butts. "The first thing I would want to do is somehow document that dunks *do* energize the crowd more than other made shots. I could believe that that's true, but I'd like to be convinced," he says. "How long does the crowd stay on their feet after a dunk? That would be the first thing that I would like to document."

Green ponders that hypothetical event where a poster slam late in the fourth quarter sends the crowd into rapturous ecstasy. But how often does that happen? I've crammed an outlier into this experiment right off the bat. It's a tell that I don't know much about statistics and Green zeroes in on the unlikeliness of it all. "You're conditioning on it being a close game," he says, "but if it is a thirty-point blowout, then maybe a first-quarter dunk is worth more than when the game has already been decided." That is also based on a specific set of conditions, namely that crowd noise actually is an endogenous response to game action.

"What does a dunk do?" Green asks. "A dunk is more effort than a layup. If you thought that crowds respond more to high-effort plays, then that's going to motivate them to make more noise. A player is exerting more effort in order to energize the crowd and maybe his teammates, and the crowd responding to that in kind." I assume a dunk boosts the dunker's own ego as well. That's certainly how it works in my dreams.

Now we are talking about a crowd as a separate closed system, a symbiotic organism that exchanges nutrients with the players on the court but still cares about its own survival. "I don't see crowd energy as being fixed. There are a number of different factors that can affect it. They kind of have a dual objective. Fans are going to try to help their team win to the extent that they can, by being energetic, but they also want to enjoy themselves. Screaming consecutively for the whole game is not going to be a very fun experience for them," Green says, clearly aware that stadiums stop serving beer after the third quarter.

Even when we drill it down to specific terms and conditions (e.g. the crowd cheers for a full minute after a dunk in a close game), the results are far from concrete. Green wisely advises against coming to any conclusions based on our chat. "If you want to say, 'Here is a reason why a dunk is not worth two points,' that makes perfect sense. Now, how much more is it worth than two points, exactly? That I don't know." We've barely scratched the surface, and there's a lot of work left to do. "Trying to quantify it is not so easy."

Still, I manage to get one quick, back-of-the-napkin equation out of him. "Let's say home court advantage is worth four points in the NBA." (Note: It varies between teams, but *The Wages of Wins Journal* found that home-court advantage in the NBA is worth between 3.17 points and 4.51 points.) "And let's say those four points are because throughout the entire game the crowd is making noise at moments when they're motivating the home team and demotivating the visiting team. One more minute divided by forty-eight times four is not very big," Green says. "But it's not zero. Maybe I'm underestimating it." According to his calculations, a dunk under these specific conditions would be worth 2.08 points. (And what about when the away team dunks? "I feel like made shots, one way or another, silence the crowd," Green says. "It's wrong to cheer following the opponent making a shot, whether it's a dunk or a layup." That's a good point.)

None of this will hold up under the slightest bit of academic scrutiny, but perhaps it was foolish for me to even try to pin down the worth of a dunk. True works of art should elicit feeling, not market analysis. Who cares if it is only worth 2.08 points while at home during a close game and with the crowd making noise at maximally motivating and demotivating moments? A dunk is exciting and looks cool, and that should be enough. It's the stuff that dreams are made of.

• • •

A LONELY TREE may or may not make sound when it clatters to the forest floor, but a dunk always deserves an audience. It is the most breathtaking visual spectacle in all of sports, and a dunk in isolation would be a waste of kinetic energy. There's a reason I always have an audience in those wonderful dreams of mine. I need to show off.

I actually have two recurring dreams. In the other, I'm racing through an infinitely huge airport to catch a flight. It's a classic stress dream, and I almost always wake up after I fail to make it to the gate in time. There are rare occasions when I actually do get to the plane before the doors close, but those dreams usually end with the plane crashing. The chaotic tumble toward earth is vivid and terrifying, but I am always comforted by the same calming thought: "At least I made my flight." I much prefer the dunk dream.

"Recurring dreams are examples of your subconscious successfully grabbing your attention," Layne Dalfen tells me. Dalfen is a professional dream interpreter. She's been untangling people's dreams for over thirty years, and I've reached out to her to learn why my sleeping brain is so obsessed with dunking.

Before our chat I checked a few dream dictionaries for information on what it could mean, and while those books contain entries for seemingly every type of subconscious sojourn, I couldn't find anything regarding dunking. There were explanations for dreams about peepholes ("symbolizes your very constricted view of things"), crabs ("suggests being aware of other people's hidden crabby behavior"), and roller coasters ("symbolizes that life is just a ride"), but the deep symbolic meaning of a rim-rattling slam remains a mystery.

According to Dalfen, I was just wasting my time. "Oh my God," she groans. "You cannot look it up in a book. You cannot tell somebody what their dream means. You can only project."

Dreams are intensely personal, and Dalfen asserts that you need proper context and information about the dreamer in order to understand the coded language of the subconscious. "At the first level, the dream is triggered by a very specific current situation in your waking life that is bugging you," she says. "The solution to the problem that you are attempting to come to a conclusion about arrives in your unconscious mind before it gets to your consciousness."

She tells me a story about Elias Howe, the man who invented the lock-stitch sewing machine. "He was so close with the invention, but he kept screwing up with the needle. He dreamt that he was captured by cannibals. They kept poking him into the pot with their spears, and in the dream he saw that there were holes on the front of their spears. Upon waking up he realized he should not be putting the hole at the top of the needle, he needed to place it near its point."

As far as visual metaphors go, understanding that spears represent sewing needles is pretty obvious. Howe's subconscious made it easy for him. My dunk dreams, on the other hand, don't seem to be connected in any meaningful way to the specific problems of my life. I've been having them for decades, and they seem to be nothing more than a periodic reminder that I would be much happier if I didn't have such a sorry vertical leap.

"There's some situation in your life that you're not looking after," Dalfen says. "Your unconscious never lies to you. If you've got a girlfriend who's cheating on you, your unconscious is either going to give you a huge night-mare or a recurring dream over a short period of time that's going to grab your attention and make you wonder what's going on." Considering I started having these dunking dreams nearly two decades before I even met my wife, I'd like to assume that I am in the clear in this regard.

"If you have a recurring dream over a number of years, that's different," says Dalfen. "That's a favorite expression." Like a phrase you frequently find yourself repeating, a recurring dream follows you through life and appears whenever you're confronted with a familiar emotion. In waking life, Dalfen's favorite expression is "Oh shit." "I could have said 'oh shit' forty-five years ago when I missed the bus. And I could have said it about an hour ago when I realized that our call wasn't at eleven thirty. I'm still saying 'oh shit,' but it's about completely different reasons."

According to Dalfen, your brain probably won't deploy a recurring dream to solve a problem. Rather, it's a way for your sleeping mind to converse with its waking counterpart. Like two tipsy airline passengers bonding over basketball at an airport bar, it's all about finding common ground.

I describe my dream in detail to Dalfen. Every time, I don't think I will be able to dunk, but I try anyway and gleefully exceed my expectations. It feels *amazing*, and when I wake up it takes a few seconds for the joy to fade into acrid nostalgia.

"It reminds me of a horny dream," Dalfen says.

"But it feels so much better than a horny dream," I say, sheepishly waving at my wife in the other room.

"Sometimes, when you have a dream that makes you feel so good, the point is to take that feeling and run with it," Dalfen says. "With you, it's more like take that feeling and jump with it. There's physical movement to dunking a basketball. You cannot dunk a basketball by sitting on the couch. The dream is providing a rehearsal for movement as opposed to procrastinating. Are you a procrastinator?"

"Of course I am," I say. "I'm a writer."

We discuss this book, and Dalfen tells me about going to summer camp in upstate New York over half a century ago. The camp was owned by Dolph Schayes, the Syracuse Nationals forward who played in that shot clock exhibition game and spoke so glowingly about its inventor, Danny Biasone.

"He was a giant, in all respects," she says of Schayes. "I remember being small enough that I was looking at his knee. That was amazing." Since then, the sport always conjures up a feeling of awe for her, like looking up at redwoods. "Basketball means different things to different people," she says.

Dalfen is herself an author, and we commiserate about deadlines. While I'm unable to tell her specifically about what was going on in my life during the other dozen or so times I've had this dream, I can confirm that I have had it recently. She listens patiently as I ramble on about my writing struggles, and I briefly forget that *I'm* the one who's supposed to be interviewing *her*. Remember, writing a book is a self-involved endeavor, just like dunking.

"The dreams are great because they give you the rehearsal to get to work," she tells me. "They make movement happen. They show you that movement creates success and you end up feeling so good. It's to inspire you to stop procrastinating, when you get those dreams."

Of course my brain turns to dunking when it needs to be inspired. If I can re-create just a fraction of that feeling by getting off my butt, then any attempts at procrastination would amount to me blocking my own dunk. How stupid is that? The sleeping mind tends to make a good amount of sense. It's a shame we can't use it all the time.

Dalfen's dive into my subconscious revealed my own childlike need for positive reinforcement, but she ends our conversation on a negative note.

"I have sort of bad news for you," she says. "Now that you understand what the image in your dream is about, you probably won't have it again. The unconscious is so conniving, it will now look for another favorite expression that will also make you feel good. It just probably won't be a dunk."

How can my unconscious be expected to find an adequate replacement for that dream? Literally nothing feels better than a dunk.

What a nightmare.

MAKING THAT DREAM WORK

TOPICS DISCUSSED IN THIS SECTION:

Oak Ridge National
   Laboratory
Assists
Arctic wolves
Flopping
The 1968 Republican
   National Convention
The Five Love Languages
Climate Orbiter *Akatsuki*
The triangle offense
Barbra Streisand

Betelgeuse
Defense
Grover Cleveland's
   reelection campaign
Yubikeys
Atmospheric science
Marlin fishing
HTTPS encryption
Molecular architecture
Superconducting islands
Sledgehammers

TOPICS NOT DISCUSSED IN THIS SECTION:

Peanut brittle
Cathy Guisewite
"Hard seltzer"
Dazzle camouflage
The Ruddington
   Framework Knitters'
   Museum
Radish roses
The Lucerne Kapellbrücke
   (Chapel Bridge)
Kevin Costner
Hydroponic farming
The reversal of the
   Chicago River

Archaeoraptor dinosaur
   hoax
"Deceptacon" by Le Tigre
Concordat of Worms
Oregano
Visual effects master Rick
   Baker
Tennis
John Kay's flying shuttle
Borborygmus
Mice

STOUT, RESOLUTE, AND SOMEWHAT INVISIBLE

Defense flies under the radar

T O BE A great defender is to disrupt and destroy a beautiful, free-flowing game. It's rude! Like a pest who gleefully stomps out sandcastles or draws mustaches on yearbook photos, you've got to be a real sicko to enjoy playing defense. I mean that as a compliment.

But what does great defense look like? The question is surprisingly difficult to answer. Individual defensive success can be easy to spot—Natasha Howard swatting a layup into the stands or Kawhi Leonard ripping the ball from a dribbler's grasp like a nasty older sibling—but effective team defense often manifests itself in the things you *don't* see. Players can't penetrate with the ball. Passes get exchanged around the parameter without purpose. Lanes are clogged, expected geometries denied.

Basketball is easy to watch when an offense dictates the pace and flow of the game, but when a defense calls the shots it can look like something invisible has broken deep inside the sport's machinery.

Bronson Messer specializes in seeing the nigh unseeable. He is a computational and theoretical astrophysicist at Oak Ridge National Laboratory in Tennessee, meaning he tries to make sense of what is happening at the farthest reaches of the universe.

"I'm wholly dependent upon visualization," he tells me. "Of course I have to know quantitative data. I need to know exactly what the temperature of an exploding star is at some point, and I need to know exactly how many neutrinos are being emitted per second and that kind of stuff. But to understand what is actually going on, to understand the physics of what is actually happening, we rely on very sophisticated visualizations of what's going on inside the boiling heart of an exploding star."

To do this, Messer relies on the help of Summit, the world's fastest supercomputer. "It's about the size of a basketball court," he says. "It's the most powerful computer ever built by human beings. A little over 200 petaflops."

If you could ask the man who controls the most powerful computer in the world any question, what would it be?

How big is the universe?

Is there a God?

When will humanity expire?

Does the computer have a screen?

(I picked the last one.)

"There's no monitor per se," Messer explains. "You log in remotely via terminal emulator, from anywhere in the world."

Messer has a thick Southern accent and a knack for describing complex phenomena with clever analogies. He is also a three-time *Jeopardy!* champion with $31,599 in lifetime winnings. (The Final Jeopardy! category that eventually ended his run was "Presidential Elections." The clue: *The only two Democratic presidents defeated for reelection since the Civil War.*)

Supernovas are Messer's specialty, and he spends his days analyzing the universe's most incredible celestial highlights. "When big stars end their life, they don't just go quietly into that good night," he says. "They blow up and feed the interstellar medium with the seeds that will become us. Every iron nucleus in your blood, every piece of gold you've ever held, everything in fact that you've ever held in your hand or seen that is heavier than hydrogen or helium was formed in a star and then dispersed into space by a supernova explosion. So we really are stardust. That's my elevator pitch for the kind of thing I do." (Oh, in case you were wondering, Cleveland and Carter were the only Democratic presidents defeated for reelection since the Civil War. Messer guessed Carter and Hoover.)

When I get in touch with Messer, he has his eye on Betelgeuse, a big red ball of gas sitting on the shoulder of Orion. "It's the star closest to us that's most likely to go supernova," he says. "It's making the news right now because it has dimmed precipitously over the last month. Used to be you could go out and you could immediately see that it was red and it looked large. Now, if you go out tonight and look, you'll have a hard time seeing it because it has dimmed." When stars dim like this, it means that a cosmos-altering boom might be imminent. Betelgeuse is the tenth-brightest star in our sky, and its potential supernova is a huge deal. "It's not going to go tonight, probably, but it could. But when it does explode, Betelgeuse will be brighter than the full moon for a few months, and it will be daylight-visible for weeks."

In order to understand what's happening inside a star 770 light-years (4,526,541,537,351,377.952755906 miles) away, Messer relies on what he calls "physical intuition," which he describes as the ability to craft a phenomenological and narrative understanding of the otherwise unknowable. "Physical intuition is something that is drilled into the heads of grad students when they're training," he says. "One of your primary responsibilities as a grad student is to, quote, 'develop your physical intuition.' And to me it wasn't that hard of a concept because I was such a big sports-head when I was a kid. It made perfect sense to me. You have to develop experience seeing patterns over and over again so you can somehow figure out what's going on."

Thanks to years of playing and watching basketball, Messer is confident in his physical intuition as it pertains to hoops. "You can see a pick-and-roll about to happen," he says. "You know what the vocabulary that's going to build up to the play is about. But on defense, you have to be thinking instead of the next sort of move, you have to be thinking two moves in advance. I think that's kind of hard for people to grok unless they've had empirical experience."

After running these rhythms and patterns through his brain—his "wetware," as he calls it—Messer managed to produce a visual analog that has stuck with him. "The best defense, I always think, looks like an iridescent turtle shell."

Can you picture it, this magical, shimmering, reptile? No? Think about a possession in which the defense creates a sort of force field around the perimeter. That's Messer's shell. "People move in these epicycles, these little convective cells that make little circles around at the edges, and it pushes everybody out."

Broadly speaking, basketball teams have two general defensive strategies they can run: man-to-man, where each player is responsible for guarding a single opponent, and zone, wherein they are tasked with defending a specific area of the floor. Long a collegiate staple, zone defenses were prohibited in the NBA until 2001. However, it was notoriously difficult to legislate, so teams were able to incorporate subtle versions of it into their game plans. Nowadays, most professional teams will play a mix of the two styles that, to at least one theoretical astrophysicist and three-time *Jeopardy!* champion, looks like an iridescent turtle shell.

"Imagine one guy with the ball," Messer says. "He probes, stepping into the top of the key with it to see if he can drive or not. He's either going to drive and shoot or he's going to drive and dish. The double-team comes, a guy peels off and goes to the center. They make these convective cells, little churnings that are little circles, two people running in a circle over and over again. A tight circle, but still a circle. It pushes all the action to the edge. Or, the two guards pinching at the top of a zone defense and not letting that guy drive into the center of the lane. They peel off and make a little circle when

Fig. a: Modern motion defense

they do that." He pauses to give his metaphor some thought. "Perhaps it's more of a snapping turtle."

Messer has a soft spot for defense. As a kid he was always the "big palooka" tasked with protecting the middle of the floor. Much like his current job observing the cosmos, that gave him an opportunity to watch and learn how bodies move through space. "Even though our star is a single star, most of the stars in the universe are in binaries or multiple systems," he tells me. "They dance around each other. There's certainly a dance that comes along with basketball offenses and basketball defenses and what they move like. This happens more in the NBA now that you don't have to play only man-to-man. There is a rhythm to a defense."

Keeping track of this rhythmic dance isn't always easy. "Every offensive move has a counter, and every defensive counter has a counter-counter," Messer says. But if you happen to get lost, just look for the luminous turtle sashaying among the stars. It'll help you find your way.

• • •

I KNOW WHAT you may be thinking: "I'm not an idiot, I know what good defense looks like." If so, that's great! (And I never called you an idiot.) But please try to allow for a moment the possibility that defense is more complicated than it might seem.

For example, few plays scream "great defense" like when a defender swats a layup into the stands. I mean, the shot was about to go in, we all saw it, and then, out of nowhere—*thwack*—a big ol' hand swings in to send that sucker into the twenty-fifth row. Two points, erased. That's what defense is all about, right?

A block is, to use an idiom literally, the last line of defense. It marks a satisfying end to a seemingly successful defensive possession, but there could have been an entire series of breakdowns leading up to that denied attempt. The on-ball defender was playing on her heels and gave the dribbler a free path to the hoop. Or, a teammate wasn't paying attention and allowed her assignment to cut into the paint and receive a pass down low. Perhaps the blocker herself, duped by a pump-fake, scrambled to recover and was lucky to get her hand on the ball at all. She managed to swat it, which you may argue is all that matters, but can it actually be considered an example of *great* defense? The best defense would have prevented the offensive player from even having a chance at a layup in the first place.

Restricting the opponent to a low-percentage shot attempt is nice, but for defensive-minded squads, forcing a shot clock violation at the end of a possession is the grandest prize of all. The way some teams celebrate, you'd think they'd just withstood the Siege of Leningrad and not the Charlotte Hornets.

Those cheers are earned. Such resolute defending only occurs when everyone commits to his or her job with physical energy and mental acuity. However, when it comes to producing a maximally desirable end product, there's actually something better than a shot clock violation. It doesn't come without its risks, but drawing an offensive foul is the ideal defensive play. Not only does your team get possession, but the opponent incurs a costly penalty as well. Under perfect circumstances, it can result in the other team's best player fouling out of the contest and a pair of free throws for you at the other end. If basketball were Uno, it would be the Draw Four card. A total screwjob.

The most common type of offensive foul is the charge. According to the rules, the defender needs to be standing still at the point of contact in order for the officials to rule in their favor. Television commentators will often describe the player in this situation as "sacrificing their body." While taking up such a rigid posture and confronting the inevitable has the effect of standing before a firing squad, sans cigarette, is it really a "sacrifice"? I've never heard of a slaughtered lamb getting a chance to shoot free throws after its own sacrifice.

Offensive fouls happen in the blink of an eye and are, like those old zone defense violations, extremely difficult for officials to adjudicate. To once again pull from the commentators' dictionary, they are "bang-bang" plays. Did the defender get there in time? Were his feet planted? These things are hard enough to spot when everybody is acting honestly and honorably, but some players are adept at (or just prone to) embellishing instances of normal contact to make them look like major infractions.

Flopping, as this is known, is technically a form of cheating. But is it wrong in a moral or ethical sense? Francisco Javier López Frías is the philosopher at Penn State who helped us with our little Ship of Theseus issue.

He teaches kinesiology and ethics, and he's dedicated much of his research to the things that threaten the fairness of sports, like performance enhancing drugs or miniature motors that cheating cyclists have been known to hide inside their bikes. As such, he's spent many ponderous hours considering *what it means* when Chris Paul flails at the slightest amount of contact. "I don't like flopping, but I see the argument for why it might have room at the professional level," he says. "Differences are so small, in terms of performance, that every tiny thing that you can do to gain an edge is in many cases going to decide a game. In those scenarios, I see flopping as an example of how we can use strategic thinking to try and take advantage of a specific situation in the game."

Whether it's ethically excusable or not, the NBA has been trying to discourage flopping for decades. The league painted a dotted line four feet from the basket in 1997 to create a charge-free zone so referees don't have to use their judgment on plays near the hoop. Players caught flopping in games are punished with technical fouls, and in 2012, the NBA began fining those who, based on video review, are judged to have flopped. They receive a warning for their first infraction, a $5,000 penalty for the second, $10,000 for the third, and so on. "There's a trade-off," Frías says. "It becomes a strategic decision. Do I try to deceive knowing that, if I get caught, I am going to get penalized?"

The Boston Celtics' Marcus Smart is perhaps the most prolific flopper in the NBA right now. Whereas most stars have YouTube videos dedicated to their best highlights, Smart is the subject of more than a dozen flop compilations featuring his most outlandish pratfalls. When the league fined him in 2016 for a particularly egregious flop, one where he went flying like a stuntman off the balcony of the O.K. Corral, Smart laughed the whole thing off. "That's a flop. Let's get that straight, that's a flop, this was hilarious," he told ESPN. "I deserved everything that came my way after that."

Frías argues that if the NBA wanted to abolish flopping completely, they'd enforce even stricter penalties. "We don't want basketball to be about trying to deceive the referee, but we acknowledge that there is *some* value in exercising this strategic thinking. So we penalize it, or we make it more difficult for players to engage in that type of behavior," he says. "We still leave the door open for them to try." That door is very much ajar. The NBA issued only fourteen fines for flopping in the first six seasons after it began fining players for the behavior. There were plenty of obvious flops after Smart's stuntman flail in 2016, but it took the league three full years before it issued another fine. The Los Angeles Clippers' Patrick Beverley was the guilty party in that instance, when he appeared to suffer a cardiac arrest after James Harden's shoulder nearly grazed his chin. The unconvincing performance cost him five grand.

It's worth noting that Smart and Beverley are two of the best defenders in the league. They don't *need* to flop. But the potential reward is often worth the risk. Smart's take on the act is similar to Frías's, in that it is a form of strategy. "I flop on defense, your favorite player flops on offense," he told ESPN. "That's the only difference. Especially in a game where the offense has nothing but the advantage, the defense has to do something to get the advantage back." He's referring to how some superstars resort to histrionics while attacking the basket in order to get a foul call. That's known as "selling contact," and it's a largely accepted way for players to get the officials' attention. As NBA referee Zach Zarba told *Business Insider* in 2018, "the selling of a call is just showing what actually happened . . . that's a legal play."

But how is it different from flopping? When the league announced its flopping guidelines in 2012, the press release stated, "The primary factor in determining whether a player committed a flop is whether his physical reaction to contact with another player is inconsistent with what would reasonably be expected given the force or direction of the contact." That is the literal definition of "selling contact." The NBA seems to be saying that the only distinction between a flop and a foul in most scenarios is whether the player manages to put on a compelling and convincing performance.

"It's a magic trick. There are people who know how to look at a camera and make love to it, if you will," Lori Wyman tells me. "There are people that really know how to come alive when you put a camera on them." Wyman is a Miami-based casting director who's worked on shows like HBO's *Ballers* and Netflix's *Bloodline*. She also has considerable experience casting for soap operas and telenovelas, which is why I reached out to her. We're talking about flopping, after all.

No one's ever put on an episode of *General Hospital* and said, "I wonder if that fellow is hurt." The emotions are immediately identifiable and, in the context of the soap opera, believable (in a manic sort of way). It is a skill that could be useful should a player want to, say, sell some contact to an otherwise distracted, whistle-toting audience.

According to Wyman, being able to cry on cue is a common requirement for soap opera casting. "They're soap operas!" she exclaims. "They're dramas. *Let's see how you cry.*"

Crying is rare in professional basketball, which is a good thing because it's an incredibly difficult thing to fake. "It's just natural talent," Wyman says. "It's truly an art, if you will." She tells me about a time she saw a woman weeping in the waiting room during a soap opera casting call. "She was listening to something on her phone with the little earphones in her ears. I went over to her and said, 'Are you ready?' And she said, 'Yeah [sniff], I'm ready, and she came in and she was still crying. But it wasn't real. There was a disconnect. I said to her, 'What were you listening to?' She said she was listening to a Barbra Streisand song that always makes her cry."

I'm dying to know: Was it "People"? "The Way We Were"? "Memory"? Wyman doesn't recall, but she clearly remembers that the woman blew the audition. "I just thought, 'You're not getting it.' You need to know how to connect to the character. You're not in the moment at all."

There's a lesson for potential floppers in this: No one is going to believe you if you force a reaction from nothing. You need to actually feel the contact you're trying to sell. Babs can't save you.

"I always say, *be*, as opposed to act," Wyman advises. "Don't act hurt, *be* hurt. You understand what I'm saying? Because when you act it, people can tell, *Oh, he's acting*. But when you actually feel it, you actually *be* it, it's more convincing."

A convincing performance gives your team the ball and, perhaps, two free throws; an unconvincing performance gets you a personal or technical foul. "A lot's riding on that," Wyman tells me. "I always use the term 'less is more.' The bigger you act, the worse it looks." The casting director is right, and the science backs her up.

Dallas Mavericks owner Mark Cuban has long been annoyed with flopping. "If you look at a high-contact sport like football, you see few pancakes, where guys end up on their behinds," he told the *Wall Street Journal* in 2013. "Yet in our sport, guys end up on their backsides all the time." Cuban

b. THE FULL-BODY FLAIL

a. THE KNOCK-OUT PUNCH

c. THE FLYING STUNTMAN

FLOPPERS

is famously outspoken, which is a nice way of saying he complains a lot. He's been made to pay millions of dollars in fines to the NBA for his repeated criticisms of its referees. But, in 2013, he decided to do something other than complain: He issued a six-figure grant to researchers at Southern Methodist University to study the physics of flopping. His aim was to "take out guessing and reduce the amount of judgment involved" in making these extremely consequential calls.

Led by biomechanics professor Peter Weyand, the team used a variety of methods—including shoving each other over while wearing force-detecting sensors—to find out the differences between genuine tumbles and embellished flops. ("We had very thick mats," Weyand told the *Guardian* regarding the shoving tests.)

SMU's research found that, when a player is completely stationary (as the charging rules dictate), then it is surprisingly easy to topple him over. "If we had found that it takes huge amounts of force, then you could assume that every time you see someone falling over in a NBA game, they're faking it," said Weyand. "But no—in many cases, if the defender just doesn't move their feet, then down they go."

According to their research, the biggest tell that someone is trying to dupe the referees can be spotted in the movement of his or her arms. You'll often see players dramatically throw their hands above their head, but the SMU study found that this is "not natural counter-movement" to contact. In non-flops, a player tends to thrust his arms out and to the side (like he's making himself into a T), which is a natural reaction to impact. It's a more subdued movement. As Lori Wyman says, "Less is more."

There's a fine line between acting natural and going completely unnoticed, both in casting and in basketball. It all comes back to talent. "If the actor is a good actor and versatile, they'll know how to turn it up," Wyman tells me. "You see that sometimes with basketball players. When they're on the court, that's when the camera's on them, and they know how to play it."

As long as flopping remains part of the game, fans have no choice but to learn how to live with and, in some cases, appreciate it when it happens. "It is a skill," Frías says. "It's not the most important skill, and if I was a coach it is not a skill that I would recommend anybody to try and develop in one's practice. But if they happen to be good at it and can on some specific occasions take advantage of it, well, it is what it is."

I ask Frías how he would react if his team won an important game due to a flop. "I'm going to celebrate," he says. "There's no doubt about it. Later on, if I were to rationalize it, I would say, 'Of course it would have been better if it happened differently.' But I'm definitely going to celebrate."

• • •

DRAWING AN OFFENSIVE foul may not always be honest work, but defense is a desperate gig. No matter how hard a team tries to prevent an opponent from scoring, it takes but a single moment of luck or talent to render all that effort moot. The basketball cliché states that "good offense beats good defense," but the sour truth is that bad offense sometimes wins, too.

The most that a team can do on defense is reduce their opponents' odds for success. It's damage mitigation, and it calls for much preparation.

As David Adrian tells me, "You've got to figure out who are your attackers, how are they going to come at you, and what are you actually trying to defend against." Adrian isn't referring to basketball, specifically, but he is talking about defense. He's a cybersecurity researcher and the cofounder of Cencys, a Michigan-based startup that protects companies from internet-based attacks.

Preparation means understanding your own strengths and weaknesses. The Milwaukee Bucks had a historically great defense before the coronavirus pandemic interrupted the 2019–20 season, and much of that was due to their adherence to that ancient aphorism: know thyself. While most teams usually want to restrict opponents' attempts at the basket, Milwaukee has three elite defenders patrolling that part of the floor (Giannis Antetokounmpo and the Lopez brothers, Brook and Robin). As *FiveThirtyEight*'s Chris Herring pointed out, "the Bucks all but roll out a red carpet to the rim, as they surrender more drives per one hundred possessions than any other club." That would be a catastrophic stat for most other teams, but for Milwaukee it just meant that the plan was going splendidly.

In cybersecurity, knowing thyself is called "threat modeling." As Adrian explains, "You don't want anyone to be able to exploit the baseline set of web vulnerabilities on your site and get access to your user database. But also maybe you're worried about your third-party dependencies. I know how to defend my code, but my code depends upon all this other code, is it secure? Am I keeping it up to date? Is that in your threat model?" It's a litany of worries, and because defense tends to be reactive, it never stops.

The threat modelling Adrian did regarding major encryption vulnerabilities while he was earning his PhD helped uncover two previously undetected cyberattacks. The attacks, nicknamed Logjam and DROWN, allowed hackers to gain access to private data that was supposed to be protected. In order to discover the weak spots, Adrian had to think like a nefarious cybercriminal. Sort of. "For the DROWN attack, we were just like, 'Well, there's this thing that someone could do that is surely incredibly, incredibly silly. No one should do this. So let's see if anyone is actually doing this."

The "silly" thing to which he's referring is the use of an outdated and obsolete encryption protocol that "only existed for like six months in the early 1990s." Not updating it would be like replacing your house's front door with strings of beads, hence Adrian's incredulousness. However, when he ran an internet-wide scan to gauge its prevalence, he found that 33 percent of all HTTPS servers were using the outdated protocol. That's a lot of bead strings.

It's unlikely that you'll ever see such a flagrant and widespread vulnerability in the defensive strategies used by high-level basketball teams. Far more common is when a momentary lapse in judgment—allowing a dribbler to cut inside, going under a screen against a deadly three-point shooter, etc.—leads to a total breakdown. Rest unassured, there's plenty of that happening in cybersecurity, too.

"Basically, Trump won the election because John Podesta clicked a link in his email and got phished," Adrian says. He's referring, of course, to the time Russian-affiliated hackers gained access to the Gmail account for Hillary Clinton's campaign chairman in 2016 and the subsequent "But her emails . . ." hell that helped sink her election chances. It was a costly defensive lapse.

"It is demoralizing that we've done all this stuff, and there are these huge security teams at companies that put in all this effort and then, at the end of the day, someone clicks a link in an email and that's an election flipped," Adrian says. "But this is also good to know." Defense is all about making adjustments. If someone burns you by faking a handoff on a pick-and-roll, you make sure you're ready in case it happens again.

There are ways to prevent human error, but, ironically, these often require the participation of humans. Adrian refers to the Yubikey, which is a 100-percent effective way to prevent phishing attacks like the one that nabbed Podesta. These are physical USB devices that make it so an online account can only be used by its rightful owner, the person in possession of the Yubikey. That way, even if your campaign chairman does get phished, the hacker sitting in Moscow won't be able to access his Gmail. "It's an organizational process to get those pushed out and required everywhere," Adrian says. Team defense requires everyone's participation.

"There are a lot of strong opinions about what makes things secure or how to go about securing an organization that tend to be pushed through without thinking that hard about them or with a weird set of assumptions," Adrian continues. "Some people might say you need to do all this phishing training to get this stop. Yeah, maybe that can make it so that phishing is only 5 percent successful instead of 50 percent successful, but guess what?"

The answer is implied: It only takes one mistake to fuck everything up. Good defense requires great discipline. Lunge for the steal and you might get crossed over. Rush a double-team and leave a shooter wide open. Bite on a pump-fake and, whoops, you just gave up a layup *and* a foul.

Take the two most important defensive plays from Game 7 of the 2016 NBA Finals, the series where LeBron James and the Cleveland Cavaliers overcame a 3–1 deficit against the seventy-three-win Golden State Warriors. You've surely seen the most famous play of that contest replayed millions of times: With two minutes remaining and the score tied at eighty-nine, Andre Iguodala rebounds a bad Cavaliers miss, outruns all but one Cleveland player, and, after a quick give-and-go with Steph Curry, goes up for the layup. But James had been trailing the entire time and, with a superhuman burst of speed, he surges into the picture and swats Iguodala's attempt off the backboard.

It is perhaps the greatest highlight of James's career, but it wouldn't have been possible were it not for the disciplined play of J. R. Smith. Yes, you read that correctly. J. R. Smith, the man whom the league has punished for untying his opponents' shoelaces during free throw attempts (among numerous other infractions) was the only Cleveland player who was disciplined enough in his positioning to sprint back to where he was supposed to be on defense. When Iguodala went for the layup, Smith acrobatically contorted his body in midair and managed to disrupt the attempt without giving up a costly foul. Because of this, Iguodala had to bring the ball down to his midriff and then back up again, giving James the opportunity and time to make his legacy-defining block.

Flash-forward one minute later. Golden State is down by three points and Draymond Green sets a pick for Stephen Curry. As former coach and current commentator Hubie Brown has said, "You set screens for one reason: to make defenders think." Do you stay with your opponent, or do you churn with your teammate like little cells inside a turtle's shell and switch assignments? The Cavs decided to switch, leaving six-foot-ten power forward Kevin Love to guard the greatest shooter humanity has ever produced.

Switching is an important tenet of modern basketball defense, as it denies three-point shooters the room to freely fire away. The catch is that, for it to work, it helps if everyone in the lineup is able to guard each of the other five positions on the floor. The Warriors brought about the NBA's switching revolution in the middle of the decade when they began doing it on every single screen they faced, and the trend helped accelerate the mass big-man extinction event originally started by the three-point line. Love entered the league in 2008 as a lumbering post player and elite rebounder, and he survived this schism by losing a ton of weight and learning how to shoot the long ball. For the majority of his basketball playing life, Love never would have had to defend a point guard mano a mano, yet here he was, facing off against the league's most deadly offensive weapon with less than a minute remaining in the biggest game of his career.

Standing thirty-five feet from the hoop, Love makes a mistake almost immediately. He lunges at a Curry pump-fake, but the point guard doesn't take advantage with a drive or a shot. Instead, Curry regroups and performs a series of moves, but Love, having learned his lesson, refuses to bite. With great discipline, he stays in front of Curry for what seems like an eternity and forces him to settle for an off-balanced three-pointer. It's the kind of shot he makes around 40 percent of the time, but that's what defense and damage mitigation is all about. The fates ruled in favor of Love, and Cleveland hung on to win its first-ever NBA Championship.

Smith and Love refused to make rash decisions, and they were rewarded for their defensive puritanism. Ironically, the stats we most commonly use to judge someone's defensive abilities (steals and blocks) will often reflect the types of gambles that should be avoided, things that would have sunk the Cavaliers had Smith and Love tried to force them in the moment. Great defense is defined by what the opponent cannot do, but this can be difficult to quantify. How is one supposed to measure the absence of something?

For David Adrian, an ideal cyber defense is completely unsexy. "If I come up with some software architecture or something that prevents a whole class of attacks, by definition, nothing is then going to happen," he tells me. "It's doing its job, so there's no reason to pay attention to it. From that sense, defense can be almost, I don't want to say boring, but you're not going to see someone walk into the [annual computer security] Black Hat Conference in Vegas every summer and be like, 'Hey, we did a good job coding this thing and we think that there are fewer vulnerabilities as a result.'"

This sentiment is echoed by Mark Eaton, the Utah Jazz's yeti of a center who won two defensive player of the year awards in the 1980s. "You know you're really changing the game as a shot blocker when your numbers go down," he told journalist Chris Ballard. "That means teams aren't even attempting certain shots because you're in there." You can't block shots if your opponents are too scared to take them near you.

As an expert in cybersecurity, one would assume Adrian is well-suited to understating the subtleties that go into its basketball analog. He tells me he's getting the hang of it, but there's quite a steep learning curve. "I started paying attention to it and reading about it more," he says before conceding that "it's hard to know what's going on on defense and actually make sense of it."

Adrian is not alone. For a long time, no one had any clue how to quantify good team defense. The most common metrics were opponents' field goal percentage and points allowed per game. The latter was especially troublesome because, well, all games are different. Some games move fast, some move slow, and scores surge or ebb depending on that flow.

A meteorologist in Utah named Ken Pomeroy noticed this quirk in the early 2000s. He was watching an Air Force game and couldn't believe the commentators were lauding the Falcons' defense. Sure, the team had been holding their opponents to low scorelines, but Pomeroy just didn't buy the hype. "It was particularly obvious because they didn't have the personnel that would lead you to believe that they had a great defense," he tells me over the phone.

In his day job with the National Weather Service, Pomeroy created and analyzed forecast models. During his free time, he started working on an equivalent for college basketball. In order to make more accurate predictions about games, Pomeroy sought to understand accurately how good teams were on both offense and defense. To do this, he recorded the number of possessions in games and adjusted his statistics in accordance with a new baseline: pace. Unlike opponents' scoring averages, these statistics ("adjusted defensive efficiency," "adjusted efficiency margin," etc.) portrayed aspects of the game as if they were occurring in a dimension where tempo remained constant.

"The same kind of storm that develops in the middle of February will do something different in June," he tells me. "College basketball is an environment. If you have a situation where everybody is shooting the ball more and shooting it better, then obviously the best offenses are going to be helped by that. Really, the way to evaluate the best offenses or defenses is not to look at raw numbers, but to also consider the environment they're playing in."

Pomeroy posts his data to KenPom.com, which has become the premiere source for advanced college basketball analytics. It's some pretty heady stuff, and he has some rather impressive readers. A member of Ohio State's coaching staff told the *New York Times* that the site was the "first thing I look at every time I go into a scout" and described it as "the Bible." When Butler University went on a Cinderella run to the National Championship game in 2010, head coach Brad Stevens prepared for the matchup against Duke by poring over Pomeroy's website. All that studying almost paid off—the Bulldogs were one missed shot away from pulling off the biggest upset in men's college basketball history.

University of Michigan fan David Adrian is another KenPom.com devotee, and he saw a connection between Pomeroy's approach to basketball and his own research that helped him better understand the elusive nature of both defense and internet security.

"I couldn't tell you the slightest about how KenPom's prediction algorithm works," Adrian says, "but the idea of tempo-free stats—*what if we had a consistent denominator for all of our comparisons? What if we divided everything by possessions so we could actually compare across games?*—this was exactly like fixing the problems I saw a lot of in internet measurement for security."

When performing internet scans to search for encryption vulnerabilities, Adrian found that organizations and researchers were all using different methodologies. Like Pomeroy struggling to come to grips with commentators' praise for air force's defense, Adrian discovered that these measurements were woefully inconsistent when he was trying to find those outdated encryption protocols. In essence, they were working with different tempos. "If you're trying to say what percentage of servers have some property, you'd better have a consistent measurement of those servers, otherwise you're just making up a percentage," he says. It left him exasperated. "Your denominator is not consistent! The numbers you are putting in don't make a lot of sense."

Whether you're analyzing basketball defenses or encryption vulnerabilities, the goal is plainly simple. "You're trying to understand how something works," Pomeroy tells me. The same can be said for weather. "Meteorology is trying to understand how the atmosphere works and the mathematical equations that govern that, and it's kind of the same thing in basketball. But in basketball it's far simpler. There's a lot of data that comes out of college basketball games, but it doesn't compare to the amount of data that is developed from the global atmosphere."

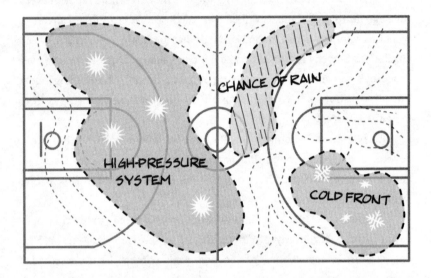

Pomeroy has less time to analyze the weather now that he's one of the most influential voices in advanced analytics. (He no longer works at the NWS, and he stopped teaching atmospheric sciences at the University of Utah in 2014 to focus on his website.) Still, he finds himself a little wistful when it comes to meteorology. "I miss it a lot," he tells me. "It's something that affects everybody. You can't really say that about basketball."

With the NCAA Men's Division I Basketball Tournament canceled due to the COVID-19 pandemic, KenPom's team ratings for 2020 were stuck in time like the gauges on a sunken shipwreck. Virginia's defense was once again the nation's top unit, but due to their plodding offense, Pomeroy had the defending champions ranked all the way down at forty-seventh overall. He has a great track record with these things, but now we would never get to see his forecasts put to the test during March Madness. The future is a mystery. "If they are playing games, then the operations of my site won't change very much," Pomeroy says. "Who knows how it's going to look? The way things are trending I'll be pretty happy if they're playing games at all." Like the weather, uncertainty reigns.

For once, Pomeroy has no way of forecasting what will happen next. It's an unnatural position for him. "For some reason, I am drawn to making predictions about things," he tells me. "I've always kind of had this dream of having a weather casino where people would bet on the high temperature or something." Things are getting desperate without basketball.

Predictions are tough, with or without reams of data. Bronson Messer is a genius who gets to work with the fastest computer in the world, yet he only managed to get one Final Four team correct in his 2019 March Madness bracket. His picks were so bad, the *Knoxville News Sentinel* wrote a story about it. (Headline: "Busted NCAA bracket? Don't worry, even a rocket scientist's predictions aren't perfect.")

Messer can laugh about it, though. He's used to dealing with the volatility of the universe. For an example, look up at the night sky. Betelgeuse is still there, fully intact.

It has been a few months since our chat about the iridescent turtle shell, and I wanted to check back in with Messer to see how the red giant was doing.

"It's brightened back up," he explains. "It got dimmer and dimmer and dimmer for many months, and it's turned around. When it got really, really dim, it got a little scary. It's not supposed to get that dim. It was a remarkable event."

To the best of Messer's knowledge, Betelgeuse was not primed to go supernova, and an explosion is not actually imminent. It was just one supergiant misunderstanding.

"It's almost back to its usual peak brightness," he says. "Best we can tell, it probably was an episode of dust ejection. It ejected some dust and that dust obscured it for a while. It's become diffuse enough that it can shine through again." Betelgeuse, at least from our perspective, keeps on churning.

"It totally pump-faked us," he laughs. "It was quite a pump-fake."

A PASSING INTEREST IN ASSISTS
The selflessness and selfishness of sharing

I **F IT WEREN'T** for eye-witness testimony and a surfeit of concrete documentary evidence, one could make a compelling argument that Wilt Chamberlain didn't actually exist. His individual statistical achievements look like typos. Or, better yet, like an imaginative prankster snuck into the NBA's offices and sprinkled this fictional character throughout the league's record books. Though, if somebody wanted to get away with that kind of jape, they really should have made the records plausible. What this "Wilt Chamberlain" fellow accomplished was anything but.

—In 1961–62, he averaged 50.4 points per game. Fifty points! A game!

—Over his career he averaged 22.9 rebounds a game. For comparison's sake, Chamberlain could expect to grab more boards on a normal evening than seven-footer Joel Embiid had in his best-ever game (22). (Embiid is no slouch, either. He averages 11.5 rebounds a contest.)

—Chamberlain had 55 rebounds in a single game in 1960. He did this against Bill Russell, the second-greatest rebounder of all time.

—Of the 3,890 total minutes of basketball played by the Philadelphia Warriors in 1961–62, Chamberlain featured in all but eight minutes and thirty-three seconds of them. He would have played every single minute that season were he not ejected in the fourth quarter of a game for arguing with the referees.

—He averaged 48.5 minutes per game that year. (Reminder: an NBA game is only 48 minutes. There were overtimes.)

Of course, I can't leave out the time Chamberlain scored one hundred points in a single game, but he didn't think much of that particular record. "A lot of people ask me if that 100-point game was my biggest thrill in sports. Frankly, it isn't even close to the top," he wrote. "[A]nyone can get lucky."

That quote comes from his 1973 autobiography, *Wilt*. (Subtitle: *Just Like Any Other 7-Foot Black Millionaire Who Lives Next Door*.) In it, he writes that, hours before he scored a hundred points against the Knicks, he also set the high score on a shooting gallery–style arcade game near the stadium. He seems more impressed with that virtual achievement than the basketball one, and he dedicates about as much space in his book to each feat.

Wilt is a bizarre autobiography. There's an entire chapter dedicated to the design and construction of his sprawling Los Angeles mansion that suddenly digresses into a lengthy defense of him not offering his dates tickets to see him play. (In regard to environmentalists' concerns about the use of nose fur from arctic wolves on the playroom furniture: "I'm deeply concerned about the environment, too . . . I hadn't ordered the wolves killed; I just bought the fur after they were already dead." And, a few paragraphs later, describing his dating strategy: "I'd rather have her appreciate my other skills in a more appropriate setting—ordering dinner in a good restaurant, talking on a sunlit beach, driving in a fine car, making love in a warm bed.") While chock-full of tales about romantic conquests, this particular book does not include the claim that he slept with twenty thousand women during his life. That appears in a later autobiography, 1991's *A View from Above*, and it should be noted that he uses some pretty specious math to reach that infamous number.

Chamberlain is a charming and erudite megalomaniac, and if you've ever wanted to read hundreds of pages detailing how great he was, then this is the book for you. Hell, I'd recommend it to those who don't care to learn about his glamorous lifestyle and various triumphs—*Wilt* is still a remarkably entertaining book. He portrays himself as both the main character of mid-century America and a bemused loner who just wants to hang out in his mansion festooned in ethically sourced arctic wolf hair. There are details about his relationship with Richard Nixon, whom he controversially endorsed for the 1968 presidential election, and his struggles courting Black delegates at the Republican National Convention after Nixon chose someone even more racist than himself, Maryland Governor Spiro Agnew, as his running mate. (Agnew was, in Chamberlain's words, a "dumb fuck." True!)

Chamberlain describes the admiration he and the president shared for each other, but he also makes it clear that their friendship was mostly a transactional one. "If Richard won, of course, I figured I'd have some input at the White House, a chance to talk to the top man about some social and political issues," he muses. Some of those issues included, but were not limited to, "the overpopulation problem," euthanasia (he's pro), and the decriminalization of gambling, pornography, prostitution, and marijuana use. It was an eclectic platform.

In the end, Chamberlain "was pleased with many of the things Richard did after he took office," but felt he surrounded himself with bad people during the ongoing Watergate scandal (a "horrible mistake"). Few things better illustrate the uniqueness of Wilt's perspective than what he perceived to be an impropriety too far from his pal in the Oval Office: "I was . . . pissed off when Richard had our astronauts put an American flag on the moon. Outer space is supposed to be for all mankind, not just Americans. I was disappointed in Richard then." Profound and unpredictable, just like the man himself.

As was the case with Nixon, Chamberlain could fairly be diagnosed with a persecution complex. He complains constantly throughout *Wilt* about being perceived as a "loser" because, despite all the records and his comic-book athleticism (he was a seven-foot-two-inch track star, for goodness sake), he "only" won two championships during his NBA career. "For damn near half my life, I'd lived with that 'loser' label stuck on me like some big, ugly scar from an operation I'd never had," he writes.

Exacerbating matters was the success of his biggest rival, Bill Russell, who won eight straight NBA Championships with the Boston Celtics during Chamberlain's first eight seasons in the league. That kind of pummeling could humble a mountain range into a valley, but Wilt Chamberlain was clinically incapable of taking responsibility for his teams' losses. "Most knowledgeable observers readily agree that Boston almost invariably had better players, better coaching, and better luck than my teams did," he writes. "The astonishing thing was not that my teams lost, but that we came so close to winning so often."

To be fair, if you were Wilt Chamberlain, you'd probably have a persecution complex, too. People really were against him. Both college and professional basketball associations changed a whole host of rules to make the game more difficult for him. We've discussed a few of these already, but I'd be remiss if I didn't include the rule forcing free throw shooters to stay behind the foul line until they've released the ball. That one came about after Chamberlain dunked from behind the line at practice as a freshman at Kansas. A rival coach saw this feat, was justifiably terrified, and lobbied the conference to make sure he could never do it in a game.

Some of Chamberlain's sourest grapes were had whenever he lost out on an individual accolade. Despite averaging more than fifty points a game in 1961–62, the league gave MVP honors to Bill Russell instead. (Russell's stats: 18.9 points per game, 23.6 rebounds per game; Chamberlain's stats: 50.4 points per game, 25.7 rebounds per game.) That'd be enough to drive anyone mad. As he writes in *Wilt*:

A lot of other players resented my scoring all those points and breaking all those records, too. I didn't even make the all-NBA team that year, if you can imagine that. Here I was, breaking every record in sight and leading the league in everything but ingrown toenails, and the other players in the NBA voted for Walt Bellamy—Walt Bellamy for Christ sake!—as the best center in the league. Maybe he did more for his team than I did for mine, you say? My team, the Warriors, went to the seventh game of the playoffs; his team, Chicago, finished in last place, with the worst record in the NBA.

Not to play armchair psychiatrist or anything, but it seems as if the snub pushed him to the point of paranoid delusions. According to league records, Chamberlain *was* named to the all-NBA team that season. Walt Bellamy, meanwhile, never made a single all-NBA team during his fourteen-year career. (Bellamy was still a terrific player and, by all accounts, a great guy. I just want to include that on the record lest *Wilt* skews your assessment of the man's life and career.)

With an unreliable narrator like Chamberlain, it helps to consult the record books for verification. But that isn't always possible with his autobiography. Do I think he actually set the record for the fastest single-person transcontinental automobile trip when he drove from New York to Los Angeles in thirty-five hours and fifty-three minutes? Maybe? What about his claim that he trounced three Russians at a drinking contest during a state dinner in the Soviet Union, an event that also happened to mark the first time Chamberlain ever drank vodka? I *want* to believe.

Nonetheless, the thing that I would argue to be his most astonishing achievement is undeniably true, and the record books back it up.

Chamberlain was bored heading into the 1967–68 season. He was also sick of being called selfish, a pejorative that followed him around even more than "loser" did, and so he resolved to do something about both issues. "I'd already proved I could outscore everyone. That was no longer much of a challenge," he writes. "I've always been the kind of person who needs specific, concrete goals and challenges . . . so I decided I'd lead the NBA in assists."

It's one thing to say you're going to be the league's top passer and another thing to actually do it, especially when you're a seven-foot-two-inch scoring machine who had been averaging twenty-nine field goal attempts per game up until that point of your career. The focus of almost every team Chamberlain had ever played for was to get him the ball as frequently as possible so he could score as many points as possible, and he wanted to invert that game plan out of boredom and spite. As he himself put it, it would be like "Babe Ruth leading the league in sacrifice bunts."

Astonishingly, Wilt did it. He actually did it.

Chamberlain finished the season with 702 assists, 23 more than the runner-up, Hall of Fame point guard Lenny Wilkens. It was the first and only time in history that a center led the NBA in assists. "I probably got more satisfaction out of winning that title than almost any other," Chamberlain writes. "It was my way of answering those people who said I was a selfish gunner and a freak who couldn't do anything but dunk." This marked a most dramatic career pivot, much like when Chamberlain's co-star from the touching period drama *Conan the Destroyer* won the California gubernatorial race in 2003.

We hail assist leaders as altruistic paragons of team ball, but Wilt Chamberlain's triumph was hilariously egocentric. "I remember a few games when I'd tell whoever was hot on my team, 'Look, I'm just going to pass the ball to you for a while. I keep setting these other guys up, and they keep blowing easy shots. How am I going to beat Wilkens that way?' "

The joy of sharing should be its own reward, but Chamberlain didn't finish the 1967–68 season leading the league in joy (at least not on the court). His year of giving ended in familiar fashion, with his 76ers bowing out of the playoffs at the hands of the Boston Celtics. This defeat was particularly frustrating, as Philadelphia blew a 3–1 series advantage. It was the first time a team had ever endured such a collapse in the postseason.

Chamberlain made a show of being unselfish and attempted only nine field goals during the deciding Game 7, which Philadelphia lost by four points. "In earlier losses to Boston—in other years—I was blamed for shooting too much and not playing team ball. This time, they said I didn't shoot enough, particularly in the second half, when I didn't take one shot from the field," he writes. "But I was playing the way we'd played—and won—all year."

It's not that Chamberlain was incapable of self-reflection—he frequently recounts moments of failure throughout *Wilt*—it's just that he almost never comes to the conclusion that he was responsible in any way. (One notable exception: "I know I was wrong," he concedes about abandoning granny-style free throws, even though you may recall that he thought they made him look "like a sissy.")

"Boston had half their team guarding me," he writes of that Game 7. "That left my teammates open for easy eight-to-ten-foot jump shots. I kept passing the ball to them, but they kept missing. Hal [Greer] hit only eight of twenty-five shots. Wali [Jones] hit eight of twenty-two. Matty [Goukas] hit two of ten. Chet [Walker] hit eight of twenty-two. Those four guys took most of our shots, and hit less than a third of them. But I got the blame." Unlike the Walt Bellamy mix-up, Chamberlain's recollection of his teammates' shooting statistics from that contest are completely accurate.

Chamberlain's year wasn't a total wash. Whereas his 50.4 points a game in 1961–62 weren't deemed worthy of MVP honors, his pass-heavy performances in 1967–68 earned him the NBA's most prestigious individual accolade. It was his fourth and final MVP Award, but it would come with a dubious distinction. That summer, he asked Philadelphia to trade him to the Los Angeles Lakers, marking the only time a team willingly parted ways with a reigning MVP. Chamberlain was thrilled—Los Angeles was the perfect home for a star as bright as himself—but it was quite the way to end a season that began with his stated intention to prove how unselfish he was.

"When couples come to therapy, the goal is often, implicitly, to stay together," couples therapist Alicia Muñoz tells me. "That's considered a win, to stay together and be happy together and feel fulfilled together and do whatever it takes for the relationship to continue." Or, they can just break up, which is the route Chamberlain and the 76ers opted to take in 1968.

Muñoz is the author of a series of relationship guides, including *No More Fighting* and *The Couples Quiz Book*. When I tell her about Chamberlain's quest for the assists title, she says his approach to performative unselfishness is actually rather common. "Oh my God, it happens all the time. I've been guilty of that early in my relationship with my husband as well," she confesses. It's the kind of thing that, if left unchecked, can take its toll. "The idea is that there really is no sacrifice in relationships, and you're not manipulating a situation, you're not trying to check the boxes, you're not trying to get kudos from your partner. You're not saying, 'Well, I did everything you asked, why are you still unhappy? Why are you still complaining?' A lot of times we—not just as couples but as human beings—have this innate sense of egotism and self-focus and self-centeredness."

In his book, Chamberlain says that Chet Walker eventually apologized for that Game 7. The two were on vacation when Walker "got all choked up one day in Stockholm" and told him, "We were wrong." Wilt seemed to think this apology was the least he could do, writing that "[t]he other guys had blown cinch shots, too, but none of them had come forward to accept the blame for the loss; they'd all let me be the whipping boy."

If true, that story makes Chet Walker seem like a dream teammate: empathetic, communicative, and willing to accompany you to Sweden after a bad loss. Was the tearful forward actually "wrong" in that situation? According to Muñoz, it doesn't even matter. She sometimes tells her couples, "You can be right, or you can be in a relationship. You can't be both, so take your pick." It's an easy thing to bristle at, and she says it often "goes in one ear and out the other until they start to see the benefits or they get hurt enough that they start to wake up." As someone who celebrates wildly whenever I win an argument, I will have to remember to rein it in the two or three times I am proven right each year.

That is not to say that being in a relationship requires acquiescent servitude. Quite the contrary. The term Muñoz uses is "enlightened self-interest," which is the ability to understand that the individual shares the success of the collective. "Even if you may not be the superstar, whatever you do in support of your team or whatever you do in support of your relationship is actually enlightened self-interest," she says. "That team is your home. It's a network of connectivity. Whatever I do that serves you and supports you truly is my best bet at success."

Passing is an unselfish act only when it is done as a means to achieve a shared goal, and one imagines Chamberlain would have taken at least one shot in the second half of that Game 7 had he truly wanted to put his teammates in the best possible position. How can we wrap our heads around this paradox of the self-serving sharer? "I think that speaks to the idea that it's not what you do, it's who you are," Muñoz says. "You can't neglect the work of who you are."

I worry that comparing romantic relationships to a basketball team is a bit of an oversimplification, but Muñoz assures me they share plenty in common. "Many of the troubles and conflicts and struggles that couples get into are about a lack of teamwork—a lack of alliance, or a sense that there are two *me*'s versus a *we*. Not only being a team, but feeling like a team. Figuring out what makes each person feel like they are in a true alliance is critical." To put this to the test, I ask how she would counsel a pair of teammates who are fighting over one's refusal to share the ball.

"I would start with them listening to each other," she says. "I would start with having one person speak and explain why he's doing what he's doing and have the other person just listen and maybe validate them, like, 'OK, it makes sense that you're not passing the ball because you think this is the best way to win.' And then I would have them switch and have the other person explain or share why they want more passes. Maybe it's, 'Hey, we're not looking at the short-term stuff, we're looking at developing a team that's relational and sustainable.' That's certainly going to get them further than just digging in their heels and judging each other."

I'm not sure that Wilt Chamberlain, by virtue of the fact that he was Wilt Chamberlain, could ever switch places with someone else, even during a hypothetical couples' therapy session. He possessed just about the precise physical specifications one needs to dominate Naismith's game, and this random bit of genetic happenstance ensured that he would lead a completely singular life full of fame and expectation. "I feel that stardom and fame really reinforce a lot of the negative aspects of our minds and our egos," Muñoz says. "You don't have that with normal couples so much."

When he enrolled at University of Kansas, Chamberlain says that Phog Allen, the school's legendary head coach, told everyone, "Wilt Chamberlain's the greatest basketball player I ever saw. With him, we'll never lose a game; we could win the national championship with Wilt, two sorority girls and two Phi Beta Kappas." During his sophomore year, famed columnist Jimmy Breslin wrote an article titled, "Can Basketball Survive Chamberlain?" He essentially was a fictional character in people's eyes, but this Paul Bunyan needed more than just a blue ox to get by. Chamberlain never won a national championship at Kansas. Basketball did, in fact, survive his existence.

"[S]ince basketball is a team sport," he writes near the end of *Wilt*, "there isn't much solace in individual accomplishments."

• • •

IF PASSING WERE a truly altruistic pursuit, we wouldn't consider assists to be an individual statistic. Teams would have to share them like they do wins and losses. There'd be no assist title, and Wilt Chamberlain would have been forced to pursue some other goal in order to prove his unselfishness and stave off boredom during the 1967–68 season. Crocheting new warm-ups for his teammates, perhaps?

What's more, the assist may be the most deceptive statistic in basketball. The NBA rulebook defines it as a subjective metric that is not only open to interpretation, but wholly reliant upon it:

An assist is a pass that directly leads to a basket. . . . In basketball, an assist is awarded only if, in the judgment of the statistician, the last player's pass contributed directly to a made basket. An assist can be awarded for a basket scored after the ball has been dribbled if the player's pass led to the field goal being made.

Sure, there are obvious assists, like when a point guard connects with a center for an alley-oop dunk. The pass in that instance made the basket—put it on a platter, if you will. But skill needn't be a prerequisite for an assist. Let's say someone makes an easy toss to Steph Curry. They, too, will be credited with an assist when he swishes a thirty-foot three-pointer. But what if I'm the person who makes that pass to Curry, and he has to dribble through a double-team to get his shot off because my defender quickly identified that I am no threat whatsoever? Do I get credited with an assist even though Curry did all the work to escape the trap and hit an off-balance runner? For a long time, the asnwer depended upon where the game was played.

Each arena has its own scorekeeping staff, meaning that a team employee is in charge of tallying the game's most subjective statistic. For years they served as autonomous judges and juries presiding over box scores, and there was a noticeable difference between overall assist numbers for players at home as compared to when they were on the road.

In the 1980s and 1990s, friendly bookkeeping accounted for a 6- to 8-percent increase in assists for teams playing on their home courts. According to *The Ringer*'s Zach Kram, Jason Kidd typically saw an 11-percent spike in assists. That's not home cooking—that's an eighteen-course tasting menu enjoyed forty-one times each year, and Kidd stuffed himself to the tune of 12,091 total career assists (the second-most in league history).

This biased fun wouldn't last forever. During the 2017–18 season, the NBA began auditing statistics from its replay center in Secaucus, New Jersey. Since then, the home-court assist discrepancy has nearly disappeared. The statistic itself is as vague as ever; the only difference now is that a league employee is trusted to make this fact a tad less obvious.

It is a shame that a beautiful act like passing gets associated with something as flighty and skewable as the assist. Ball movement is the connective tissue that turns five individual kinetic entities into a harmonious system. It's the signature of aesthetically pleasing team play.

When Emily Lakdawalla played basketball in high school, she spent most of her time on the bench pulling double duty as the team's manager. One of her responsibilities was to log statistics, and she enjoyed the game's most subjective stat more than the others. "I really appreciated the assists," she tells me. As a planetary geologist and writer, Lakdawalla is a walking encyclopedia on rover and orbiter missions, and, when I initially reached out to her, I wanted to talk about jump shots. Given the prevalence of the three-pointer in today's NBA, I figured someone so familiar with aiming objects onto faraway targets would understand the joys and pitfalls of long-range shooting, but as I've discovered repeatedly while working on this book, we all see the game differently.

"I think that interplanetary travel is more like passing in basketball," Lakdawalla says. She is waiting on the cable guy when I call her, confounding my assumptions yet again. (I figured her for a satellite customer.)

"When you're launching something from a planet, say Earth, to another one, like Mars, neither Earth nor Mars is stationary," she tells me. "When you're designing a trajectory, you are accounting for the speed, motion, and trajectory that Earth already has as its starting point. Similarly, we're launching it to a spot where Mars is not yet but *will be* once the spacecraft gets there. That's what passing is all about, getting the ball to the place where they're going to be. That aspect of both the passer and the recipient having to account for both their own and the other's motion, and then the ball is in motion, I think that's a perfect analogy right there."

Further helping the comparison is the fact that pass attempts, like space travel, have a decent track record for success. Sure, there are the occasional disasters, but the odds of completing a pass are far greater than they are for hitting a three-pointer, which, even in the most capable hands, is about a 40 percent proposition, at best. "Early in the space age there was a much lower success rate," Lakdawalla tells me. "For obvious reasons. It was new. You'll often hear that only half of all Mars landing attempts have succeeded. While that's technically true, the success rate on recent missions is a lot higher. Most missions these days are successful. It's very rare to have a complete failure." Of the past ten Mars orbital or landing missions, only one has been a dud. A joint attempt from Russia and China in 2011 got stuck in Earth's orbit and eventually disintegrated above the Pacific Ocean. It was a costly turnover.

One reason passes are so much more dependable than shots is because, unlike rims, humans have arms that can reach out and grab the ball. Similarly, a planet's gravitational pull can pluck a well-positioned spacecraft from the void. As is the case with a bullet pass to a lumbering center, however, a certain level of accuracy is needed for the object to arrive safely at its destination. "Basketball players are tall, but their reach isn't that long compared to the size of the court," Lakdawalla says. "The gravity of that planet really doesn't matter a whole lot until you get really close. The timing needs to be perfect. If you miss, that's it. That actually happened to a Venus mission called *Akatsuki*. The nozzle of its rocket engine broke and Venus failed to catch it, basically. It went out of bounds." You hate to blame your teammates, but Venus really blew it on that one.

While surprises aren't always welcome during a fine-tuned space mission, Lakdawalla's favorite basketball passes are the ones she can't see coming. "I really do appreciate the assists where the passer has this clairvoyance about where his teammate is going to be," she says. "They'll rocket these passes, and it's amazing."

Los Angeles Lakers legend Magic Johnson was a maestro in this regard. "He's so smart on the floor that it sometimes gets him in trouble," his former rival Isiah Thomas said when Johnson was in the process of winning his third assist title. "He'll be thinking two or three plays ahead, while most guys just aren't on that level." Michael Cooper, Johnson's teammate on the Lakers, had to learn to adjust to basketballs entering his orbit unannounced when he first started playing alongside the point guard. "It was difficult my first year," he told the *New York Times* in 1986. "I'd be running down the floor thinking that there's no way he'd be able to get a pass to me and all of a sudden—*whack*—I'd get it in the side of the head, or if I caught it, I'd be so off guard that I'd take a bad shot. I've learned to know where I'm at on the floor and concentrate until the ball leaves his hands, then I can relax."

Lakdawalla loves going to Lakers games, but Magic Johnson isn't pulling the strings for the home team anymore. Instead, she gets to watch LeBron James, Los Angeles' heir apparent, do his thing with similar style and clairvoyance.

To say that LeBron has eyes on the back of his head would undersell his court vision. If I didn't know any better, I'd say eyes cover every inch of his cranium like mirrors on a disco ball. "A lot of times, when guys come here, they're not really used to having wide-open shots. That's something that he supplies for us," Lakers guard Kyle Kuzma told reporters regarding James's ability to find teammates in space. It's an ironic sort of learning curve, one where players must learn how to take easy, unguarded jumpers.

A basketball court is 4,700 square feet, and every inch of that area is fair game for one of James's passes. He is six-foot-nine, the same height as Magic

Johnson, and he surveys the floor like a galloping air traffic control tower. Whereas teams devise elaborate plays full of weaving movement in order to work a pass to a shooter waiting in the corner, LeBron can achieve the same result with a casual flick of the wrist. Driving or stationary, looking or not looking, he can get the ball wherever it needs to be. It's painless teleportation, like if Jeff Goldblum had quit while he was ahead in *The Fly*.

According to DraftExpress, the average wingspan of all the players selected in the previous three decades of NBA Drafts is about six feet, nine inches long. Doing some rudimentary geometry **(A = πr²)**, we find that thanks to those long limbs, an individual player can cover and defend an area of nearly thirty-six square feet, which is slightly larger than a queen-size mattress. Now, picture the court from above and plop five of those stately, spacious beds across different sections of one half of the floor. That's a pretty crowded sleepover LeBron must navigate.

Moriba Jah can relate. He is an aerospace engineer, and during his career at the NASA Jet Propulsion Lab, Jah served as spacecraft navigator for the Mars Global Surveyor, Mars Odyssey, and Mars Exploration Rover missions (among others). He also says he was quite the baller back in the day. "In my best experiences in basketball, I had the ability to understand what's going on on the court and to predict given outcomes," he tells me. "I didn't shy away from being able to drive the ball at will. I had a very good crossover." Jah does issue one caveat, however: "I was not a good long-distance shooter." Ironically, the guy is more accurate from sixty-four million miles away than he is from twenty-five feet.

Like Lakdawalla, Jah counts a successful interplanetary mission as an assist. "It is like passing," he says. "Like a half-court kind of thing, through several people. Either on the bounce or in the air, when you time it just right and, all of a sudden, it's like, *whoa*. Somebody just got a whole pelvic thrust on a major dunk." Apologies if you can't follow all that technical aerospace terminology.

Jah teaches Advanced Sciences and Technology Research in Astronautics at the University of Texas at Austin. He is also the brains behind AstriaGraph, a crowd-sourced, three-dimensional map plotting the locations of the many objects currently orbiting Earth. There is *a ton* of crap up there.

"We don't fully understand what the consequences are—intended and even unintended—of launching stuff into space," he tells me. "You got people like Elon Musk launching something like sixty satellites every few weeks. What are the unintended consequences of pumping all those objects into orbit? The answer is we don't know."

Jah's mission is to collect the most accurate information possible so he can predict and prevent any potentially catastrophic accidents. In one hypothetical (but plausible) scenario, a stray paint chip from a decommissioned spacecraft hits an important telecommunications satellite. At 17,000 miles per hour, a speck of paint might as well be a cannonball, and the collision could theoretically knock out mobile communications for an entire hemisphere. "People have no idea," Jah says of the possible repercussions. "They have no idea how vulnerable their technology is to this stuff."

The AstriaGraph project collects data from international and private space programs, and getting these often competing entities to comply is one of Jah's greatest challenges. "I'm trying to tell them, at the end of the day, there are people in space behaving maliciously toward each other. For now you may like not being overly regulated, but at the same time it means that you are in an environment that is a lot more vulnerable for you," he says. "It's my job to show them that, even though they didn't really collaborate with me, I can still figure out what they're doing anyway."

NASA estimates there are more than half a million pieces of space debris careening throughout low Earth orbit. It may seem like a big place, but so are the oceans, and look what humans did to them. "I see space as being analogous to lands that need to be protected, environmentally," Jah says. "That's what keeps me up at night, trying to do the science to motivate the policy and regulation that can be enforced to hold people accountable for their behaviors and make space more predictable and transparent."

Remember that 1892 game at Cornell when a hundred students played all at once because the five-person-per-team limit was not yet codified? Pity the naive fools who tried to squeeze passes through such a dense thicket of spastic Ithacans. It simply could not be done. Jah's fear is that, one day, space might look like that Ivy League gym. "You want the orbital ecosystem as it were to be long-term sustainable," he says. "The ability to predict how things evolve and what the reactions between objects are going to be, to navigate and move around, this is very similar to a basketball game in many ways." It's like LeBron understanding the exact spot his teammate is going to be at a given moment on offense, except the teammate in this scenario is a five-ton Soviet satellite with no court awareness. (Though, to be fair, James does play with JaVale McGee.)

The goal for Jah's AstriaGraph is akin to total court vision, though it's not quite as simple as knowing the locations of five long-armed defenders at all times. AstriaGraph tracks over 20,000 orbital spacecrafts and bits of debris and plots their most likely routes through space. "I have all these objects moving around in different orbits, some of them are controlled by people, most of them are garbage, and people have to make decisions. Do I get out of the way? How do I launch? People want to be safe."

AstriaGraph is free and open for the public to access. It's worth checking out, even if you aren't a spacecraft navigator responsible for the launch of a multibillion dollar communications satellite. It helps grant some perspective on the amount of junk we've stored in our planet's attic. All that crap is represented in AstriaGraph as a rather intimidating cloud of dots, but Jah has experience weaving through crowds. "There were times when it didn't matter what I'd do," he says of his days playing point guard, "I'd find a way to help other people get the ball in the basket. It's almost like *The Matrix*. Beyond just being able to feel what was around me, it was the ability to predict."

Jah believes this sort of intuition essential to learning about our relationship with the cosmos. "One of the things that I tell my students is if you want to know something, you have to measure it, and if you want to understand something, you have to predict it," he says. "When I've felt in the zone in my own work, there are times when I can just kind of close my eyes and picture all these things in space moving around in different ways. It's a very powerful experience to tap in and connect to that."

• • •

LEBRON JAMES IS an interesting case study in how objects travel through space. He has skipped around the league, from Cleveland to Miami, back to Cleveland, and then off to Los Angeles. Fairly or unfairly, this has earned him a reputation, much like Wilt Chamberlain, as a self-absorbed superstar willing to abandon his teammates at the drop of a hat. Moriba Jah doesn't much care for it. "There's been a shift in the whole NBA thing to me. Players play a few years here, make their mark and go somewhere else," he says. "They used to pick a specific franchise and be dedicated to that franchise. Do or die. It was like being brought into a family."

It's odd, then, that LeBron is also one of the more unselfish players to have ever stepped on a basketball court. He is eighth on the list of the NBA's all-time assist leaders, but you needn't put your faith in that subjective statistic. Just watch him play and it's clear that his approach to passing is pure and altruistic.

LeBron doesn't simply pass to his teammates—he serves the ball to them à la carte. "It's my responsibility to know how my guys want the ball," he told ESPN's Brian Windhorst. "If they like it with no seams or with the seams. I know that might not make sense—some guys like it different ways. I get the ball right in my hand before I throw it." "Seamless," as he puts it, likely means that the ball will land in their hands with the three main, parallel lines facing toward the hoop. It's not a common term in the sport because few players are so aware of their teammates' wants and needs as to align the seams of the basketball to fit those individual preferences.

Emily Lakdawalla tells me about how voyages to Mars require careful planning for the sake and health of the planet itself. "It is a place we want to protect from Earth bacteria. When we send a lander there, the landers are highly sterilized. We are very careful. It's called planetary protection." But while the lander is clean, the launch vehicle that guides it is not, and so scientists devise ways to ensure that only the preferred components of the craft touch down. A seamless pass, some would call it.

Being considerate is a form of versatility. Sure, LeBron has made a habit of switching teams, but on the court he goes to great lengths to ensure that everybody is comfortable and catered to. "I know the guys on my team like seams or guys who like the ball high when they catch it. I know guys who like it low or midsection. I know where everyone wants the ball, and I just try to put it there on time and on target," he told ESPN. "All they have to do is catch and fire. It's those guys working on their craft that allows me to do that."

James averaged 10.6 assists a game during the 2019–20 season, the best mark of his career and good enough to lead the league. Unlike Chamberlain, James's relationship with passing isn't a fleeting affair. Sharing the ball has been his MO since his days as the most-hyped teenager in the world, back when he was tossing no-look assists on ESPN's live broadcasts of his high school games. By the age of thirty-five he won his first-ever assist title. (The NBA no longer bases this award on total assists, but rather assists per game. That change was made in 1968–69, right after Chamberlain won with the most total assists but not the highest per-game average. Maybe the world really was against him.)

"The assist has always been my favorite because it gives my teammates an opportunity to score, and that's what's always mattered to me," James told reporters in 2019. "I don't get the assists if my teammates don't make the shots, that's what it all boils down to. So they deserve all the credit." If you swap the word "credit" for "blame," then James's quote sounds like an excerpt from *Wilt*. LeBron's passes are gifts; Chamberlain's were loans.

You may not be surprised to learn that couples therapist Alicia Muñoz is a big LeBron James fan. She likens the way he studies his teammates' preferences to "The Five Love Languages," a framework on how to communicate affection that was made famous by relationship guru Gary Chapman. "The idea is that you are trying to have partners understand what feels like love," Muñoz says. That quintet includes "words of affirmation," "quality time," "giving gifts," "acts of service," and "physical touch." I won't try to break down LeBron's game and how it relates to each one, but I will note that he flew to Cleveland to attend former teammate Zydrunas Ilgauskas's retirement ceremony in March 2014 on a day when, according to records, the temperature barely rose above freezing. True love or not, I'd call that an act of service.

James practically hosts a couples' therapy workshop every time he steps on the court. "I'm thinking about LeBron figuring out how somebody likes for him to pass them the ball," Muñoz says. "He's not assuming there's a right way to pass the ball, or that there's a best way to pass the ball at all. Not, 'I like passing the ball one way and it feels comfortable to me and it's how I learned how to do it.' People do that with love. They're like, 'Well, I just bought you this amazing birthday present and you're still complaining that you don't feel loved.' Or, 'I just had the most amazing sex with you last night and you're still saying you're not feeling loved.' Or, 'I spent all this time with you without looking at my phone and gazed at you in the eyes and you still say that you want me to wash the dishes and that's what's going to make you feel loved.'" She's right. I have never heard LeBron say any of those things about his teammates.

"We tend to judge the way our partners want us to love them as wrong or bad because it's not our way," she continues. "And then of course that completely does not work. The relationship is conflictual. No fun. LeBron is just, oh my God," she sighs. "I just love him."

Muñoz uses a meditation app that features occasional affirmations narrated by James (he partnered with the company as one of his many business ventures). "He talks about stuff like the humility of being on the court and developing as an athlete," Muñoz says. "You get your ass kicked over and over again. And you get your ass kicked in relationships over and over again until you are humbled." Sounds nice, but one's own humility doesn't always make for the most entertaining subject. I'd much rather listen to excerpts from *Wilt*'s audiobook. (Chapter 13: "Once I started playing volleyball regularly, I stopped carrying large sums of money on me. I still enjoy an occasional foray into haute cuisine, and I have a couple of antelope suits that cost me $3,000, but I don't go in that much for expensive food and clothes any more either.")

While we celebrate LeBron for his eagerness to share on the court, he endured plenty of criticism early in his career for this same kind of unselfishness. When he reached his first Eastern Conference Finals with the Cleveland

Cavaliers in 2007, James had a chance to manufacture a moment of playoff immortality during Game 1. Down two points with twelve seconds remaining against the Detroit Pistons, he received the inbounds pass at the top of the key. The Pistons' defense collapsed as he drove to his left through the lane and surrounded him in a forest of arms. Instinctively, he flicked a pinpoint pass to teammate Donyell Marshall, who was standing alone in the corner because his defender had sprinted to meet James under the rim. Marshall had ages to line up his shot—"he could have sat and had a cup of coffee and a sandwich," his coach said after the game—but the attempt careened off the heel of the rim and Detroit held on for the win.

"I go for the winning play," James said after the game. "If two guys come at you and your teammate is open, then give it up. Simple as that."

"The play wasn't designed for me to get the shot," Marshall said. "Me not having made a three all night, they probably didn't even know I was in the game." It was a marvelous bit of improvisation from James, one that impressed Pistons point guard Chauncey Billups. "I thought it was a great play," he said. "It was horrible defense by us, but it was a great play." He's right, of course, but the pass sparked a ridiculous-yet-persistent narrative that LeBron is afraid of big moments. (As someone who *is* afraid of big moments, let me tell you: I would have been en route to the hospital and faking appendicitis to avoid the situation entirely.)

To many, passing in that scenario was a sign of weakness. Charles Barkley hit out at James from his bully pulpit on TNT's *Inside the NBA*. "I've got a problem with the best player on the floor not taking any of these shots down the stretch," he said. "If I'm the best player on the court, I've got to get a shot. That's not a criticism, that's a fact."

Stephen A. Smith, then a syndicated columnist, argued that the decision to pass the ball to Marshall "stained a legacy sprinkled with greatness, pausing to remind us all that, perhaps, you've got to actually win something before adopting such illustrious titles as 'The Chosen One' or 'King James.' " Keep in mind that LeBron was just twenty-two years old at the time of this legacy-staining transgression.

Even the relentlessly saccharine Mitch Albom couldn't find it in his heart to cut LeBron some slack. "Help me out here. This is LeBron, right?" the *Tuesdays with Morrie* author asked in the *Detroit Free Press*. "The superstar's superstar? And those other guys he's talking about . . . I mean, he was dishing to Donyell Marshall. The guy had one basket all night."

You know things are bad when Mitch Albom is roasting you. That's like getting a wedgie at a Model UN conference.

LeBron said that his decision to pass to Marshall at the end of that game earned him more criticism than he had ever endured at that point in his career. Like Chamberlain, he was getting blamed for his teammates' misses, but he refused to denounce them in public and resisted the temptation to change his playing style.

The following year, James must have experienced a twinge of déjà vu while facing the Washington Wizards in the first round of the playoffs. With the score tied and a little more than five seconds remaining at the end of a tense Game 4, James received the ball and drove into the lane. Presented with a nearly identical situation to the one he faced in Detroit, LeBron made the same exact decision. He passed to a teammate—Delonte West, this time— who was standing alone in the corner. Unlike Marshall, however, West hit the three-pointer and sealed the win.

"I've always been a guy who trusted my teammates," James said after that game. "Even before I got to the NBA, I've always been a guy who has put my teammates first and in front of me as an individual. This is a team game and I know that I can't win without my teammates." It'd be easy to dismiss this as clichéd jock-speak were it not for the fact that he's put the fate of his own reputation in his teammates' hands time and time again. That's called trust, and it's couples' therapy 101.

"It takes a lot of maturity to get to the point where you're not acting out of self-interest," Alicia Muñoz tells me. "Nobody gets socialized into being an adult without going through trauma and pain and challenges. If you're not truly coming from a place of wholeheartedness then it's going to bite you in the butt."

As Wilt Chamberlain laments in his autobiography, "Even Wilt can't do it alone."

THE PHENOMENAL SHAPE OF CHEMISTRY
When things work

ON ONE END you have Wilt Chamberlain, who only decided to pass the ball because he wanted to set a record for Wilt Chamberlain. Standing across from him on the other side of the spectrum is LeBron James, a guy who's so willing to pass that even Mitch Album made fun of him for it. Place a point in between those two extremes and you'll get Michael Jordan, who famously had to learn to share with his teammates in order to win. Of course, because he's Jordan, we'll have to put him on a higher plane of existence than the others.

Huh, would you look at that? We've made a triangle.

The story of basketball's most famous shape has been told countless times, but here's a basic outline should you need a reminder:

1984–89: Jordan is the NBA's most exciting star and the most prolific scorer since Chamberlain. However, like Chamberlain, he can't seem to win the Big One and is made to wear the Scarlet S. (It stands for "selfish," though, I gotta say, a scarlet S would look a lot like Superman's logo. It works better in the metaphorical sense than as a literal patch.)

1989–90: The Chicago Bulls promote Phil Jackson to head coach. Tex Winter, his assistant, implements the triangle offense, a system reliant on passing and movement. Jordan is skeptical, as it requires him to share the ball, but he agrees to learn the secrets of the triangle and trust his teammates.

1991–Onward: Jordan ascends to demigod status and the Bulls lay waste to everyone in their path. Decades later, in the midst of a plague, the world gathers to watch a ten-hour documentary canonizing these heroes. The whole thing is extremely biblical.

After leaving the Bulls, Jackson and Winter brought the triangle with them to Los Angeles, and its magic helped facilitate a dynastic Lakers run. That would be the triangle's last hurrah. Winter suffered a stroke in 2009 and couldn't physically carry on coaching. In 2014, the New York Knicks hired Jackson as team president, and his attempt to use the offense to revitalize that beleaguered franchise was an unmitigated disaster. "At this point I'm getting tired of hearing about the triangle," Carmelo Anthony, the team's marquee star, said in 2016. "Just getting tired of hearing about it."

The triangle offense has all the makings of a mystic relic. For one thing, it doesn't really exist anymore. The last successful, big-name coach to run the system was Tara VanDerveer, at Stanford, but she ditched it for good in 2014. VanDerveer, an elite-level chess player, came to the conclusion that she lacked the proper pieces to complete Winter's vision. "We did not feel running the triangle would help them," she said.

So, what is the triangle, you ask? That's a good question. "If the triangle hit me upside the head, I wouldn't know what it was," said Houston Rockets head coach Mike D'Antoni in 2017. D'Antoni is responsible for implementing two of the most influential offenses of the twenty-first century—the run-and-gun "Seven Seconds or Less" system with the Phoenix Suns in the mid-aughts and the Rockets' sprawlball experiment—but even he couldn't make heads or tails of Winter's polygon.

"Basketball is a game of geometry," Winter once said. "The court is a rectangle. The ball is a sphere. The rim and net form a cylinder. And an offense, when run properly, will produce triangles." In this system, the triangles are formed by a post player, who acts as a pivot, and two perimeter players on his or her side of the floor. The genius of the triangle is (or was) that it can be run without the coach calling any specific planned plays from the sideline. The players must instead practice relentlessly and learn one another's tendencies so they can make instinctive decisions—passes, hand-offs, cuts—to take advantage of any weaknesses they notice in an opponents' defense. As Kobe Bryant said of his time running the triangle in Los Angeles, "Our teams were hard to play against because the opposition didn't know what we were going to do. Why? Because we didn't know what we were going to do from moment to moment."

Bryant was entering his fourth year in the NBA when Jackson took over as the Lakers head coach and brought Winter along to be his assistant. The young guard missed the first six weeks of that season with a broken hand, and the brief setback proved to be an invaluable opportunity for Bryant as he watched games alongside Winter on the bench. The situation was, to Bryant, "like Luke Skywalker sitting next to Yoda and Yoda hitting him upside the head—he'd think out loud about what he'd see, and we'd discuss it."

Besides Yoda, Morice Fredrick "Tex" Winter has been described as something of a John Steinbeck character, but there's a little Flannery O'Connor in there, too. When Winter was a boy in Texas, his father, Ernest, died of sepsis on Christmas Day after a marlin speared him during a deep-sea fishing trip in the Gulf of Mexico. The entire family soon packed up and moved to California, where Winter worked on a farm and performed odd jobs.

Tex joined the navy in World War II and served as a test pilot. (Add some Tom Wolfe to that Steinbeck and O'Connor while you're at it.) He also studied architectural draftsmanship during enlistment, picking up skills that would come in handy when it came time to engineer shapes into complex systems on the basketball court.

After the navy, Winter attended the University of Southern California. It was there that he learned the precepts of the triangle offense from its originator, Trojans head coach Sam Barry. As a post-grad, Winter landed an assistant coaching gig at Kansas State, and he dedicated the next seven decades of his life to the study of basketball.

Whereas Sam Barry established the triangle as a basic jumping-off point for an offense, Winter obsessed over all the possibilities it presented and pursued them with monkish devotion. As head coach at Kansas State, Winter detailed his theories in a book that he wrote out in longhand and peppered with hand-drawn, navy-grade diagrams. His wife, Nancy, typed up and helped polish the manuscript for publication in 1962. Part Bible, part Voynich manuscript, readers have described *The Triple-Post Offense* as a dense and enigmatic study of motion, space, and power forwards. It is the triangle's holy scripture.

When a scout for the Washington Bullets named Jerry Krause visited Kansas State in the 1960s, Winter gave him his book. Winter also mentioned that he had sent copies of *The Triple-Post Offense* to all the rival coaches in his conference, a move Krause found crazy.

"Why are you giving away your secrets?" he asked.

"I'm not," Winter replied. "It'll only confuse them."

Krause frequently described Winter as a "basketball genius" and, decades later, in his role as Chicago Bulls GM, the former scout hired the triangle guru to be an assistant coach.

In many ways, *The Triple-Post Offense* is the opposite of James Naismith's book. There is no narrative or wistful recollection. It's just pure, uncut basketball. Much of the text is laid out like a simple instruction manual, but it is far from an easy read. When an editor at the *New York Times Magazine* assigned writer Nicholas Dawidoff to produce a story on the triangle during Phil Jackson's doomed stint with the Knicks, he turned in ten thousand words about his obsessive quest to understand the book. Dawidoff was magna cum laude at Harvard and a Guggenheim Fellow, but even he found Winter's work intimidating. "The system is basketball's Gödel, Escher, Bach, renowned for being highbrow and difficult to understand," he writes. "Yet trying to get through an abstruse book about the essence of cognition is one thing; that basketball could be over our heads is somehow harder to take." He nevertheless came away a convert. "By the end of his book, Winter had me convinced that the triangle offense was the most comprehensive system ever devised for playing basketball."

Out of print for decades, Dawidoff ponied up more than $160 for a copy of *The Triple-Post Offense*, but notes he was lucky—used editions could fetch as much as $700 or so. Dawidoff's ode must have raised some interest in Winter's text, for a small press has since revived the book and is promoting it on Amazon with a pull quote from his article. Despite this edition's flimsy, Kinkos-style spiral binding, I consider it $36 well spent. Should the triangle ever return, I'll have a guide at the ready.

The part of *The Triple-Post Offense* that instructs Winter's specific system is relatively slim, and it only takes up a small chunk of my edition's 216 pages. There are four basic offensive patterns, and within each of these exist twelve novel play options. Winter drew diagrams for all of them, and the descriptions read like choose-your-own-adventure stories because that's exactly what they are. ("If the defensive man covering 3 is sagging off, 1 cuts between him and 3 . . . If 3 does not pass to 1 on an inside cut or on front hand off, he attempts to penetrate into the free throw area.") There are no specific set plays in the triangle, just movement, choices, and trust. Learning all of this takes practice, and so the bulk of Winter's book is dedicated to training and fundamentals, the things a player needs to master before he can begin to comprehend the complexities of the offense.

"Believe me, with the Bulls, we started running [the triangle]—we thought that it was Stephen Hawking talking to us," Horace Grant told Dawidoff. "If you never, ever spoke Mandarin in your life, it was trying to learn Mandarin in the first year." Grant was Chicago's power forward during the first half of the Bulls' dynasty, which is a position of key importance in the triangle.

For a team running the triangle, post players are pivotal in the most literal sense. The offense often flows through and around them like rocks in a stream, and the decisions they make spark an infinite fractal of branching eddies. To do this effectively, players need to understand exactly what their teammates' next moves will be. It's an instinct that is drilled into you through practice. "Every day we began with passing, cutting, and screening," Grant said. "Every day. Every single day. Fundamental basketball. We weren't bored. It was so intriguing to us. We wanted to learn something different."

Game 6 of the 1993 NBA Finals. Fourteen seconds remain on the clock and the Bulls trail the Phoenix Suns by two points. Point guard B. J. Armstrong inbounds the ball to Michael Jordan in Chicago's backcourt. When

Jordan nears the centerline, he passes to Scottie Pippen, who had sprinted from the baseline to the top of the three-point arc.

"The ball has to be moved. Moving the ball keeps the defense occupied, thereby creating passing lanes and scoring opportunities."
—Principle No. 6 of the "Seven Principles of Passing," The Triple-Post Offense

Suns forward Charles Barkley correctly reads that the play is supposed to be a give-and-go between Jordan and Pippen, so he leaves Pippen and attempts a steal. Pippen senses his defender's gamble, however, and improvises with a drive to the hoop.

"The offense should provide a counter to the defense."
—Principle No. 6 of the "Seven Principles of Sound Offense" (not to be confused with the "Seven Principles of Passing"), The Triple-Post Offense

As Pippen enters the lane, Phoenix's Mark West and Danny Ainge collapse to cut him off. This leaves Grant open near the baseline, where Pippen feeds him the ball.

"All good teams have one thing in common; they keep the basketball moving."
—Page 136, The Triple-Post Offense

Grant takes a step toward the hoop, forcing West to scramble back to guard him. Ainge also races to the low block, leaving Bulls guard John Paxson wide open behind the three-point arc.

"Anticipate when you may receive the ball and develop enough basketball intuition to know beforehand the best places to pass the ball. The outstanding basketball player has this instinct."
—Principle No. 7 of the "Seven Principles of Passing," The Triple-Post Offense

Grant is keenly aware that Paxson is standing behind him, so he stops on a dime and hits him with a pinpoint pass. Ainge knows he's fucked up, and he hangs his head in anguish while stumbling toward the wing. It's the third different errand the Bulls have sent him on in a matter of seconds.

"See your passing lane and your receiver, but do not look at him. . . . There is a big difference between seeing and looking."
—*Principle No. 3 of the "Seven Principles of Passing,"* The Triple-Post Offense

Paxson nails the shot, Chicago wins, and the visiting locker room in Phoenix smells like stale champagne all off-season.

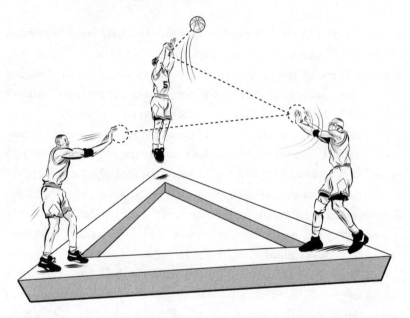

"The ball was not supposed to come to me," Paxson recalled during *The Last Dance*, ESPN's mega-documentary about the Bulls. "But as a player, you're always ready. For me personally, it was pretty special."

The play was meant for Michael Jordan, who up until Paxson's shot had scored all of the Bulls' points in that quarter. But the most important possession of the season unfolded in such a way that he didn't even get to touch the ball on the offensive side of the floor. The plan simultaneously broke down and worked to perfection.

I vividly remember watching that Finals as a kid in Chicago and feeling like the game was supposed to end that way, even if it wasn't. Much of this can be attributed to me having spent nearly half my life watching the Bulls win championships and being a basketball Calvinist who presumed triumph was predestined, but the specific manner in which it happened was too elegant to suggest that anything else would have been possible. When your favorite team works in such wonderful harmony, the world can't help but make sense.

• • •

EVEN AFTER READING Winter's book, I'm not entirely sure whether that championship-winning play was unique to the triangle in any specific way. It involved some of its most basic principles, like spacing, improvisation, and incisive playmaking from the post position, but none of those are exclusive to this particular offense. It was just a neat way to score a basket.

Watch a game on television, and the ball looks like a snug fit for the hoop. But, as Winter explains, this isn't exactly true: "The diameter of a basketball is between 9.125 and 9.25 inches. Since the inside diameter of the rim is 18 inches, two basketballs will go into the basket at once. The basket is twice as big as the ball. It's important for the players to understand this; otherwise they may get the idea that *one* won't even fit. Every coach will agree there have been occasions when he wondered."

The game is interesting not because the ball goes through a comfortably-sized hoop, but because of all the different things a team must do in order to reach that final step. Every offensive basketball play is a Rube Goldberg machine.

I had always assumed that a Rube Goldberg machine had to be pains-takingly plotted out before its construction. How else can you explain such whimsical precision and detail? But then I actually spoke with someone who makes Rube Goldberg machines and learned otherwise.

"I'm not very good at planning," says Brett Doar. "I don't do that very well, but what I do do very well is, you know, throwing a bunch of shit on the floor and then seeing how I can fit it all together."

Doar is responsible for some of the largest and most impressive Rube Goldberg contraptions ever conceived. He was the primary engineer for the machine that was featured in the "This Too Shall Pass" music video by the band OK Go. It begins when a toy truck topples a row of dominos which releases a Hot Wheels car down a track that nudges a billiard ball into a vinyl record that releases a small seesaw that hits play on an iPod connected to a speaker whose bass fires a marble into a funnel that leads to . . . you know what? You should probably go and watch it yourself. More than a month's worth of work went into building the machine, and whenever something went wrong during filming it took thirty people about an hour to reset the contraption.

All told, it took more than sixty takes to get it right, but the end result is four straight minutes of wonder. I only described the first twenty-three seconds of the journey. After that there's a falling piano, paint cannons, and a flying television set attached to a trapeze. Oh, there are a bunch of sledge-hammers, too.

"I think I have like fourteen sledgehammers," Doar tells me. "I always end up buying new sledgehammers. Every time I buy a new sledgehammer, I go, 'I am never buying another sledgehammer. Surely I have as many sledge-hammers as I will ever need.' Then a job will come up and I can't believe I need a different sledgehammer."

The section of the OK Go video I find most impressive is when a set of spoons, hanging by strings from a rotating guitar, hits a series of bottles with the precise timing and pitch to match the song's percussion. It was especially satisfying for Doar, too. "I've always liked playing music, but I don't have the patience to practice guitar," he says. "The thing about machines is that they're repetitive. They do the same things over and over again. I can build something that can do those repetitive things, and if I can sequence those things in a physical way, then I can create music. I don't actually have to know how to play the instrument."

He may not have perfect pitch, but Doar is attuned to picking out unconventional compositions when he hears them. "I had a real revelation once watching a basketball game," he tells me. "You've got this structure that sort of hems in everything, but within that structure you've got these guys dancing around those notes."

The same can be said for Doar's own work. Rather than stick to a specific plan when making his contraptions, he leaves all his options open. "What I do is really iterative," he says. "It's also very improvisational." His strategy involves filling up shopping carts at sporting goods stores and hardware shops and then turning those heaps of junk into something magnificent. In operation, the joy of a Rube Goldberg machine comes from its cascade of surprising triggers and interactions, and for Doar, the same can be said for the construction process. "One of the most exciting things is when you're running in this one direction but something else happens," he tells me. "How are you going to respond to that thing?"

Doar's preferred strategy when building his structures is a linear one. "I can pay very close attention to one thing, one thread," he says. "If I'm trying to look at many other things that are happening at the same time, I really get lost." He tells me about when he was working as a stagehand during a school play. His job was to hit a light switch at a specific point during the production, but he kept messing up. "I would always miss that cue. I just don't have the attention span for those kinds of things, or the discipline. But if I can get a machine to do it, then I don't have to."

When Doar built a Rube Goldberg machine to be used during the opening of a *Colbert Report* episode, he only had a limited time frame in which to make it work. The series taped daily, and so the entire construction process, from start to finish, had to be completed over the course of a single night in the show's studio. "There's a part where there's a stuffed eagle on a zipline that comes out of the rafters and flies down and hits an electric switch that turns on a little motorized car." At three in the morning, that switch broke. "It's New York, but electric stores aren't open," he says. "There's not a RadioShack I can go to at that hour. What the hell am I going to do?" The solution was a microcosm for the machine in general: "I realized that if I tied a wire around the head of a hammer and had it slam down on a penny, that was all I needed." This whimsical interaction between two household objects performed the task of a specialized piece of equipment, and it did it in a far more entertaining way.

"That's the most exciting part," Doar says. "You're able to take a step back and be surprised by what you've done."

For a Rube Goldberg machine to work, it doesn't matter what the components are—what's important is that they do their job without error. For Tex Winter, that was the very definition of good basketball. "Systems can succeed or fail on the execution of the minute details of the basic fundamentals," wrote the coach. This shouldn't be confused with micromanaging or meddling, as his entire offensive system was predicated on improvisation and surprise. Remember what Kobe Bryant had to say about the triangle: "The

opposition didn't know what we were going to do . . . because we didn't know what we were going to do."

Of the diagrams visualizing the triangle's many patterns and options in Winter's book, none include the final step—getting the ball in the basket. The focus is always on how a team should start the play. Winter pushed the toy truck into the dominos to spark the machine; it was up to the players themselves to build the rest.

Starting a play is not easy, mind you. In the triangle, this often means getting the ball into the post, and Winter spends a considerable portion of his book detailing all the things teams can do in order to ensure this opening salvo is successful. "This important phase of the game should be emphasized early in the practice season," he writes. Here, Winter includes little diagrams that look like waltz instructions, complete with cute little outlines of shoes, as a way to instruct forwards and centers on how to establish position in that crowded area of the court. It doesn't matter how brilliant or intricate your offense is—if that entry pass fails, nothing is going to work.

Likewise, Rube Goldberg inventors know how important it is to get off on the right foot. "You always want to put the most finicky stuff in the beginning," Doar tells me. That way, when it fails, you only have to reset that one element and not the entire machine. "All the stuff that happens downstream should be really, really reliable."

For some contraptions, failure is bad no matter where it occurs along the chain of operations. In 2012, Doar was the lead engineer on a comically large project for Red Bull dubbed the "kluge," which is a rough synonym, likely Germanic in origin, for "Rube Goldberg." The machine revolved around and depended upon the participation of a group of athletes, who at different stations triggered its many moving parts. (For example, a skateboarder glides down a ramp that compresses under his weight and releases a tricycle; a hurdler crosses a finish line that's tied to a row of collapsible shelves, etc.)

Red Bull reserved an entire marine base in the desert for this project and, due to the busy schedules of all the athletes involved, Doar and company only had seven hours to make it work. To kick off the kluge, a skydiver jumped from a helicopter and landed on a platform that . . . did nothing. It was supposed to trigger a pinwheel that would start the entire machine, but the wood bent under the skydiver's feet and failed to make proper contact.

"That was exasperating," Doar says. "Those are huge stakes when you have a helicopter that costs probably ten thousand dollars, if not more, to operate." It wasn't a one-time failure, either, and the skydiver spent much of his morning repacking his chute and hitching rides back up to altitude. "It happened a lot because that section wasn't built very well."

All it takes is one soggy board or a misplaced pass to sabotage an entire team's effort before it even begins. Tex Winter knew this both as an architectural draftsman and a basketball coach, and his favorite proverb, one that he frequently recited for his players, reflected this belief. He included it in his book, where it sticks out like an island of verse in a sea of dense basketball argot:

Everything turns upon a trifle;
For want of a nail the shoe was lost,
For want of a shoe the horse was lost,
And for want of a horse the rider was lost,
Being overtaken and slain by the enemy;
All for want or care about a horseshoe nail.

Winter was a devout pragmatist and stickler for fundamentals. He'd repeatedly harangue Michael Jordan because he thought the star didn't know how to throw a proper chest pass. So much of *The Triple-Post Offense* is a gospel for doing the little things right, but then, on page 180, he slips in a most vital bit of heterodoxy: "[B]e prepared to accept marked individual deviations from what is recommended by the so-called experts." The machine can be weird. What matters is that it works.

• • •

WHY DID A system that helped win eleven NBA Championships in a span of two decades go extinct? There are a number of theories, and because the triangle has always lent itself to interpretation, I'm inclined to believe most of them. The triangle depends on constant motion to create space, but modern teams achieve similar results by loitering behind the three-point arc. And, now that the game has migrated to the perimeter, initiating the offense through the post is an extraneous step. "Today's game is so ball dominant," Golden State Warriors head coach Steve Kerr told Nicholas Dawidoff for his *New York Times Magazine* story about *The Triple-Post Offense*. "Players grow up with the pick-and-roll, so they don't naturally play without the ball." (Playing without the ball is mentioned in both Principle No. 4 of Winter's "Seven Principles of Sound Offense" and Principle No. 7 of his "Seven Principles of Passing.") The triangle is also extremely difficult to master. Developing that extrasensory understanding with your teammates takes time, something that isn't available in the modern NBA, where players switch clubs every offseason.

However, the most convincing explanation for the triangle's demise is that it actually hasn't gone away. At least not completely. Some elements have been absorbed and disseminated throughout the game. If you squint, you might be able to make them out.

During the 2015 NBA Finals, Kerr told reporters, "We don't run the triangle, but we do have some concepts of the triangle within what we do." Kerr is intensely familiar with the system, and he took over John Paxson's role in the Bulls' triangle the season after Paxson's game-winning shot against Phoenix.

Luke Walton was Kerr's assistant coach from 2014–16, and he learned the triple-post offense directly from Winter when he played for the Los Angeles Lakers in the 2000s. "What was great about Tex with the triangle offense was, if the defense would work hard to take something away from you, then something else has to be open," Walton told *Vice* journalist Roland Lazenby in 2015. When asked about Winter's famously strict adherence to fundamentals, he joked, "We definitely try our best to get these guys to use Tex's two-handed chest pass, even though our guys prefer the behind the back."

Regarding specific triangle elements the Warriors incorporated, Walton said, "We run the corner series that was part of the triangle." Winter preached a myriad of ways to get a player in the corner of the court by the baseline, and he diagramed many of these plays in *The Triple-Post Offense*.

It looked as if that's what the Warriors were doing in Game 7 of the following year's Finals, the game where J. R. Smith and Kevin Love came to Cleveland's rescue on defense. Clinging to a one-point lead with about five minutes remaining, Stephen Curry brought the ball up as Klay Thompson cut to the wing on the strong side. According to *The Triple-Post Offense*, this move could have initiated a whole series of options, and by my count, seven of those would have ended with Curry running to the right corner, a spot where he made 50 percent of his shots that season.

The play never got that far. When Curry tried to hit Thompson, he opted for a left-handed behind-the-back pass and the ball flew out of bounds. The Warriors lost their lead in the very next possession and would never regain it. Somewhere, Tex Winter was fuming. *For want of a nail . . .*

• • •

DR. TENDAI GADZIKWA teaches inorganic chemistry at Kansas State University, the school where Winter first made his name as a coach. She describes herself as a molecular architect, though she laughs when I ask whether this is a specific scientific field. "Actually, the story is that it comes from a friend of mine when I was in Amsterdam," she says. "I guess the field of chemistry that we're in is kind of difficult to explain to laypeople. Whenever he tried to pick up a girl at a bar, when he would describe what we do they would give him these blank faces and not want to talk to him anymore. And so he came up with this term, 'molecular architecture.' It was this running joke that we had. But the work that I do now, to me, it really embodies that. I've taken the term to describe what I do."

What Gadzikwa does is combine organic molecules with metals to make supramolecular structures—Frankenstein structures, if you will. "You're not making a molecule, because they're not bonding together," she says. "They're more, like, interacting. So you've got multiple molecules interacting to make a bigger structure." She compares it to Tinkertoy, the children's play kits where rods are fitted into spools to create different types of frames. "For the spool, the thing that joins everything together, we choose specific metals. You're making these frameworks and the metals are the corners that join everything together, and the linkers are organic molecules." Once built, these structures can be modified to different specifications, and Gadzikwa's team is focused on producing catalytic sites that can mimic and dictate certain chemical reactions.

I guess you could call Gadzikwa a coach. Or, at the very least a general manager. When GMs assemble a team, they must make a series of extremely important decisions regarding personnel and then sit back and hope for the best. Likewise, a coach has to formulate a game plan and train the players, but they are helpless to do anything once the ball is in play. In her field of research, Gadzikwa similarly forfeits that sense of agency every time she combines molecules. "You decide what parts need to make your structure, but then you don't have that much control about how they assemble," she says. "You basically set up the pieces as best as you can so that they assemble in a specific way." When the ball is tipped, the chemistry's out of your hands.

Basketball is unpredictable, and any attempts to build a "perfect offense" will undoubtedly come undone because the game's design depends on things going wrong. Passes will go astray. Shots are going to miss. Shit happens. Naismith created the sport to be just orderly enough so as to prevent violence. Nothing more, nothing less. "You can do all this planning up front, and you can do all this designing and put all the pieces that need to be on the court together, but once they are there, you really have no control over it," Gadzikwa says. "I guess when people talk about how people have 'good chemistry,' whether there's like a team or a relationship or whatever, to be honest I never picture actual chemistry," she continues. "Because actual chemistry is very messy, you know? There's too many things going on. It's never clean."

In basketball, 50 percent represents a great field goal percentage, so the best a team can hope is to miss as many shots as they make. That's why you almost never see a happy coach. "I am not sure I have found the answer on how to control tension during the course of a game itself," wrote Tex Winter. "It has been said that a good way to get rid of tension is to 'blow your top.' There may be something to this." From where coaches sit, basketball is brutal to watch.

"With a team you have all these moving parts," Gadzikwa says. "That's actually something that's very difficult for chemists to do. That's how biology and nature work, where multiple processes and a whole bunch of things are going on in the same parts and at the same time. Different reactions, everything. In chemistry we don't really have that level of control."

Perfect chemistry may not exist. But if it does, we're just as likely to call it a miracle.

• • •

THE SECRET TO the triangle's success didn't lie in any specifically dia-grammed play, but in its general ethos. It is a form of indoctrinated teamwork and instinct, something Phil Jackson called "five-man tai chi." As he wrote in his book, the humbly titled *Eleven Rings*, "The idea is not to go head to head against the defense but to read what the defense is doing and respond accordingly. . . . But they all need to be acutely aware of what's happening and coordinated enough to move together in unison. . . . That's where the music comes in."

When you watch the triangle, you are watching a team watch basketball. It is the Droste effect, a picture of a woman taking a picture of a woman tak-ing a picture of a woman taking a picture of a woman taking a jump shot. As the Bulls were preparing for the 1993 Finals against Phoenix, John Paxson told reporters that the team's insistent practicing and study meant that the game was "a matter of reacting instead of thinking." At the end of that decid-ing Game 6, he watched the play unfold and automatically went to the part of the floor where Horace Grant knew he would be.

Fluid, instinctive basketball might be a miracle. No matter the rules, skill level, or court size, if a team plays well together, then the game is going to be fun to watch. Extremely smart basketball fans are able to identify specific sequences and plays (*they're running elevators!*) but most of us get to enjoy these elegant interchanges and movements like children watching a Rube Goldberg machine. There's a visual vocabulary for what we're seeing (player sets a pick; bowling ball falls off a table and onto a spring), but all the work that went into facilitating these interactions is invisible. "That's the thing that makes sports exciting," Brett Doar, our Rube Goldberg maker, says. "You don't know what's going to happen."

Teamwork occurs at all levels of nature; we just call it different things depending on the make-up of the team. Nadya Mason is concerned with some of the smallest players in the known universe (not Muggsy Bogues). She is a materials scientist and physics professor at the University of Illinois. She also leads the school's Mason Group, which uses nanoscale structures to further our understanding of the way things work together in the natural world. "Physics is all about understanding the fundamentals of how things interact," she says. "How one particle behaves when in the presence of another particle, for example."

To put it broadly, materials science is the study of how matter behaves. "That's what allows us to understand how a cell phone works and how to design them," Mason says. "I love going to the gem collections. They have chunks of silicon and chunks of germanium and chunks of gold and chunks of aluminum and they're all embedded in rock. They're just chunks of material. You'd think nothing of them if you just passed by. And yet, somehow we managed to extract them from these pieces of rock and melt them down and structure them and form them and grow them and turn them into our cell phones. Without the knowledge of the fundamental things, we couldn't design it."

Combining basic elements into a grander design is a key function of discovery. It's how we got basketball, and it's also responsible for every successful play you've ever seen on the court. The smaller things get, however, the more difficult they are to diagram.

"There are basic interactions between particles that on a microscopic level can lead to more macroscopic behavior," Mason says. "That's really hard to predict in advance until you see it happen. We understand the rules on the microscopic level, but we might not have been able to predict what happens on the macroscopic level because there are so many particles involved. In one gram of material, there's something like 10^{21} atoms or more. 10^{28}, I think. Some ridiculously huge number. So if you try to figure out what every atom is doing with respect to every other atom, it's an impossible calculation. That's the sort of thing we're talking about."

Mason's research revolves around superconductivity, which is an ideal form of teamwork. The term describes an electrical interaction where there is no friction or resistance. It's pure efficiency, the kind of thing that would make Tex Winter drool. "Superconductivity is a really unique phenomena where the electrons are interacting with each other," she says. "They pair up on a very large scale. And when they pair up, they move in these pairs in a way that there's no energy lost to heat or anything. They move at perfect conductivity. That's a collective phenomena."

Mason is developing and testing a strategy called "superconducting islands." This uses networks of nanoscopic materials like graphene, which is so tiny it is actually two-dimensional. "In this case, each individual particle was a superconductor by itself but the properties were just unique to that particle," she tells me. "When we made arrays of thousands of these and had them interact using electrical interactions, you got different sorts of behavior that you could control. You could modify the properties of the bulk superconductor in ways that you couldn't modify the individual particles." Scientists use that term "collective phenomena" to describe when microscopic behaviors create new macroscopic phases, though it could just as easily be called teamwork.

While describing superconducting islands, Mason helpfully uses a basketball analogy. "You have one person try to make a play by themselves, but if you actually space them out and then control their spacing, you can move the ball across the court in a totally different way than you would have before." Coincidentally, spacing is the crux of the triangle offense; one could even argue that the system exists only as a means of keeping teammates fifteen to eighteen feet away from one another, the geometric distance Winter believed was ideal for facilitating ball movement.

Like teamwork, collective phenomena exist throughout nature. "In particles, they can be electric interactions or electronic charges," Mason says. "In ants, they can be emissions of smells or things they emit that leave traces about where they've been. In people, I think there are subtle signals, the way that they move so their teammates can know what that means and then act collectively on that."

Fluid, instinctive basketball really is miraculous. "It's interesting because it's not that everyone has decided on what to do beforehand," Mason says, "It's that when they see someone start moving in a certain way, based on their knowledge of the rules and based on the way that this person is doing something, they automatically know how to follow." Like electrons dancing in a frozen vacuum, it is a literal phenomenon.

Basketball, it must be said, allows for plenty of individual phenomena, too. He might not have taken the last shot in the 1993 NBA Finals, but Michael Jordan was a one-man superconductor when he needed to be. In fact, the triangle had a special release valve for him. If all that weaving and ball movement didn't produce anything after twenty seconds, it was Jordan's job to make something happen on his own. The key, though, was limiting the need for those four-second bursts of individual brilliance. "It's a very delicate balance," Winter told reporters before the 1993 NBA Finals. "It's a thing we continually work with because we want isolation for Michael in certain parts of the game. . . . But we want to develop out of the offense. We don't want him or Pippen—or anyone—to feel they are going to go out and take over the game one-on-one, because our idea is a team concept. We want to involve all five players."

The challenge for a coach is not just getting all the pieces to fit, but to make each individual understand his or her function as part of the greater whole. As Phil Jackson wrote, "The beauty of the system—and this applies to all kinds of systems, not just the triangle—was that it turned the whole team into a *learning organization*. Everybody from Michael on down had something to learn, no matter how talented or untalented he was." Basketball, which is itself a system, works in a similar way.

As an extremely talented gymnast in the 1980s, Nadya Mason earned a spot on the U.S. National Team, and she maintains an acute awareness of team dynamics to this day. "I'm definitely familiar with how coaches interact with people," she says. "On the one hand, materials follow fundamental rules in a way that people don't have to. If I take a material like gold and I try to make it not conduct electricity, the way the atoms are structured inside of it makes it conduct electricity very well. To prevent that I would have to do something really crazy to it. Make it atomically thin or hammer it down to where you can barely see it. You have to modify it in extreme ways to get it to not do the thing it naturally does. My hope for people is that we're a little bit more malleable. If you want a person to change a habit, I think people's natures are more malleable than materials."

This reminds me of something Tex Winter wrote in the last chapter of *The Triple-Post Offense*, titled "Philosophy of Coaching." The section is uncharacteristic for Winter; it is meandering and referential in a way that the rest of the book most certainly is not. There are quotes from Sigmund Freud, Dr. Edmund Jacobson ("one of the foremost experts on relaxation"), and a lengthy excerpt from *Psychiatry in Modern Warfare*. The whole thing is very entertaining and doesn't tell you anything about how to actually play basketball, which may be why Winter stuck it at the very end of his book, as a way to ensure that readers would glean all the utilitarian info first. But it would be a shame to skip this chapter, for he makes some keen observations about the nature of, well, life. "In order to realize real happiness," writes Winter, "a coach must recognize that true victories come from the satisfaction of having done the best job possible with the material available."

EPILOGUE
Bouncing Back

I DID NOT FORGET about rebounding. How could I? With remarkably few exceptions, you will always see more rebounds in a basketball game than made field goals. They are an essential feature of the sport, albeit one that's easy to take for granted. Hence, the rebound's place in this epilogue. A literal afterthought.

Think back to that first-ever game in Springfield. In thirty minutes of frantic action, the students combined to only make a single basket. There would have been a flurry of rebounds, yet rebounding is not mentioned by name in Naismith's book. Under the *R* section of the index you'll find "Roosevelt, Theodore" and "Rumania, basketball in," but not "rebounding." It is ubiquitous to the point of near invisibility. To paraphrase Jorge Luis Borges, "There are no camels in the Koran."

Rebounds both power basketball's perpetual motion machine and account for its directional flow. Nevertheless, the NBA didn't think to record offensive rebounds as a separate statistic until the 1973–74 season. Prior to that, the league indiscriminately lumped all rebounds together, like ballot counters in a dictatorship. But this dereliction of accounting never stopped anyone from actually trying to grab a rebound. It's just something you have to do.

"The rebound keeps things going," Colleen Macklin tells me. Macklin is the game designer who helped explain the inherent paradox of games, which is that they use rules to generate fun. When we first spoke, the NBA was gearing up for the 2020 regular season. Come March, the coronavirus pandemic put everything on hold. There would be no basketball for months. There certainly would be no fun.

June marked a breakthrough, however. The pandemic was still very much raging throughout the country, but the league sealed itself inside a "bubble" at Walt Disney World in Orlando, Florida. There, it could implement the features of a competent virus response that America itself had failed to enact during the months-long crisis. Basketball rebounded, even if the country didn't.

Watching these "bubble" games was an odd experience. As potential disease vectors, normal citizens were not allowed to attend. Instead, housebound fans live-streamed themselves onto giant screens surrounding the court and rooted for the "home" team (albeit with a slight lag, depending on their internet speeds). The whole thing fit the definition of a terrifying dystopia but for one exception: The basketball was fantastic.

Macklin had helped explain why games were fun in the first place. But as I watched these hermetically sealed NBA players competing and diving for loose balls during a pandemic, a new question emerged: Why do we return to games?

"Replayabilty in basketball is about scaling up, right?" Macklin says. "Certainly there is player progression. It's about developing your abilities." But self-improvement isn't why fans tune in. We watch because we don't know what's going to happen next. "When you're playing against other humans, there's just something fun and unpredictable about that. The real world has truly unique features. The way a ball bounces off the rim is going to be different every time. Physics and the laws of the universe are consistently unpredictable. You never know." And no matter where the ball bounces, somebody's got to grab it.

It may seem like mindless grunt work, but every rebound requires a plan. There is no better example for this than Dennis Rodman, who won seven straight rebounding titles between 1992 and 1998. The Hall of Famer may be known for his untethered aggressiveness (and foreign relations work with North Korea), but his brain is what made him one of history's greatest rebounders. During pregame warmups, he would stand to the side and stare at the action going on near the baskets. When his Detroit Pistons teammate Isiah Thomas chastised him early in his career for not participating, Rodman explained, "I'm just watching the rotations on the basketball." He then told Thomas that his shots usually spun three times in the air before hitting the rim.

"He knew the rotation of every person that shot on our team," Thomas told the *Detroit Free Press*. "If it spins sideways, where it would bounce, how often it would bounce left or right. He had rebounding down to a science." Thomas never bugged Rodman to practice his jumper during those pregame shootarounds again.

Rodman's studious approach to rebounding was a lifelong commitment. While with the Chicago Bulls, he stuffed his mental filing cabinets with all the information he could retain about his new teammates. "Anytime I see Scottie or Michael shoot from the top of the key, I know the ball will come off the rim to the right," he told *Sports Illustrated* in 1996. "Take somebody like Steve Kerr. He has a high arc on his shots, so I know his rebounds are either going to go straight up or off to the opposite side. Either way, they're going to be pretty close to the rim." Patterns emerge in the careening chaos if you know what to look for.

Rodman also considered rebounding to be a form of expression, and he pledged that he would tear off his uniform and run around the court naked if he ever grabbed fifty boards in a single game. Much to the relief of the NBA's broadcast partners, his career high topped out at thirty-four.

Wilt Chamberlain managed to keep his clothes on after his record-setting fifty-five rebound effort against the Boston Celtics in 1960, but I'm sure he still found a way to celebrate. He adored grabbing boards, stating that he "always thought rebounding was more important than scoring." As basketball's ultimate hedonist, he only pursued things that made him feel good, and rebounding fit the bill just fine. He made a habit of slapping the ball after each one to let everybody in the arena know what he had just accomplished. "It sounded like a gunshot, and it gave me a sense of power, of fighting back against these guys who were harassing me," he writes in his wonderfully odd autobiography. "In a sense, I was saying, 'This is my kingdom; stay out.'"

Overlooked or not, rebounds are still fun for players who have a special knack for hauling them in. There's reward in keeping the game going.

"Another thing that makes something inherently playable is that it just happens to be pleasurable," Macklin says. "In game design, we call the little elements of interaction that make up the feel of a game 'mechanics.' " She mentions *Super Mario Bros.*, which only offers players a few mechanics, but each one happens to be insanely fun. "When you're jumping in *Super Mario* it has got to feel good. If it doesn't feel right, you're going to not want to come back to it. These little atoms of interactive things that you're doing have to have a feel that you want to keep experiencing."

Combining both athleticism and geometric acuity, rebounding is a mechanic of real purpose. Each one benefits the game itself, for it manages to turn failure—a missed shot—into opportunity.

Here, Macklin asserts that there are *two* central paradoxes to game design. We already know the first paradox, which is that rules and restrictions can facilitate fun. "The other one," she says, "is that, in a game, failure can feel satisfying or good." As one of the worst coaches of his era, James Naismith would have been familiar with this contradiction. The only loss he worried about was a loss of interest.

"You want to calibrate failure so it isn't too discouraging," Macklin says. "You're constantly trying to make failure feel OK for the player and to be an opportunity to learn how the system works. In fact, if you lose a game, you should probably want to play it more."

• • •

IN READING ABOUT James Naismith, you get the sense that he would have led a perfectly happy and fulfilling life had he not invented basketball. It's not like he played it all that often (two times, to be precise). He also didn't make any money from the game, which, to his credit, was never his intent. The whole thing was an accidental phenomenon, wherein a peculiar man combined a certain set of rules with an unlikely group of players in the right environment and at the correct time.

What if Naismith had failed with his class of incorrigibles? What if the dubious melee he described during that 1939 radio interview actually happened, and all his students were either too hurt, too concussed, or too dead to continue with his experiment? Would somebody else have created a similar enough set of rules to spark a different sport that would become basketball? Or did Naismith get it just right, including in all the things he got wrong?

Thankfully, we don't have to worry about any of that. Basketball exists. And, now that it exists, it always will exist. Too many different people love it for too many different reasons. Despite all its changes, and because of them.

In his book, Naismith reminisces about coming up with that first rule, that ultimately stupid decision to prohibit players from moving with the ball. "On looking back, it was hard to see why I was so elated," he writes. "I had as yet nothing but a single idea, but I was sure the rest would work out correctly."

Somehow, he was right.

SOURCES

Statistics via basketball-reference.com and NBA.com/stats. *Dream Dictionary* excerpts via dreamdictionary.org.

Adande, J.A. "Klay Thompson's stroke of genius." ESPN. February 13, 2015. espn.com/nba/allstar2015/story/_/id/12322332/nba-how-klay-thompson-developed-shooting-form.

Albom, Mitch. "Why was James passing at the end?" *Detroit Free Press*, May 22, 2007.

Allen, Forrest Claire. *Better Basketball*. New York: McGraw-Hill Book Company, 1937.

Arace, Michael. "Barkley plays through elbow injury to score 32." *Hartford Courant*, June 17, 1993.

"Army Teams to Be Guinea Pigs for New Basketball Scoring." *Clovis News-Journal*, February 8, 1945.

Associated Press. "Joe Fortenberry, Olympic Captain, 82." *New York Times*, June 5, 1993.

———. "LeBron criticized for passing ball." *Deseret News*, May 23, 2007.

———. "Texan's 6 Foot 7. Looks Clumsy, But—." *Fort Worth Star-Telegram*, January 4, 1933.

Babwin, Don. "Globetrotters played for real in a game that altered history." *SFGATE*, February 2008.

Baker, Chris. "Truly Foul Shooters: There's No Defense on Free Throws, So Why Are So Many in the NBA So Bad?" *Los Angeles Times*, February 10, 1996.

Baker, William J. "Introduction." In *Basketball, Its Origin and Development*, 5–17. Lincoln and London: University of Nebraska Press, 1996.

Ballard, Chris. *The Art of a Beautiful Game: The Thinking Fan's Tour of the NBA*. New York: Simon & Schuster, 2009.

Barnas, Jo-Ann. "The Story of Rodman." *Detroit Free-Press*, March 31, 2011.

Barry, Dan. "The Triangle Offense, a Simple Yet Perplexing System, Dies." *New York Times*, June 28, 2017.

Becque, Fran. "Lillian Copeland, Alpha Epsilon Phi, #NotableSororityWomen, #WHM2019." FranBecque.com. March 28, 2019. franbecque.com/lillian-copeland-alpha-epsilon-phi-notablesororitywomen-whm2019/.

"Big Instant Replay Technological Advances." *San Francisco Examiner*, January 27, 1980.

Blumenthal, Ralph, and Leslie Kean. "Do We Believe in U.F.O.s? That's the Wrong Question." *New York Times*, July 28, 2020.

——. "No Longer in Shadows, Pentagon's U.F.O. Unit Will Make Some Findings Public." *New York Times*, July 23, 2020.

Branch, John. "For Free Throws, 50 Years of Practice Is No Help." *New York Times*, March 3, 2009.

Broussard, Chris. "A Game Played Above the Rim, Above All Else." *New York Times*, February 15, 2004.

Cacciola, Scott. "Three Sides to This Story." *New York Times*, October 27, 2014.

Chamberlain, Wilt. "Wilt: Just like any other 7-foot black millionaire who lives next door." New York: Macmillan, 1973.

Cohen, Ben. "How George Steinbrenner and the Harlem Globetrotters Changed the NBA Forever." *Wall Street Journal*, February 13, 2020.

——. "Physics of Flopping: Cuban Backs a Study." *Wall Street Journal*, June 7, 2013.

Cooney, Frank. "Dr. Albo's Magic World." *San Francisco Examiner*, March 12, 1991. Craig, Jack. "Olympics. Face Over-Exposure?" *Boston Globe*, February 12, 1968.

Craig, Jack. "On TV, an isolated sensation." *Boston Globe*, October 7, 1993.

Daley, Arthur J. "Awesome Kansas Giants Reverse Basketball Lay-Up Shot Process." *New York Times*, March 10, 1936.

Dawidoff, Nicholas. "The Obtuse Triangle." *New York Times*, June 23, 2015.

Deprisco, Michael. "Marcus Smart defends flopping." NBC Sports Boston. July 29, 2019. nbcsports.com/boston/celtics/marcus-smart-defends-flopping-i-flop-defense-your-favorite-player-flops-offense.

Downey, Meg. "The Weird and Wonderful History of Kryptonite." DCComics.com. April 5, 2018. dccomics.com/blog/2018/04/05/the-weird-and-wonderful-history-of-kryptonite.

Drummond, Andre, "Let me make this clear . . . . I'm not shooting free throws underhand. . #Relax." Twitter, August 17, 2013. twitter.com/andredrummond/status/368833109904482304.

Dupree, David. "For LeBron, the play's the thing." *Sports Illustrated*, April 28, 2008.

Effrat, Louis. "Columbia Defeats Fordham, 73 to 58." *New York Times*, February 8, 1945.

Ellis, Vince. "Pistons exploring ways to boost Drummond's FT shooting." *Detroit Free Press*, January 26, 2016.

"Explanation of Anti-Flopping Rule." NBA.com. October 5, 2012. official.nba.com/explanation-of-anti-flopping-rule/.

Fairchild, Paul. "Kryptonite Is Crap." *Atlantic*, June 20, 2013.

Feng, Ed. "Home Court Advantage in the NBA Playoffs." *The Wages of Wins Journal*, April 19, 2013. wagesofwins.com/2013/04/19/home-court-advantage-in-the-nba-playoffs/.

Fisher, Bob. *Straight Shooter: A game-changing new approach to basketball shooting*. Dublin, Ohio: Telemachus Press, 2018.

Fleming, David. "Sports' perfect 0.4 seconds." ESPN. April 1, 2014. espn.com/nba/story/_/id/10703246/golden-state-warriors-stephen-curry-reinventing-shooting-espn-magazine.

Friedell, Nick. "The secret to Andre Drummond's dramatic free throw improvement." ESPN. November 7, 2017. espn.com/nba/story/_/id/21332122/nba-andre-drummond-dramatic-free-throw-improvement-driven-back-basics-approach.

"From the Beginning." Spalding Basketball. spalding-basketball.com/de/about-spalding/history/.

Fury, Shawn. "Long Shot: How Basketball's Three-Pointer Was Launched from Morningside Heights." *Columbia Magazine*, Spring 2017.

——. *Rise and Fire: The Origins, Science, and Evolution of the Jump Shot—and How It Transformed Basketball Forever*. New York: Flatiron Books, 2016.

Goldsberry, Kirk. *SprawlBall: A Visual Tour of the New Era of the NBA*. Boston: Houghton Mifflin Harcourt, 2019.

Gopnik, Adam. "The Real Work." *New Yorker*, July 28, 2008.

Guerra, Denise, and Michel Martin. "Why Rick and Canyon Barry Stay True to the 'Granny Shot'." *All Things Considered*. NPR, May 28, 2017.

Gutman, Bill. *Tales from the 1969–1970 New York Knicks*. Champaign, IL: Sports Publishing L.L.C., 2005.

Haberstroh, Tom. "The Year of Steph Curry." ESPN. May 10, 2016. espn.com/espn/feature/story/_/id/15492948/the-numbers-steph-curry-incredible-mvp-season

Haggar, Jeff. "The NBA on CBS late night and tape delay playoff era." *Classic TV Sports*, May 14, 2013.

Hall, Donald. "Basketball: The Purest Sport of Bodies." In *Basketball: Great Writing About America's Game*, edited by Alexander Wolff, 187–191. New York: Library of America, 2018.

Henderson, John. "Wooden's Wisdom." *Denver Post*, May 8, 2016.

Herring, Chris. "Few Teams Have Ever Defended Like These Milwaukee Bucks." FiveThirtyEight. February 27, 2020. fivethirtyeight.com/features/few-teams-have-ever-defended-like-these-milwaukee-bucks/.

———. "LeBron and Harden Are the NBA's Best Quarterbacks." FiveThirtyEight. March 10, 2017. fivethirtyeight.com/features/lebron-and-harden-are-the-nbas-best-quarterbacks/.

———. "The Warriors and Rockets Have Reinvented Modern NBA Defense. Yes, Defense." FiveThirtyEight. May 14, 2018. fivethirtyeight.com/features/the-warriors-and-rockets-have-reinvented-modern-nba-defense-yes-defense/.

Hickey, Dave. *Air Guitar: Essays on Art and Democracy*. New York: Art Issues Press, 2012.

Holman, Nat. *Scientific Basketball*. University of Iowa: Incra Publishing Company, 1922.

Hruby, Patrick. "Inside the six-figure project to solve the mystery of NBA flopping." *Guardian*, October 30, 2019.

"Instant Replay." *Fort Worth Star-Telegram*, August 31, 1994.

Jackson, Phil. *Eleven Rings: The Soul of Success*. New York: The Penguin Press, 2013.

Jemail, Jimmy. "THE QUESTION: Do you think that old-time, low-scoring basketball—before Hank Luisetti popularized the one-hand jump shot—was a better and more interesting game than it is today?" *Sports Illustrated*, December 9, 1957.

Jenkins, Lee. "Reason No. 1: This. Dunk." *Sports Illustrated*, February 18, 2013.

Jenkins, Sally. "Tara VanDerveer is a Stanford educator—with 1,000 basketball coaching wins." *Washington Post*, February 3, 2017.

Johnson, Roy S. "Magic on Court: Pass Master." *New York Times*, February 3, 1986.

Jones, Gordie. "New or Old, This Magic's Valuable." *Intelligencer Journal* (Lancaster, Pennsylvania), February 23, 1987.

Jordan, Michael. "For the Love of the Game." New York: Crown, 1998.

Kerkhoff, Blair. "Kansas roots in U.S. hoops." *Kansas City Star*, July 29, 2012.

Kast, Monica. "Busted NCAA bracket? Don't worry, even a rocket scientist's predictions aren't perfect." *Knoxville News Sentinel*, March 26, 2019.

Kram, Zach. "The NBA's Home-Court Assist Advantage Is No More." The Ringer. January 21, 2020. theringer.com/nba/2020/1/21/21074724/nba-home-court-assist-advantage.

Krugel, Mitchell. "1993 NBA Finals: Bulls' success a take of the tape." *Times of Northwest Indiana*, June 8, 1993.

Lazenby, Roland. "How Tex Winter Has Influenced the Golden State Warriors." *Vice*, June 14, 2015.

"Legends profile: George Mikan." NBA.com. August 23, 2017. nba.com/history/legends/profiles/george-mikan.

"LILLIAN COPELAND." So Cal Jewish Sports Hall of Fame. scjewishsportshof.com/copeland.html.

Litsky, Frank. "King of the Court Clowns." *Boys' Life*, February 1968.

Mandell, Nina. "Shaq believes 'the man way upstairs' was to blame for his bad free throw shooting." *USA Today*, August 4, 2017.

McDill, Kent. "Female referees don't concern Rodman." *Daily Herald*, October 29, 1997.

McDill, Kent, and Mike McGraw. "Maintenance crew deserves assist on Malone's misses." *Daily Herald*, June 2, 1997.

McKnight, Michael. "Learn to Dunk." *Sports Illustrated*, 2015.

McLuhan, Marshall. "Interview with Marshall McLuhan." By Edwin Newman. *Speaking Freely*. Public Broadcasting, N.E.T., January 4, 1971.

McMenamin, Dave. "Dime King: The Lakers are benefiting from peak playmaker LeBron James." ESPN. November 14, 2019. espn.com/nba/story/_/id/28076196/dime-king-lakers-benefiting-peak-playmaker-lebron-james.

McNicol, Andrew. "How the NBA became China's most popular sports league, with a boost from tech giants such as Weibo and Tencent." *South China Morning Post*, September 27, 2017.

Metivier, Don A. "Mikhail Baryshnikov Triumphant at Spa." *Post-Star*, July 10, 1978.

Montee, Kristy. "TO AIR, DIVINE." *South Florida Sun Sentinel*, April 17, 1995.

Naismith, James. *Basketball, Its Origin and Development*. New York: Association Press, 1941.

———. "Interview with James Naismith." By Gabriel Heatter. *We the People*. WOR-AM, January 31, 1938. exhibits.lib.ku.edu/exhibits/show/naismith150/collections/radio-interview.

NBA India. "Shoot with great form." YouTube. January 14, 2017. youtube.com/watch?v=8-7JVqPlUJ4.

"NBA players complain new ball hurts." *Globe and Mail*, December 8, 2006.

Nelson, Megan Kate. "A Brief History of the Stoplight." *Smithsonian*, May 2018.

Ocbazghi, Emmanuel, Noah Friedman, and Graham Flanagan. "Shaq reveals why he never tried the underhand free throw technique." *Business Insider*, December 11, 2017.

O'Donnell, Ricky. "NBA All-Stars loved the new format and want to see it continue." *SB Nation*, February 17, 2020. sbnation.com/nba/2020/2/17/21140832/nba-all-star-game-2020-quotes-format-rule-changes-players-thoughts.

Parsons, Louella O. "Film Producers Yearn for College Athletic Tales, Asserts Critic." *El Paso Times*, October 2, 1927.

Partnow, Seth. "About that 'Elam Ending': A Q&A with its creator, Nick Elam, about strategy and gameplay." The Athletic. February 15, 2020. theathletic.com/1609152/2020/02/15/about-that-elam-ending-a-qa-with-its-creator-nick-elam-about-strategy-and-gameplay/.

Paterno, Vincent. "Hobson's choice." *Morning News* (Paterson, New Jersey), June 18, 1979.

Peeler, Tim. *Legends of N.C. State Basketball: Dick Dickey, Tommy Burleson, David Thompson, Jim Valvano, and Other Wolfpack Stars*. Champaign, IL: Sports Publishing L.L.C., 2015.

Penner, Mike. "Wooden Remains a Winner." *Los Angeles Times*, December 9, 1995.

Petchesky, Barry. "How Grinnell College Bastardizes Basketball to Set Records." *Deadspin*, November 18, 2013. deadspin.com/how-grinnell-college-bastardizes-basketball-to-set-reco-1466714609.

Pluto, Terry. *Loose Balls: The Short, Wild Life of the American Basketball Association*. New York: Simon & Schuster, 1990.

———. *Tall Tales: The Glory Years of the NBA*. New York: Simon & Schuster, 1992.

Powers, Charles T. "Ballet Star Caught Up in Whirl of Work, Fame." *Los Angeles Times*, August 25, 1976.

Prada, Mike. "There's a new dribble move taking the NBA by storm." SB Nation. February 15, 2015. sbnation.com/nba/2015/2/15/8037121/nba-yo-yo-dribble-chris-paul-john-wall

Preston, Ross. *The Road to 138: The Inside Story of the Insanely Fast, Record-Breaking Grinnell Pioneers:* Overland Park, KS: Curiosity Publishing, 2014.

Price, S.L. "High-flying Jordan jams his way to dunk crown." *Sacramento Bee,* February 8, 1987.

Rains, Rob. *James Naismith: The Man Who Invented Basketball.* Philadelphia: Temple University Press, 2009.

Sachare, Alex. "24-Second Clock Revived the Game." NBA.com. archive.nba.com/ history/24secondclock.html.

Scholick, Jennie. "Baryshnikov on Brodsky." The Poetry Foundation. January 29, 2018. poetryfoundation.org/articles/145539/baryshnikov-on-brodsky.

Schuhmann, John. "The Best Dunk Contest Ever." NBA.com. 2006. archive.nba.com/allstar2006/ moments_88dunkcontest.html.

Shea, Bill. "It's the future of basketball': How the 'Elam Ending' was born and why the NBA is adopting it for the All-Star Game." The Athletic. February 13, 2020. theathletic. com/1606367/2020/02/13/its-the-future-of-basketball-how-the-elam-ending-was-born-and-why-the-nba-is-adopting-it-for-the-all-star-game/.

Sheridan, Chris. "Should LeBron have passed?" ESPN. May 23, 2007. espn.com/nba/ dailydime?page=dailydime-070522&lpos=tv1&lid=tab1pos2.

Silverberg, Larry, Chau Tran, and Kit Adcock. "Numerical Analysis of the Basketball Shot." *Journal of Dynamic Systems, Measurement, and Control,* December 2003.

Singer, Mark. "Secrets of the Magus." *New Yorker,* April 5, 1993.

Smith, Stephen A. "Time for LeBron to live up to the hype and do something." *Philadelphia Inquirer,* May 27, 2007.

Sohi, Seerat. "How the NBA Was Saved on the Back of a Napkin." *Sports Illustrated,* August 28, 2017.

"Special Interest to Basketball Fans." *Daily Reporter* (Greenfield, Indiana), January 26, 1928.

Stein, Marc. "NBA ball controversy reaches new level." ESPN. December 7, 2006. espn.com/nba/ columns/story?columnist=stein_marc&id=2689744.

———. "NBA discussed new court, 4-pointer." ESPN. February 25, 2014. espn.com/blog/marc-stein/ post/_/id/1661/nba-explores-new-court-4-pointer.

———. "The N.B.A. Embraces a 'Trash' Defense." *New York Times,* January 17, 2020.

Swiss, Jamy Ian. *Shattering Illusions.* Vanishing Inc. Magic, 2002.

Tarazano, Lawrence D. "The Patents Behind Basketball." Smithsonianmag.com. March 29, 2019. smithsonianmag.com/sponsored/patents-behind-basketball-180971830/.

Tasty. "The Art of Making Noodles by Hand." YouTube. May 16, 2018. youtube.com/ watch?v=f2kesmAO8VU.

Taylor, Phil. "Tricks of the Trade." *Sports Illustrated,* March 4, 1996.

Teacher, Jordan. "Where the Triangle Offense Lives." *New Yorker,* September 14, 2017.

Telander, Rick. "Ready . . . Set . . . Levitate!" *Sports Illustrated,* November 17, 1986.

———. "The weekend Michael Jordan really became MJ." *Chicago Sun-Times,* February 15, 2020.

Thamel, Pete. "Meteorologist Becomes a Go-To Guy." *New York Times,* March 23, 2011.

Thanawalla, Ali. "Klay Thompson's Four-Dribble Night Really Impressed LeBron James." NBC Sports Bay Area. January 9, 2019. nbcbayarea.com/news/sports/klay_thompson_s_four-dribble_night_ really_impressed_lebron_james_bay/5610/.

TMZ Sports. "Roy Hibbert on NBA Future, 'It's Just Time to Move On.'" YouTube. July 17, 2018. youtube.com/watch?v=6eBFcmrlrfc.

Tran, Chau, and Larry Silverberg. "Optimal release conditions for the free throw in men's basketball." *Journal of Sports Sciences,* 2008.

UPI. "3-Point Basket Could Help End NBA Violence." *St. Louis Post-Dispatch*, July 16, 1978.

Verrier, Justin. "You Can't Stop NBA Offenses—and Now, You Can't Even Hope to Contain Them." The Ringer. October 30, 2018. theringer.com/nba/2018/10/30/18038802/nba-defense-offensive-boom.

Walks, Matt. "Flashback: 20 years ago today, Anderson forces MJ back to No. 23." ESPN. May 7, 2015. espn.com/blog/nba/post/_/id/2648/flashback-20-years-ago-today-anderson-forces-mj-back-to-no-23.

Weinreb, Michael. "How Ken Pomeroy Became College Basketball's Favorite Number-Cruncher." *Vice*, March 10, 2016.

Windhorst, Brian. "LeBron James' unprecedented season of sharing has arrived." ESPN. November 29, 2016. espn.com/nba/story/_/id/18159427/why-lebron-james-cooking-more-dishes.

Winfield, Kristian. "Klay Thompson held the ball for just 90 seconds in his 60-point Performance of the Year." SB Nation. June 26, 2017. sbnation.com/2016/12/6/13854272/klay-thompson-highlights-stats-scoring-60-points.

Winfrey, Lee. "Will NBA finals be season's final straw?" *Philadelphia Inquirer*, May 29, 1984.

Winter, Fred "Tex." *The Triple-Post Offense*. Manhattan, KS: Ag Press, 1997.

Withers, Tom. "The Debate on James' Pass Heats Up." *Ledger*, May 23, 2007.

Woike, Dan. "Appreciation: Tex Winter was about more than the triangle offense; he was a stickler for details." *Los Angeles Times*, October 11, 2018.

ACKNOWLEDGMENTS

Writing this book was an incredibly fun experience, and there are many, many people to whom I owe that pleasure. I need to first thank all the experts and geniuses who agreed to speak with me. These are extremely busy folks who took time out of their schedules to shoot the shit about hoops. Their participation was invaluable, and I will always appreciate it.

A million thanks to Samantha Weiner for shepherding this through with enthusiasm and confidence at every step. She and everyone at Abrams have been fantastic teammates.

It was always a joy whenever I saw J.O. Applegate's marvelous illustrations pop up in my e-mail inbox, and I am grateful to him and the Abrams art department for all their hard work.

William LoTurco was the one who first reached out to me about writing a book, and his sage and steady navigation throughout the process made the whole thing possible.

I can't forget Dru-Ann Chuckran, whose fact-checking was an immense help.

I also owe a debt of gratitude to Josh Levin for his wisdom and encouragement. It means a lot to me.

Then there are all the incredibly smart and insightful basketball writers and reporters whose work continues to help me learn about and appreciate the game. May your deadlines be spacious and overtimes few.

I have so many friends I need to thank for their support, but I want to single out Robert and Frannie and Allie and Ethan and Jen and Camille and Alex and William and Beata and Charlie ... the list goes on and on. (And yes, I'm aware that's not "singling out.")

I'm going to put my family last, but that's only because I know they're the ones I can count on to actually read this far. Dad, Martha, Amanda, Mike, Amelia, Henry, Stevie, Ruby—you're the best. And Laura, you are the most supportive and wonderful partner I could ever ask for. This book really is for you.

INDEX

ABOUT THE AUTHOR

NICK GREENE is a contributing writer for *Slate*, prior to which he worked as editor at large at *Mental Floss* and as web editor at the *Village Voice*. His work has been published in *Vice*, *Men's Health*, and *Chicago* magazine. He lives in the San Francisco Bay Area.